Lecture Notes
in Business Information Processing   **461**

Series Editors

Wil van der Aalst ⓘ
  RWTH Aachen University, Aachen, Germany
John Mylopoulos ⓘ
  University of Trento, Trento, Italy
Sudha Ram ⓘ
  University of Arizona, Tucson, AZ, USA
Michael Rosemann ⓘ
  Queensland University of Technology, Brisbane, QLD, Australia
Clemens Szyperski
  Microsoft Research, Redmond, WA, USA

More information about this series at http://www.springer.com/bookseries/7911

Mohamed Anis Bach Tobji · Rim Jallouli ·
Vasile Alecsandru Strat · Ana Maria Soares ·
Adriana Anamaria Davidescu (Eds.)

Digital Economy

Emerging Technologies and Business Innovation

7th International Conference on Digital Economy, ICDEc 2022
Bucharest, Romania, May 9–11, 2022
Proceedings

Springer

Editors
Mohamed Anis Bach Tobji 🄳
University of Manouba
Manouba, Tunisia

Rim Jallouli 🄳
University of Manouba
Manouba, Tunisia

Vasile Alecsandru Strat 🄳
Bucharest Business School
Bucharest, Romania

Ana Maria Soares 🄳
University of Minho and CICS.NOVA.
UMinho
Braga, Portugal

Adriana Anamaria Davidescu 🄳
Bucharest University of Economic Studies
Bucharest, Romania

ISSN 1865-1348   ISSN 1865-1356   (electronic)
Lecture Notes in Business Information Processing
ISBN 978-3-031-17036-2   ISBN 978-3-031-17037-9   (eBook)
https://doi.org/10.1007/978-3-031-17037-9

This Springer imprint is published by the registered company Springer Nature Switzerland AG
The registered company address is: Gewerbestrasse 11, 6330 Cham, Switzerland

Preface

Digitalization and technological innovations are driving unprecedented changes in the economy and society, continuously changing life as we know it. The digital economy and across-the-board digital transformation, significantly accelerated by COVID-19, pose a number of opportunities and challenges to practitioners, academics, and policy-makers.

In this context, addressing and understanding the multi-faceted, multi-disciplinary, and multi-sectorial implications of digital transformation processes for users, systems, processes, and consumers is crucial. This is the focus of the International Conference on Digital Economy (IDCEc), which aims at establishing itself as a key forum for researchers in this area, including junior researchers and doctoral students. The conference encourages a constructive reviewing process at the submission stage and rich discussion among participants during the conference, which may help authors to further develop their ideas and grow as researchers.

This book, entitled "Digital Economy: Emerging Technologies and Business Innovation" gathers the contributions presented at the seventh edition of the conference (ICDEc 2022), which took place during May 9–11, 2022, in Bucharest, Romania (https://www.aten.tn/ICDEc2022). The intended audience of this book mainly consists of researchers and practitioners in the following domains: digital transformation, digital business models, digital marketing, e-health, and e-learning.

The call for papers invited submissions addressing the requirements of a multi-sectorial approach when studying the digital transformation process. The Program Committee received a number of exciting contributions from a diverse range of research contexts and countries, relating to the impact of digitalizationin different sectors. These submissions were XX-blind reviewed by at least two peers, but more often three, four, and even five peers. In fact, we would like to take this opportunity to thank the Program Committee who were invaluable in providing helpful and insightful comments for authors.

This review process led to the acceptance of 15 papers that were presented at this year's edition of ICDEc, which constitutes an acceptance rate of 34%. The conference was held in a mixed format. While we look forward to a safe return to live events, we wanted to accommodate the participation of authors who still faced travel restrictions.

This book gathers those 15 papers, which address different angles of digitalization, including the impact of COVID-19 on digitalization, digital models for education and healthcare, information technology user behavior and satisfaction, and digital marketing and digital transformation.

Special thanks go to the organizers, sponsors, and scientific partners of the conference, in particular the hosting organizations: Bucharest Business School and the Bucharest University of Economic Studies.

August 2022

Mohamed Anis Bach Tobji
Rim Jallouli
Vasile Alecsandru Strat
Ana Maria Soares
Adriana Davidescu

Organization

General Chair

Adriana Davidescu   Bucharest University of Economic Studies, Romania

Program Chair

Ana Maria Soares   University of Minho, Portugal

Steering Committee

Rim Jallouli   University of Manouba, Tunisia
Mohamed Anis Bach Tobji   University of Manouba, Tunisia

Advisory Board

Olfa Nasraoui   University of Louisville, USA
Osmar Zaïane   University of Alberta, Canada
Anton Nijholt   University of Twente, The Netherlands
Vasile Alecsandru Strat   Bucharest University of Economic Studies, Romania
Farid Abdallah   Australian College of Kuwait, Kuwait
Sehl Mellouli   Université Laval, Canada
Deny Bélisle   Université de Sherbrooke, Canada
Leith Campbell   RMIT University, Australia
Gunnar Piho   Tallinn University of Technology

Organization Chair

Vasile Alecsandru Strat   Bucharest University of Economic Studies, Romania

Organization Committee

Mirela Nichita   Bucharest University of Economic Studies, Romania
Cătălina Radu   Bucharest University of Economic Studies, Romania
Zeineb Ayachi   University of Manouba, Tunisia
Meriam Belkhir   University of Sfax, Tunisia
Teissir Ben Slema   University of Manouba, Tunisia
Roula Jabado   Lebanese International University, Lebanon
Wided Guezguez   University of Tunis, Tunisia

Finance Chair

Ismehene Chahbi   University of Manouba, Tunisia

Publication Chair

Meriam Belkhir   University of Sfax, Tunisia

IT Chair

Nassim Bahri   One Way IT, Tunisia

Country Chairs

Hamish Simmonds   Monitor Deloitte, Australia
Hamid Mcheick   Université du Québec à Chicoutimi, Canada
Kristian Dokic   Polytechnic in Pozega, Croatia
Jean-François Berthevas   University of La Rochelle, France
Hamid Doost   FHM University of Applied Sciences, Germany
  Mohammadian
Dyah Ismoyowati   University of Gadjah Mada, Indonesia
Ali Afshar   Eqbal Lahoori Institute of Higher Education, Iran
Mohammad Makki   International University of Beirut, Lebanon
Javier Rodriguez Ruiz   University of Guadalajara, Mexico
Ana Maria Soares   University of Minho, Portugal
Codruta Mare   Babes-Bolyai University, Romania
Tatiana Lezina   National Research University Higher School
                                  of Economics, Russia
Sayda Elmi   University of Singapore, Singapore
Thabo Gopane   University of Johannesburg, South Africa
Mohammed El Amine   University of Salamanca and Technical University
  Abdelli   of Cartagena, Spain
Emrah Bilgic   Iskenderun Technical University, Turkey

Program Committee

Afef Belghith   University of Manouba, Tunisia
Afef Herelli   University of Manouba, Tunisia
Amine Dhraief   University of Manouba, Tunisia
Amna Abidi   Inetum, France
Anton Nijholt   University of Twente, The Netherlands
António Azevedo   University of Minho, Portugal
Barbara Pisker   Polytechnic in Pozega, Croatia
Beatriz Casais   University of Minho, Portugal

Tharwa Najjar	University of Gafsa, Tunisia
Wael Louhichi	ESSCA School of Management, Paris, France
Yamna Ettarres	University of Manouba, Tunisia
Zeineb Ayachi	University of Manouba, Tunisia

Organizers

Association Tunisienne D'économie Numérique

Academie D'études Écnomiques de Bucharest

Bukharest Business School

Scientific Partners

École Supérieure D'économie Numérique

Université de la Manouba

Universite de la Manouba

Laboratoire de Recherche Opérationnelle, de Décision et de Contrôle de Processus

Laboratoireinterdisciplinaire de Gestion
Universite-Entreprise

Journal of Telecommunication and the
Digital Economy

Lebanese International University

Wess E-Commerce

Abstracts of Keynote Talks

Two Faces of the Same Coin: Exploring the Multilateral Perspective of Informality in Relation to Sustainable Development Goals. Fostering Formal Work with Digital Tools

Adriana Davidescu

Department of Statistics and Econometrics, Bucharest University of Economic Studies, Romania

Digital transformation of the labour market is challenging the notion of decent work with new forms of informality. There is an increasing trend to apply digital tools in policy design and implementation for accelerating the transition to formality. The pandemic shows how digitalisation can affect the precarity of informal work.

Mankind is going through a crucial stage of awareness of responsibilities for its own actions that have generated serious imbalances both in society and at the environmental level, overwhelming its future. Achieving a fair, prosperous and sustainable future is realised through the adoption of the 2030 Development Agenda, which includes 17 Sustainable Development Goals (SDGs) and has 169 goals.

According to the 2030 Agenda, the concept of "leaving no one behind" (Samman et al. 2019) focuses on reducing social and economic cleavages and including discriminated and marginalized groups, including those participating in informal activities. In the light of the recent global situation, international organizations are strengthening the relevance of considering informality in various concepts, including resilience, sustainable development, social economy or circular economy.

Therefore, the presentation is focused on the one hand, on the presentation of the research field of informality from a dual perspective—unilateral versus multilateral—in relation to Sustainable Development Goals, based on research publications extracted from Web of Science published between 1978–2021 and on the other hand, on highlighting the relevance of knowing the main determinants of the phenomenon, emphasizing that keeping the incidence of the shadow economy and its causes under control could offer an alternative in the process of achieving the sustainable development. Last, but not least the presentation highlights some approaches on fostering formal work with digital tools. Digitalisation is redefining work in the informal labour market. Digitalisation is remaking the world of work, not least in the vast informal economy that provides livelihoods for more than 2 billion people worldwide.

Spreading the Word on the Digital Economy

Leith Campbell

School of Engineering at RMIT University Australia
Managing Editor of Journal of Telecommunication and Digital Economy

The concept of the digital economy has been around since the 1990s and its ever-expanding reach is leading to more and more activities being conducted online. This, in turn, is leading to an expansion of the digital society with its attendant benefits and issues. The Journal of Telecommunications and the Digital Economy (JTDE), for example, is seeing more papers evaluating the acceptance of, or resistance to, the introduction of new online services. It is important, therefore, as ICDEc is doing, to promote research and discussion on the digital economy and the digital society.

This talk is based on a new initiative by ICDEc and the JTDE to encourage expanded research papers on a wide range of aspects of the digital economy. It will describe in broad terms the topics that have been accepted for publication and provide some indications of what has not been accepted. It will attempt to draw some lessons on what is important for future studies of the digital economy and where gaps may exist in research interests.

Contents

Digital Marketing

Digital Transformation

Digitalization and COVID 19

The Impact of Digitalization on Unemployment During Covid-19 Pandemic

Sarah Hariri Haykal(iD) and Mohammad Makki(✉)(iD)

Universite Saint-Joseph De Beyrouth, Beirut, Lebanon
sarah.haykal@usj.edu.lb, mohammad.makki@net.usj.edu.lb

Abstract. The Covid19 pandemic that hit the world turned to be far more than a health crisis; the lock downs and the untraditional measures that were taken by most of the countries of the world to decrease the spread of the virus changed the form of our daily activities, and resulted in major socio-economic challenges. Although many businesses and institutions shifted to online mode in several sectors and industries, the lack of solid digital technologies and communications infrastructure made it hard for other countries to cope with the new global reality [1]. This paper claims that digitalized countries; countries with higher Digital Quality of Life (DQL) Index that is developed by the cyber security Company Surfshark in 2019, reported lower increase in their unemployment rate. The paper also claims that higher Covid19 annual cases lead to higher increase in unemployment rates. A Generalized Linear Model, for a sample of 59 countries including 118 panel data observations, was adopted to test the paper's claims. The regression results revealed that there is a significant inverse relationship between DQL index and the percentage change in the unemployment rate, yet the positive coefficient between the percentage change in Covid19 cases and the percentage change in the unemployment rate is insignificant.

Keywords: Unemployment rate · Digital quality of life index · Covid19 cases · Digitalization · Socio-economic challenges

1 Introduction

Covid19 viral pandemic is an unforgettable health shock that changed the way we live on earth; the daily physical activities that we were used to, have witnessed an untraditional transformation to heavily depend on online platforms especially when the countries of the world had to activate measures to reduce the transmission of the virus. The preventive measures to control social distancing and to avoid gathering made many economic activities impossible; economic activity contracted worldwide to bring the global economic growth rate down from 2.9% in 2019 to -3% in 2020. The world major advanced economies that constitute around sixty percent of the global economic activity are forecasted to operate under their potential levels through at least the end of 2024 [2]. As a consequence of the workplace closures, the supply chains and labor productivity were disrupted which led to massive employees' layoffs, income reduction, future uncertainty and lower spending; resulting in higher unemployment rates and higher poverty levels [3].

To ensure their survival, many businesses shifted to online mode to perform their daily operations; information technology played an important role in sustaining many sectors and industries by reimbursing for economic, social and business losses [4]. However, the socio-economic and demographic conditions of many countries including the lack of economic opportunities and other inequalities have made it difficult for those countries to cope with the existing health shock and have resulted in collateral damages [5]. The digital technologies and the communications infrastructure as well as the development of digital capabilities were and are still essential elements for a successful digital transformation, but the lack of those elements has increased the costs in terms of isolation, health and opportunities for the billions of unconnected people [6].

This paper intends to examine the significance and the impact of digitalization, measured by the Digital Quality of Life index (DQL) on the percentage change in unemployment rate during the Covid19 health crisis. DQL index is developed by the cyber security Company Surfshark in 2019, and it measures internet affordability, internet quality, e-infrastructure, e-security and e-government. The paper postulates that countries with higher DQL index recorded lower increases in their unemployment rate which indicates an inverse relationship between the two variables. The paper also tests the impact of the percentage change in Covid19 cases on the percentage change in unemployment rate while predicting a direct relationship between the two variables. The following sections of the paper present the available literature in the field of digitalization and health shocks, the methodology being adapted to test the proposed claims, and analyze the regression results and the conclusions.

2 Literature Review

Health shocks are illnesses that prevent households from performing their normal daily activities [7]. They have negative economic implications where the risks are greater in the countries that lack public healthcare and sanitations systems, and that have high population densities [8]. Health shocks significantly affect the income, consumption patterns and asset accumulation in developing countries, and they also decrease individual savings [9]. The close history showed that the outbreak of a similar virus namely the "SARS" have resulted in a decrease in travel and tourism income of most of the infected countries [10]. It has affected the demand and supply sides of the labor market with significant Human Resource Management consequences mainly on hotel employment in China and Singapore [11].

Lenhart (2018) investigated the impact of a sudden health shock on the productivity of labor, household income and employment status, as well as on the working hours to prove that sudden health shocks reduce earnings, especially for highly educated males in managerial jobs. The results also indicate that health shocks cause lower productivity in the labor market [12]. Furthermore, adverse health shocks negatively affect employment and income especially for the less educated males and for those in middle-ranking positions [13]. The remaining part of the literature review addresses two major issues: the consequences of the Covid19 pandemic on unemployment rate and poverty levels, and the importance of Digitalization in sustaining businesses in several sectors and industries and in preventing job losses.

The Covid19 is labeled as the "Great Equalizer", which indicates that everyone is equally exposed to the virus, and that the economic activity of most of the people, especially low-income groups, is similarly affected [14, 15]. Although Covid19 vaccination has started, economic recovery varies between the countries of the world; the pandemic has divided the world into two major blocs: the countries that created the vaccines and the rest of the world. Given the production capacities and the distribution inequalities, it will be very hard to maintain equal and fast recovery among all [16]. The spread prevention and control measures implemented by most of the countries of the world have resulted in an extraordinary decline in people's movement along with a reduction in energy and fuel demand [17]. Many businesses and SMEs were forced to shut down. Employees' layoffs increased, supply value chains and cash flows were interrupted, and the spending and demand behaviors of people endangered migrants and displaced populations and heightened unemployment rates and poverty levels [18]. Although digital transformation is regarded as a catalyst in bringing in business sustainability and in ensuring a survival mode [19], the lack of digital infrastructure, digital awareness and the weak internet connectivity pose critical questions regarding jobs and unemployment rates in many countries.

According to the International Labor Organization (ILO), around 255 million full-time jobs were lost across the world [20]. In the focus on urgent action to save lives and to repair livelihoods, many businesses had to shut down where the largest job losses took place during April 2020, and the major sectors and industries that were negatively affected by the pandemic are entertainment and hospitality, travel and transportation, support jobs for mining and oil and gas extraction, construction, food manufacturing, and retail, as well as the self-employed workers [21].

The shutdowns of many small to medium businesses which are financially-fragile have induced higher poverty levels among both genders, yet women were highly affected than men. Covid19 pandemic is predicted to deepen the economic disparities and inequalities among people and to add further financial stress to businesses and to consumers [22]. Cyzmara et al. (2020) stated that women had to quit their jobs to stay with their children during the school lockdowns and to control their social contacts [23]. Hai-Anh et al. (2021) indicated that women are 24% more likely to permanently lose their jobs than men which would result in 50% fall in their income and would lead to lower consumption patterns [24]. While the worldwide efforts were successfully able to decrease poverty in 2019, the Covid19 pandemic has reformed the decreasing trend and is estimated to add to the existing figures an additional 49 million people [25].

The rolling consequences of the rising unemployment and poverty in most of the countries of the world have deepened income inequality and created vaccine inequity. It has also caused food insecurity, adverse individual and public health outcomes [26], and has pushed millions of students out of the education systems especially in low-income countries [27]. Since lower paid workers, mainly women, alongside the poor, elderly, disabled and migrant populations, serve in essential services' sectors like transportation, teaching, cleaning, hotels and restaurants, policing and others, they bared the harmful consequences more than others [28].

As many businesses turn to an online mode in several sectors and industries, the Covid19 pandemic proved that digital connectivity is crucial for their survival and for social resilience especially during the peak times of the health crisis [29]. Organizations in all sectors are transforming most of their possible physical daily activities digitally to respond to the needs of their customers, patients, citizens and all other beneficiaries in their communities; yet many other companies and businesses were unable to transform their workforce digitally due to the lack of digital infrastructure and due to the shortage of skilled employees who can facilitate the process [30]. It is indicated that while digitalization can reduce human errors, retain customers and jobs and create innovative opportunities, the process might be difficult for many businesses due to limited resources, bureaucratic processes, and deficient commitment from senior administration [31].

The companies that were able to transform many of their physical activities into digital ones were able to save their employees and to serve their customers especially those who face mobility restrictions [32]. E-commerce and telecommuting proved to be very helpful in absorbing the health shock and its economic consequences; the firms that stepped rapidly into the information and communication technologies and have transformed their activities digitally were able to survive and stay in the market. Wang et al. (2021) indicated that the Covid19 pandemic has changed the labor market parameters after the rapid shift to online modes; the investment in human capital digital-skills is now an essential element for the sustainability of the workers and the enterprises [33]. Based on Dell's Digital Transformation Index that surveyed more than 4000 business leaders across the world, it was clear that 80% of the organizations tracked rapidly their digital transformation programs in 2020. The report shows that technology and digitalization is no longer a choice; it is a business strategy that shall be set as part of the strategic planning of every organization, since it can lead to effective collaboration within and between organizations, higher employee innovation and productivity, business growth and job creation [34].

Although digital transformation have a great potential in boosting growth and in preserving jobs and businesses, many countries witnessed network congestion, decline in average internet speed and failing of service quality even in relatively developed markets. In addition to that the unequal access to quality broadband connectivity risked the stability and increased social inequality between those who can use digital connectivity to ensure business continuity and observe social distancing and those who are unable to do so, mainly refugees, the poor and the minorities [35]. According to a report by the International Fund for Agricultural Development, millions of rural families will stay in poverty due to the lack of digital infrastructure; in many rural areas of many countries, people are still living under tough conditions where the access to banking services or mobile connectivity is limited if not impossible. During the pandemic many families stopped receiving the money that usually arrives with migrant workers which made them unable to cover their basic needs such as food, schooling, medical bills, and housing [36].

Based on the above-mentioned literature, it is evident that digitalization; mainly transforming the business activities, where possible, to digital ones is an important element that can smoothen the negative impacts of the pandemic, sustain the businesses and decrease the rate of losing jobs; thus, decreasing the possibility of losing income and entering into poverty.

3 Research Methodology

The main purpose of this paper is to examine the significance and the directional impact of digitalization, measured by the Digital Quality of Life Index, on the percentage change in unemployment rate during the Covid19 pandemic. Furthermore, the paper tests the significance and the directional relationship between the percentage change in unemployment rate and the percentage change in Covid19 annual cases. To achieve the purpose of the paper; a sample of 118 observations for 59 countries was selected. The countries that were considered in the study - are all countries that have DQL index in years 2020, and 2021 since the cyber security Surfshark Company have cancelled few and added others - are Australia, France, Singapore, Norway, Japan, Canada, Denmark, Italy, Sweden, United States, Netherlands, Israel, Switzerland, Spain, United Kingdom, Finland, Germany, New Zealand, Belgium, Austria, Lithuania, Hungary, Portugal, Poland, Russia, Estonia, Slovenia, Ireland, United Arab Emirates, India, Romania, Qatar, Turkey, Slovakia, Mexico, Croatia, Latvia, South Africa, Malaysia, Uruguay, Chile, Czech Republic, Albania, China, Greece, Georgia, Azerbaijan, Philippines, Brazil, Argentina, Armenia, Iran, Morocco, Indonesia, Thailand, Nepal, Pakistan, and Algeria.

The panel data sample included 118 observations for the following variables: the Unemployment rate, Digital Quality of Life Index, Covid19 annual cases, electronic government index, and per capita GDP. The Covid19 annual cases were gathered from the Worldmeter website [37], and the annual observations of the year 2021 were calculated by deducting the total number of the accumulated cases reported on December 31, 2021 from those reported on December 31, 2020. All 2019 cases reported zero values and were not considered in the data set. The Digital Quality of Life Index, developed by the cyber security company Surfshark based in British Virgin Islands, ranks countries based on five fundamental digital well-being pillars: internet affordability, internet quality, electronic infrastructure, electronic security, and electronic government. The Index was first developed in year 2019 and it included 65 countries, then the company removed few countries and added others to calculate the index for a total of 112 countries in 2020 and in 2021. The data on DQL and on the electronic government index were gathered from the homepage of Surfshark [38].

The natural logs were applied to unemployment rates since the change in natural logs are equivalent to percentage change in the variable. Natural logs were also applied to Covid19 cases to linearize the variable as Covid19 cases (count variable) are assumed to follow a power law function [39, 40]. Per capita GDP was calculated by dividing GDP by population and the data on GDP, population and unemployment rate were gathered from the World Bank development indicators [41], Statistica [42], and Macrotrends [43] websites. E-Views software was used to generate the results.

Since the number of observations N (118) is greater than the selected time period for each country T (2), stationarity testing is not an essential pre-requisite [44], thus unit root testing was not performed. Scatter diagrams were generated to provide a preliminary view on the relationship between several variable, especially for the variables that were included in the regression. Descriptive statistics are provided, Ordinary Least Squared method was used to regress the percentage change in unemployment rate on DQL index and on the percentage change in Covid19 annual cases, residual normality, and heteroskedasticity tests were conducted. The Generalized Linear Model was later used to regress unemployment rate on the considered independent variables due to the major reasons: the residuals are not normally distributed, heteroskedasticity was detected and Covid19 cases follow a power law function.

4   Results and Analysis

Box-plots were generated for the considered variables to detect the existence of any outliers; LnU data showed outliers as provided in in Fig. 1 below.

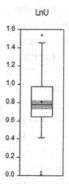

Fig. 1. Box-plot for Ln unemployment

The outliers corresponded to three observations related to South Africa and Thailand and the two countries were removed from the sample data set to avoid high variability and to ensure that the regression results are statistically significant. The scatter diagrams in Fig. 2 below were determined to provide preliminary visual figures to detect the relationship between DQL index and the percentage change in unemployment rate; provided as LnU, as well as between LnCovid19 and LnU.

The first two diagrams concern the mentioned variables and it can be concluded that the plots are inversely scattered for DQL index and LnU while they tend to directly scatter between LnCovid19 and LnU. The third diagram shows that the plots are inversely scattered, thus there is an inverse relationship between electronic government index and LnU. The last diagram clearly presents a direct relationship between DQL index and the per capita GDP.

Table 1 below provides the correlation matrix that was generated to detect any high correlation between any of the considered independent variables. The matrix shows a high correlation between DQL index and the Electronic Government Index since the latter is used to construct DQL along with other variables. Thus Electronic government index will not be used in the regression function. On the other side DQL index and LnCovid19 are not correlated.

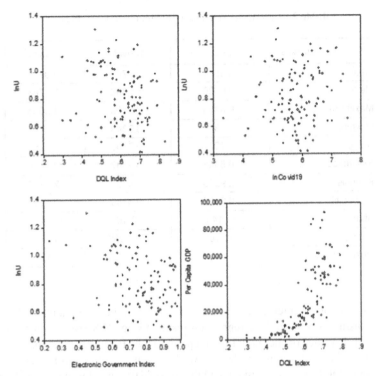

Fig. 2. Scatter diagrams

Table 1. Correlation matrix of exogenous variables.

Correlation Matrix	DQL	LnCovid19	Electronic Government Index
DQL	1	-0.0498	0.8258
LnCovid19	-0.0498	1	0.0521
Electronic Government Index	0.8258	0.0521	1

Descriptive statistics for the three variables that were used in the regression model are provided in Table 2 below. As indicated, the total number of observations considered in the sample is 114, and according to the P-value of the associated Jarque-Bera, all variables are normally distributed with a P-value higher than 5% level of significance.

Since the main purpose of the paper is to determine the partial slope coefficients of DQL index and LnCovid19 and to test their significance in affecting the percentage change in Unemployment rate, the regression function stated in Eq. (1) was regressed using Ordinary Least Squares method.

$$LnU = \beta_1 + \beta_2 DQL\,Index + \beta_3 LnCovid\,19 + u_i \qquad (1)$$

Table 2. Descriptive statistics of the regression variables.

Descriptive Statistics	DQL	LnCovid19	LnU
Mean	0.6064	5.7760	0.8088
Median	0.6200	5.7898	0.7788
Maximum	0.8300	7.5393	1.3055
Minimum	0.30	3.3348	0.4149
Std. Dev.	0.1079	0.7367	0.2052
Skewness	-0.5348	-0.2447	0.1686
Kurtosis	2.9875	3.4702	2.1391
Probability	0.0659	0.3348	0.1313
Sum	69.1400	658.4672	92.2081
Sum Sq. Dev.	1.3169	61.3368	4.7589
Observations	114	114	114

where β_1 is the model intercept, β_2 and β_3 are partial slope coefficients and u_i is the stochastic disturbance term. The regression results using OLS are presented in Table 3 below. The P-values of the model intercept and DQL Index partial slope coefficient are lower than the 5% level of significance while that of LnCovid19 is higher. Thus, the intercept and DQL Index are significant while LnCovid19 is not. Furthermore, the partial slope of DQL index is negative indicating an inverse relationship between DQL index and LnU. The Overall model is significant with an F-Statistic corresponding P-value of 0.0077 which is lower than 5% level of significance. R^2 is 8.3% indicating that 8.3% of the variation in LnU is due to the variation in DQL index. The value of R^2 is low indicating that other structural and cyclical variables like GDP, healthcare insurance, government intervention, etc. can be added to the equation to explain the variation in the unemployment rate. This is to note that the unemployment rate is a structural and cyclical variable, while DQL index is a structural variable, measuring the long-term investment in digitalization, and that Covid19 annual cases' is a circumstantial one [45].

The normality of residuals was also checked taking into consideration that the null hypothesis states that residuals are normally distributed. The P-value of the Jarque-Bera, that is 0.2161 appeared to be greater than 5% level of significance, which provides enough evidence to retain the null hypothesis. The heteroskedasticity test couldn't not be carried out due to near singular matrix error although DQL and LnCovid19 are not correlated. The auxiliary regressions between DQL and LnCovid19 were performed and the coefficients are insignificant. As a result, the constant term in the equation was dropped and heteroskedasticity was evident with a P-value of 0.0010 which is lower than 5% level of significance. The null hypothesis is rejected, and the problem of heteroskedasticity exists.

The Generalized Linear Model (GLM), which assumes homoscedasticity, allows for different error distributions and permits the dependent variable to have different relationships with the independent variables [46]. Since the residuals in the previously

Table 3. Regression results using OLS

Regression Results using Panel Least Squares			
Dependent Variable: LnU (2 periods and 57 cross-sections)			
Variable	Coefficient	Std. Error	P-value
C	0.9816	0.1851	0
DQL	-0.5165	0.1729	0.0035
LnCovid19	0.0243	0.0253	0.3394
R-squared	0.0838	Mean dependent var	0.809
Adjusted R-squared	0.0673	S.D. dependent var	0.205
S.E. of regression	0.1981	Akaike info criterion	-0.373
Sum squared resid	4.3600	Schwarz criterion	-0.301
Log likelihood	24.2722	Hannan-Quinn criterion	-0.344
F-statistic	5.0770	Durbin-Watson stat	0.591
Prob(F-statistic)	0.0077	Total Panel	114

regressed model are not normally distributed, and since the problem of heteroskedasticity was detected, the paper utilizes the GLM [47] to regress LnU on the considered independent variables. The GLM regression results are provided in Table 4 below.

The P-values of the model intercept and DQL Index partial slope coefficient are lower than the 5% level of significance while that of LnCovid19 remains higher. Thus, the intercept and DQL Index are significant while LnCovid19 is not. Furthermore, the partial slope of DQL index is negative indicating an inverse relationship between DQL index and lnU; as DQL index increases by 1 point on average, the percentage change in the unemployment rate decreases by 0.516 points.

Regarding the Likelihood ratio test, the null hypothesis sates that there is no difference between the full and reduced model, while the alternative hypothesis states that the full model is better. With P-value of 0.0062 for the LR statistic indicates that the null hypothesis is rejected at the level of significance of 5% and that additional variable(s) should be added to increase the predictive power of the model.

The regression results presented in Table 4 indicate that digitalization including internet affordability, internet quality, e-infrastructure, e-security, and e-government is a determinant factor that leads to lower surges in unemployment rate during shocks like the Covid-19 pandemic. Countries with higher Digital Quality of Life index can better respond to lockdowns and health control measures by shifting to online operations and hence preventing people from losing their jobs. Digital transformation became vital for all the sectors of the economy especially after the pandemic. The rise of digital currencies, digital technologies, and digital innovation are changing business processes, products and services and are driving business leaders to restructure their operations and their business relationships [48]. Thus, the future of the economies is expected to

Table 4. Regression results using GLM.

Regression Results using Generalized Linear Model (Newton-Raphson / Marquardt steps)			
Dependent Variable: LnU			
Variable	Coefficient	Std. Error	P-value
C	0.9816	0.1851	0
DQL	-0.5165	0.1729	0.0028
LnCovid19	0.0243	0.0253	0.3373
Mean dependent var	0.8088	S.D. dependent var	0.2052
Sum squared resid	4.36	Log likelihood	24.2521
Akaike info criterion	-0.3728	Schwarz criterion	-0.3008
Hannan-Quinn criter.	-0.3436	Deviance	4.36
Deviance statistic	0.0392	Restr. deviance	4.7589
LR statistic	10.154	Prob (LR statistic)	0.0062
Pearson SSR	4.36	Pearson statistic	0.0392
Dispersion	0.0392	Total Panel	114

follow the digital trend where international cooperation for regulating digital relations and digital operations is urged to guarantee efficient global macroeconomic results [49].

5   Conclusion

Covid19 pandemic is a health shock that hit the world during the last quarter of 2019 and outbreak in 2020 while endangering the lives of millions. The negative consequences of the Covid19 pandemic were plentiful; millions of people lost their jobs, and millions entered into poverty levels. The official measures undertaken by the authorities in most of the countries of the world to contain the virus, threatened the existence of the businesses and have led to many shutdowns. For many businesses, shifting to online modes and digitalizing their daily activities where possible was a needed action to ensure their survival. This paper succeeded in providing evidence on the significance and the inverse effects of the Digital Quality of Life index on the change in unemployment rate but it failed to prove that the percentage change in Covid19 cases directly affect the percentage change in the unemployment rate.

United Arab Emirates, Sweden, Denmark, Qatar and Norway were the top five countries with the most developed E-infrastructure, the highest DQL index [38], and with high Human Development index values in 2020 [50], while Nigeria, Nepal, Bangladesh, Kenya and Pakistan were the last five countries with the least developed E-infrastructure, the lowest DQL index, and with low Human Development index in the same year. This helps in explaining how the Covid19 health shock differently impacted the countries of the world; for example, Denmark was able to bring unemployment rate from 5.66% in

2020 to 3.1% in 2021, while Pakistan's unemployment rate increased by around 1% in 2021 [41].

The paper's results open the door for public and private sectors to set and activate predictive plans to absorb any unexpected future shocks by incorporating digital transformation into daily activities and business strategies. Furthermore, countries that are facing lack of digital infrastructure should invest more resources in the sector to prevent businesses and their citizens from the negative effects of similar future and unexpected shocks.

References

1. OECD: Digital Transformation in the age of Covid 19. https://www.oecd.org/digital/digital-economy-outlook-covid.pdf (2020). Last accessed 5 Dec 2021
2. Jackson, J., Weiss, M., Schwarzenberg, A., Nelson, R., Sutter, K., Sutherland, M.: Global Economic Effects of Covid-19. Congressional Research Service Report, Library of Congress (2021)
3. Mou, J.: Research on the impact of Covid-19 on global economy. IOP Conf.: Earth Environ. Sci. Ser. **546**, 032043 (2020)
4. Xiang, S., Rasool, S., Hang, Y., Javid, K., Javed, T., Artene, A.E.: The effect of COVID-19 pandemic on service sector sustainability and growth. Front. Psychol. **12**, 633597 (2021). https://doi.org/10.3389/fpsyg.2021.633597. Last accessed 8 Dec 2021
5. Cénat, J.M., Dalexis, R.D., Kokou-Kpolou, C.K., Mukunzi, J.N., Rousseau, C.: Social inequalities and collateral damages of the COVID-19 pandemic: when basic needs challenge mental health care. Int. J. Public Health **65**, 717–718 (2020)
6. Melhem, S., Carugati, A., Jackobsen, A., Cassabgui, J., Khanji, T., Khoury, Z.: Shaping the Future of Work: Three Challenges for SMART work transformation in the Post Covid-19 era (2021). https://blogs.worldbank.org/digital-development/shaping-future-work-three-challenges-smart-work-transformation-post-covid-19. Last accessed 1 Jan 2022
7. Morudu, P., Kollamparambil, U.: Health shocks, medical insurance and household vulnerability: evidence from South Africa. PLoS ONE **15**(2), e0228034 (2020). https://doi.org/10.1371/journal.pone.0228034
8. Hanna, D., Huang, Y.: The Impact of SARS on Asian Economies. Asian Econ. Papers **3**, 102–112 (2004)
9. Islam, A., Parasnis, J.: Heterogeneous Effects of Health Shocks in Developed Countries: Evidence from Australia. Monash Business School, Australia (2017)
10. Brown, K., Richard, M., Smith, R.: The economic impact of SARS: how does the reality match the predictions? Health Policy **88**(1), 110–120 (2008)
11. Lee, G., Warner, M.: Unemployment: the impact of the SARS epidemic on the service sector in Singapore. Asian Pac. Bus. Rev. **12**, 507–527 (2007)
12. Lenhart, O.: The effects of health shocks on labor market outcomes: evidence from UK panel data. Eur. J. Health Econ. **20**(1), 83–98 (2018)
13. Aleksandrova, E., Bagranova, V., Gerry, C.: The effect of health shocks on labour market outcomes in Russia. Camb. J. Econ. **45**, 1319–1336 (2021)
14. Mein, S.A.: COVID-19 and health disparities: the reality of "the great equalizer." J. Gen. Intern. Med. **35**, 2439–2440 (2020)
15. Singh, B., Chattu, V.K.: Prioritizing 'equity' in COVID-19 vaccine distribution through Global Health Diplomacy. Health Promot. Perspect. **11**(3), 281–287 (2021)

16. Jones, B., Jones, J.: Gov. Cuomo is wrong; covid-19 is anything but an equalizer Washington Post. https://www.washingtonpost.com/outlook/2020/04/05/gov-cuomo-is-wrong-covid-19-is-anything-an-equalizer/ (2020). Last accessed 20 Dec 2021

17. Azzam, A.-R., Ibrahim, D.: Analysis of mobility trends during the COVID-19 coronavirus pandemic: exploring the impacts on global aviation and travel in selected cities. Energy Res. Soc. Sci. **68**, 101693 (2020)

18. Al-Fadly, A.: Impact of COVID-19 on SMEs and employment. Entrepreneurship Sustain. Issues **8**(2), 629–648 (2020)

19. Uvarova, E., Pobol, P.: SMEs Digital Transformation in the EaP countries in COVID-19 Time: Challenges and Digital Solutions. https://eap-csf.eu/wp-content/uploads/SMEs-digital-transf ormation-in-the-EaP-countries-during-COVID-19.pdf (2021). Last accessed 28 Dec 2021

20. World Economic Forum Homepage (2021). https://www.weforum.org/agenda/2021/07/pan demic-damaged-youth-employment/. Last accessed 22 Dec 2021

21. AARP Homepage (2021). https://www.aarp.org/work/job-search/info-2020/job-losses-dur ing-covid.html. Last accessed 4 Jan 2021

22. Thebault, R., Tran, A., Williams, V.: African Americans are the higher risk of deaths from coronavirus, The Washington Post. https://www.washingtonpost.com/nation/2020/04/07/cor onavirus-is-infecting-killing-black-americans-an-alarmingly-high-rate-post-analysis-shows/ (2020). Last accessed 22 Dec 2021

23. Christian, S.C., Alexander, L., Tomás, C.: Cause for concerns: gender inequality in experiencing the COVID-19 lockdown in Germany. Eur. Soc. J. **23**, 68–81 (2020)

24. Dang, H.-A.H., Nguyen, C.V.: Gender inequality during the COVID-19 pandemic: Income, expenditure, savings, and job loss. World Dev. **140**, 105296 (2021). https://doi.org/10.1016/j.worlddev.2020.105296

25. Pereira, M., Oliveira, A.M.: Poverty and food insecurity may increase as the threat of COVID-19 spreads. Public Health Nutr. **23**(17), 3236–3240 (2020)

26. Niles, M.T., Bertmann, F., Belarmino, E.H., Wentworth, T., Biehl, E., Neff, R.: The early food insecurity impacts of COVID-19. Nutrients **12**, 2096 (2020)

27. Emon, E.K.H., Alif, A.R., Shahanul Islam, M.: Impact of COVID-19 on the institutional education system and its associated students in Bangladesh. Asian J. Educ. Soc. Stud. **11**(2), 34–46 (2020)

28. World Economic Forum Homepage (2020). https://www.weforum.org/agenda/2020/12/cov id19-education-innovation-outcomes/. Last accessed 2 Jan 2022

29. Strusani, D., Houngbonon, G.V.: What COVID-19 Means for Digital Infrastructure in Emerging Markets. EMCompass; No. 83. International Finance Corporation, Washington, DC. https://openknowledge.worldbank.org/handle/10986/34306 (2020). License: CC BY-NC-ND 3.0 IGO, Last accessed 18 Dec 2021

30. Version 1: The importance of Digital Transformation During Covd-19 (2021). https://www.version1.com/blog-digital-transformation-covid-19/. Last accessed 13 Dec 2021

31. Amankwah-Amoah, J., Khan, Z., Wood, G., Knight, G.: Covid-19 and digitalization: the great acceleration. J. Bus. Res. **136**, 602–611 (2021)

32. Baig, A., Hall, B., Jenkins, P., Lamarre, E., McCarthy, B.: The covid-19 recovery will be digital: A plan for the first 90 days (2020). https://www.mckinsey.com/business-functions/mckinsey-digital/our-insights/the-covid-19-recovery-will-be-digital-a-plan-for-the-first-90-days. Last accessed 11 Dec 2021

33. Wang, B., Liu, Y., Qian, J., Parker, S.K.: Achieving effective remote working during the COVID-19 pandemic: a work design perspective. Appl. Psychol. **70**, 16–59 (2021)

34. Cooper, Z.: Five reasons why digital transformation is essential for business growth. https://www.itpro.co.uk/strategy/29899/three-reasons-why-digital-transformation-is-essential-for-business-growth (2021). Last accessed 7 Dec 2021

35. Guermazi, B.: Digital Transformation in the time of COVID-19: the case of MENA. https://blogs.worldbank.org/arabvoices/digital-transformation-time-covid-19-case-mena (2020). Last accessed 19 Dec 2021

36. International Fund for Agricultural Development Homepage: https://www.ifad.org/en/covid19. Last accessed 5 Jan 2022

37. Worldometer Homepage: https://www.worldometers.info/coronavirus/. Last accessed 31 Dec 2021

38. Surfshark Homepage. https://www.surfshark.com/. Last accessed 10 Dec 2021

39. Blasius, B.: Power-law distribution in the number of confirmed COVID-19 cases. https://www.ncbi.nlm.nih.gov/pmc/articles/PMC7519452/ (2020). Last accessed 5 Jan 2022

40. World Bank Development Indicators Homepage: https://databank.worldbank.org/source/world-development-indicators. Last accessed 7 Dec 2021

41. Statistica Homepage: https://www.statista.com/. Last accessed 23 Dec 2021

42. Macrotrends Homepage: https://www.macrotrends.net/. Last accessed 14 Dec 2021

43. Baltagi, B.: Econometric Analysis of Panel Data, 4th edn. Wiley, USA (2008)

44. Wei, M.: Social distancing and lockdown - an introvert's paradise? an empirical investigation on the association between introversion and the psychological impact of COVID19-related circumstantial changes. Front. Psychol. J. 11, 561609 (2020)

45. Brouste, A.: Generalized linear model. https://www.sciencedirect.com/topics/economics-econometrics-and-finance/generalized-linear-model (2018). Last accessed 5 Jan 2022

46. Kundu, A.: What is so general about generalized linear model? https://towardsdatascience.com/what-is-so-general-about-generalized-linear-model-15dde9be2640 (2021). Last accessed 5 Jan 2022

47. Vasconcelos, G., Macedo, A., Filho, G., Brum, A., Ospina, R., Almeida, F.: Power law behaviour in the saturation regime of fatality curves of the covid-19 pandemic. Sci. Rep. 11, 4619 (2021). https://doi.org/10.1038/s41598-021-84165-1

48. Hai, T.N., Van, Q.N., Tuyet, M.N.T.: Digital transformation: opportunities and challenges for leaders in the emerging countries in response to COVID-19 pandemic. Emerg. Sci. J. 5, 21–36 (2021)

49. Brynjolfsson, E., McAfee, A.: Race against the machine: How the digital revolution is accelerating innovation, driving productivity, and irreversibly transforming employment and the economy (2011)

50. Human Development Report Homepage: https://hdr.undp.org/. Last accessed 8 Jan 2022

Digital Gender Gap in EU-27 ICT Employment During COVID-19 Impact

Barbara Pisker , Mirjana Radman-Funarić , and Kristian Dokic(✉)

Polytechnic in Pozega, 34000 Pozega, Croatia
{bpisker,radmanfunaric,kdjokic}@vup.hr

Abstract. This paper focuses on the impact of the COVID-19 pandemic on ICT sector employment through the prism of digital gender gap divide change in 2020 as a comparative analysis of EU-27 country's performance. The paper aims to examine the share of employed women and men ICT professionals in total employment in the ICT sector, aged 15 to 74, from 2011 to 2020 in the EU-27, highlighting annual national disparities in the 2020 pandemic year. The standard deviations (Z-score) and percentage deviations of the European Union countries from the EU-27 average in 2020 were calculated. The data used for the analysis have been obtained from Eurostat (2021): Employed ICT specialists by sex.

The analysis results show that in the pandemic 2020, the deviation of women's employment in the ICT sector of the EU-27 from the EU-27 average ranges from 2.4 σ to -1.6 σ. The deviation of employed men in the ICT sector from the EU-27 average is in the same range but opposite.

Peak differences and their causes have been explained. Conclusively, limitations and further research orientations within the wider topic frame are elaborated.

Keywords: Digital gender gap · ICT employment · European union · COVID-19

1 Introduction

The early 2020 outbreak of the COVID-19 pandemic has brought about years of change in the ubiquity of digitization. How our lives have changed has not left space untouched, including all business sectors in all world regions. According to the McKinsey Global Survey, business companies have accelerated the digitization of their customer interactions, supply chain and internal operations in three to four years. The share of digital or digitally enabled products in their portfolios has accelerated almost twice as fast: in a shocking seven years [1].

Besides the digital acceleration, the pandemic outbreak also exposed and further reinforced our existing traditional divides between north and south, east and west, developed and underdeveloped, rich and poor, transforming them into connected and disconnected. Various social, cultural and individual modifications in the frequency of ICT presence worldwide have been defined through the term digital divide (inequalities in access, capacity to use and ways of engaging with ICTs) throughout the research literature.

© The Author(s), under exclusive license to Springer Nature Switzerland AG 2022
M. A. Bach Tobji et al. (Eds.): ICDEc 2022, LNBIP 461, pp. 16–32, 2022.
https://doi.org/10.1007/978-3-031-17037-9_2

The digital divide problem appears as an obvious obstacle, a measurable gap between different areas of ICT implementation, integration, use, education, and employment availability for other social groups. The gap in prosperity between those who have access to ICT and the digitally excluded, if not corrected, will further widen and thus increase inequalities in all other social inclusion areas, resulting in even more significant societal deviations. The digital gender gap has been under European Commission policy closer loop recently due to EUs "Digital Compass: the European way for the Digital Decade" [2] and "Path to the Digital Decade" [3] enabling complex, structured, multilevel approach in achieving digital societal transformation in EU. Among numerous tools Digital Economy and Society Index (DESI) specific area Women in Digital Scoreboard [4] aims to place focus on woman's path in digital environments indicating how persisting extensive underrepresentation of women in digital indicators is present across EU-27 countries with only 19% of women ICT specialist whose role in digital transition acceleration is of the most importance. Digital Compass, therefore, set a target of gender balance (convergence) in ICT specialists by 2030 [2].

The main focus of this research paper is to investigate the digital gender gap between employed women and men ICT specialists, as defined by the ISCO-08 classification and including jobs like ICT service managers, ICT professionals, ICT technicians, ICT installers and servicers in the total number of employees in the ICT sector, aged 15 to 74, from 2011 to 2020 in the EU-27, highlighting annual national differences in the pandemic year 2020.

2 Literature Review

In a recent information society [5], digitalization is undeniably a total social fact [6] Its power, embedded in a technological process as a fundamental societal developmental driver, transforms the world as we know it at the speed of a mouse click. Global socio-economic stakes of digital social transformation reinforced by a COVID-19 pandemic outbreak are dizzyingly high while provoking further enforcements of inherited societal gaps (demographic and climate change, environmental degradation and social inequality growth) defined as a digital divide [7].

The digital divide is a part of the wide topic of social inequality placed in a focus of a contemporary society due to its rapid technological progress upon all other parts of today's existence lay upon. The digital divide of today can reinforce and build upon traditionally existing poles rooted in several fundamental aspects: economic resources availability, geographical distinction between urban and rural, inter-generational approach obstacles where elderly are subordinated, gender where women are severely underrepresented and suppressed, language obstacles due to the predominance of English language in ICT service and industry, educational achievement and long-life learning opportunities, social and cultural environment and support, employment rate and other forms of social exclusions (as minority, invalidity, ethnicity, religion, race, class, socially excluded and underrepresented groups). All of the above factors (or their multi-combination) can be understood as a source, cause and consequence of unequal digital attainability, reinforcing and deepening further socio-economic divisions and discrepancies [8].

2.1   Overall Frame and Literature Inputs

The term digital gender gap itself is identified when women access and use ICTs less than men, thus exacerbating and widening further gender inequalities [9] Gender characteristics of the digital divide have been of a wider interest lately due to socio-economic and demographic specificities with the exponential growth of the ICT sector worldwide as authors reinvent empowering forces of women's presence in the ICT sector [10–12] Gender bias has been often masked in the traditional binary legacy of established social norms, statuses, roles and prejudices. Mainstream was thou gender blindness as a tool for the maintenance of male privilege [13, 14], reinforcing and supporting further deeply rooted social structure of gender bias through gender pay gap and glass ceiling existence [15–19].

Berger and Luckmann, in a theory of social constructionism, explained the essence of the existing gender gap in a contemporary digitalized society considering social systems as based on interaction. Eventually, interactions develop into accustomed norms and roles while they become institutionalized and embedded in society as standardized terms of cultural expectations. Therefore, the social construction perspective could contribute to understanding cross-cultural variation in social gender roles and expectations, including the digital gender gap [20] Additionally, Crenshaw interprets gender norms in societies through intersectional theory, in which she discusses the multidimensional experience and identities as fluid and susceptible to changes through microcultural frames present [21] Cultural differences, as explained by Hofstede (2001) who has provided a powerful tool for cultural comparisons in defining culture as the "collective programming of the mind which distinguishes the members of one group from the other' and helps in understanding the difference between national cultures" can be a starting point in understanding the digital gender gap in EU-27 ICT employment [22].

UN's sustainable development goals empowered in 2016 set targets for goal 5 to achieve gender equality and empower women as a necessary foundation for a peaceful, prosperous and sustainable world by 2030. Latest reports show limited progress that has been made is now endangered due to the COVID-19 pandemic, while structural gender inequalities have been further amplified [23, 24].

Although the EU can be seen as a world leader in its dedication to gender equality, the Strategy 2020–2025 proves complete balance equilibrium is still a goal to be reached in numerous spheres of digitalized social life [25] Focusing closely on recent EU-27 policy development as a response toward pandemic outbreak relevant research have shown negative trends overspill towards women labour force in general, followed by a drastic gender gap widening, especially in female-dominated occupational sectors, while delicate growth of women appearance in traditionally male-dominated sectors, especially ICT has risen, although this result needs to be taken into consideration precisely as a direct result of enlarged e-services usage in all sectors due to the pandemic restrictions. Additionally, "women were more at risk of financial fragility than men, with 58% of women (compared with 48% of men) reporting that they would not be able to maintain the same standard of living" during the pandemic outbreak [26] Overall, long-term consequences consequently will trigger women harder than man, while attracting women to ICT is a matter of socio-economic developmental frames related to broad industry deficiencies [27] European Institute for Gender Equality (EIGE) has estimated benefits of woman's full and equal participation in STEM sector could contribute towards 820 billion EUR GDP and 1.2 million more jobs in EU-27 by 2050 [28], additionally slowing down the odds for EU the keep up the leading societies in the world digital primacy [29].

Numerous studies have shown how crises generally change priorities [30], while reductions consequently reinforce the gender gap widening, as shown in Greece, Korea and Turkey [31–33] The study conducted by Jaba, E., et al. (2021) proved that the crisis influenced the employment gender gap in the EU, reviling overall convergence, with significant variation among regions and depending on educational level [34].

Socio-economic consequences regarding the digital gender gap are numerous and diverse. They include women's exclusion from higher-paid jobs, access to knowledge, skills and information, quality and diversity of products with limitations to creative potential, reduction of ideas and innovation, ability to spread their influence wide and affect developmental and policy-shaping, lack of authority. Gender biased practices lack competitiveness and are unable to supply labour markets in demand for qualified specialists as the potential of more than half of the population is unused [35–37]. Further on, as shown by Ferrant & Kolev (2016), the income loss associated with the gender gap amounts to USD 12 trillion, or 16% of global world income [38].

Reports of tiny improvements on women's progress in ICT sector have been shattered by proven declining trends throughout Western and Northern EU countries in a couple of last decades [39] provoked by women's need for flexibility in work-life balance [40], especially for women with children [41] is partly explained through the leaky pipeline theory [42] Occupational preferences related to gender thou, are confirmed to be culture influenced and different throughout the world [43] In research analyses from China, India, Saudi Arabia and Malaysia [44, 45] where indoors working spaces (including ICT sector) are prescribed as female [19], confirming Hofstede's cultural theory.

Thinking in terms of wellbeing and Sustainability, out of the growth and profit box in ICT as a new developmental driver towards degrowth and environmental transformation [46] with ICT in a critical transformative role in bridging the digital gender gap is essential [47] to avoid the transformative process of female perspective deprivation in this equity paradox as women indeed represent over half of the total population. Enabling full population potential can undoubtedly lead to fair digital societies of tomorrow overcoming contemporary, binary stereotypes.

Additionally, ICTs are seen as a cornerstone of further socio-economic and environmental transformation toward sustainable development goals [48, 49], although it may not be seen as a magic wand but need careful planning, implementation, monitoring and cross-cultural adaptation [50, 51].

2.2 Characteristics and Employment Trends in the EU-27 ICT Sector

UN Policy Brief on COVID-19 Impact on Women exposed emerging evidence on women's socio-economic lives and participation during pandemic breakdown. Women are being affected disproportionately and differently than men as their capacities to absorb socio-economic shocks are less than men. Women traditionally take on greater care demands at unpaid home labour, so cuts and layoffs will affect their jobs. Such impacts risk rolling back the fragile gains made in female labour force participation throughout different employment sectors, including ICT [52].

According to Eurostat's (2021) data, overall employment in the ICT sector in EU-27 countries is increasing annually. The absolute increase of employed persons with ICT education is shown in Fig. 1.

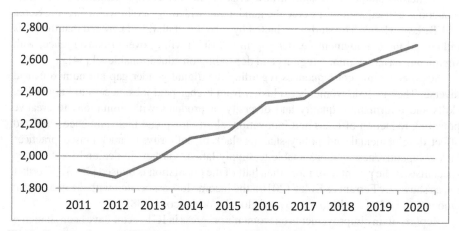

Fig. 1. Employed persons with ICT education in EU-27 2011–2020, in thousand. Source: Authors according to Eurostat (2021)

Calculated absolute and relative rates of change show an increase in total employment (men and women) with ICT education in EU-27 from 2012. The average increase from 2012 until 2020 amounts to 4.72% annually. To examine whether the pandemic year 2020, due to greater use of digital technology, increased employees with ICT education, relative changes in the number of employees from year to year were calculated, i.e. the

Table 1. EU-27 ICT employment 2011 until 2020

Year	Employed persons with ICT education in 000	Absolute rates of change in 000	Relative rates of change, %
2011	1.913,0	–	
2012	1.868,5	−45	−2,33
2013	1.971,2	103	5,50
2014	2.116,5	145	7,37
2015	2.158,9	42	2,00
2016	2.338,7	180	8,33
2017	2.367,2	29	1,22
2018	2.527,6	160	6,78
2019	2.622,4	95	3,75
2020	2.703,0	81	3,07

Source: Authors according to Eurostat (2021)

dynamics of change are shown (Table 1). The most significant annual increase is evident in 2014, 2016 and 2018 compared to the previous year. The growing linear trend shown in Fig. 1 and the dynamics of change in the number of employees shown in Table 1 from 2012 do not offer a more considerable increase in 2020 compared to the previous year's annual growth.

Female ICT specialist employment in 2020 is the same as in previous years, amounting to less than 20% of overall ICT specialist employment. Exceptions are evident in Denmark (32.9%), Greece (30.6%), Cyprus (27.5%), Bulgaria (27.4%), Romania (27.0%), Sweden (24.5%), Ireland (23.2%), Spain (20.9%) and Lithuania (20.7%) as shown in Fig. 2.

The trend in EU-27 was more deeply presented in a research paper by Pisker, Radman-Funarić, and Sudarić [53]. Pandemic 2020 did not provoke significant changes

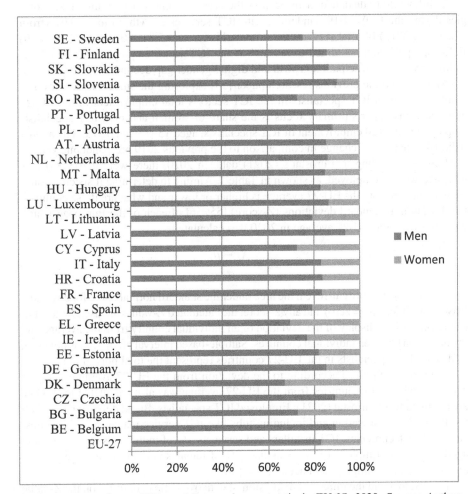

Fig. 2. Women and men ICT specialist employment ratio in EU-27, 2020. Source: Authors according to Eurostat (2021)

in the ratio of employed men and women ICT specialists, i.e. the employment of men still follows the default trend keeping men employment in the sector 4 to 5 times higher than the employment of women.

3   Data and Methodology

In the first step, the paper analyses the annual dynamics of ICT specialists' employment change in the 2020 pandemic and 2019 pre-pandemic year, aiming to determine if the overall employment increase dynamics have scaled up.

Secondly, besides the overall dynamics of change, the paper also analyses if there has happened a gender conditioned change in the ratio of women and men ICT specialists employed in EU-27 countries and their national specificities.

Third, world trade data dynamics show the growing importance of digital technologies during the COVID-19 pandemic, with ICT services growth up to 14,97% (from 12,51% in 2019) of total services exports worldwide and 5,34% (from 4,1% in 2019) in Europe [54], authors aimed to research if the ICT sector employment demand has followed women participation growth and digital gender gap decline.

Modelled on the previous research paper [53] exploring the share and deviation of employed women ICT specialists in the ICT sector's total employment in the EU-27 countries, this paper's primary focus is the share of women and men ICT specialists employed in the full employment of ICT specialists, aged 15–74, in 2020 and its annual national dynamics of change in comparison to the previous 2019 pre-pandemic year.

Fourth, according to Eurostat's (2021) data, in 2020, there were 2.703.000 ICT educated women employed, as shown in Table 1. Aiming to determine if specific countries' deviation from the EU-27 average is higher or lower and what are those countries the deviation in standard deviations (Z-score) [55, 56] of each of the European Union countries from the EU-27 average in 2020 was calculated.

$$Z_i = \frac{X_i - \mu}{\sigma} \tag{1}$$

Besides the Z-score can reveal the area under the standard normal curve for any value between the mean ($\sigma =$ zero) and any z-score, the calculated Z-values are used for a better (more accessible) display of the deviation of an individual country from the average and the deviation between individual countries. Sample-based interval prediction is not used, as data on ICT specialists in the EU-27 countries represent the total population.

Countries are ranked according to the deviation from the EU-27 average. The percentage deviation of countries from the EU-27 average was also calculated [57]. Data are obtained from Eurostat (2021): Employed ICT specialists. Broad definition based on the ISCO-08 classification and including jobs like ICT service managers, ICT professionals, ICT technicians, ICT installers and servicers - % of individuals in employment aged 15–74, and Employed ICT specialists - % of females in employment aged 15–74 and % of males in employment aged 15–74 [58].

Finally, to avoid the impact of dispersion of data from other countries on the Z-value of each country, we calculated the change in the percentage of employed women in the ICT sector, with the mean and standard deviation calculated for 2011–2019 for that country. We expressed this change as Z values, and we observed whether a difference greater than one or two standard deviations in both directions was present in the pandemic year.

4   Result and Discussion

The average deviation of the EU-27 countries from the EU-27 average in the employment of women ICT specialists is 6.68 p.p., calculated by geometric mean [56] Although the average deviations of women and men ICT specialists' employment 2020 data compared to 2019 show a significant similarity in the deviation ICT specialist of the EU-27 countries from the average, observing the EU-27 countries individually, numerous national differences are evident from country to country and by gender as shown in Fig. 3.

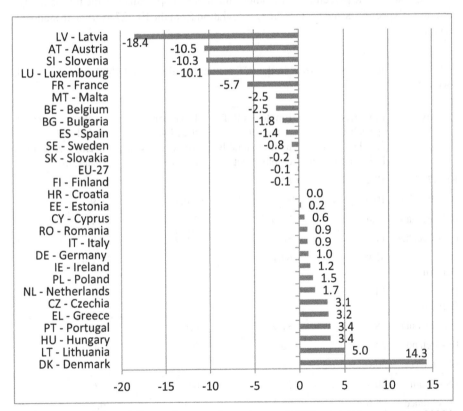

Fig. 3. Women ICT specialist employment change in overall ICT specialist employment 2020 in regards to 2019. in p.p. Source: Authors according to Eurostat (2021)

Women ICT specialist employment in 2020 in overall ICT specialist employment has fallen compared to 2019 by 0.1 percentage points. Latvia has recorded the most significant decline with a drop of 18.4 percentage points (down from 24.8% to 6.4%).

Austria, Slovenia and Luxembourg recorded a drop of about ten percentage points, and France by 5.7 percentage points. The most significant increase in women ICT specialist employment in 2020 is present in Denmark, 14.3 p.p., followed by Lithuania with five p.p. Other countries record minor changes, except Croatia, where the number of employed women ICT specialists has not changed. It is essential also to emphasize how each percentage point of change in the employment of women ICT specialists represents a change in male ICT specialists with the opposite sign.

Unlike the previous analysis, which shows the percentage change in the employment of ICT female specialists in 2020 compared to 2019 in each EU-27 country, the following shows the percentage of employed women and men ICT specialists in the total population of ICT specialists in 2020. From these data, the deviation of each country from the EU-27 average was calculated. The deviation was calculated in standard deviations to illustrate the deviation from the normal Gaussian distribution.

Table 2 shows the percentage of women and men ICT specialists in the total employment of ICT specialists and each country's deviation from the EU-27 average in standard deviations.

Table 2. Share of women employed in the ICT sector, deviation from EU-27 average in 2020, Z-score, in σ

Country	Employed ICT specialists - % of females in total ICT employment	Employed ICT specialists - % of males in total ICT employment	Deviation from the EU-27 average, Z-score, females, in σ	Deviation from the EU-27 average, Z-score, males, in σ
EU-27	**17,2**	**82,8**		
BE - Belgium	10,9	89,1	−0,9	0,9
BG - Bulgaria	27,4	72,6	1,5	−1,5
CZ - Czechia	11,1	88,9	−0,9	0,9
DK - Denmark	32,9	67,1	2,4	−2,4
DE - Germany	14,8	85,2	−0,4	0,4
EE - Estonia	18,1	81,9	0,1	−0,1
IE - Ireland	23,2	76,8	0,9	−0,9
EL - Greece	30,6	69,4	2,0	−2,0
ES - Spain	20,9	79,1	0,6	−0,6
FR - France	16,6	83,4	−0,1	0,1
HR - Croatia	16,4	83,6	−0,1	0,1
IT - Italy	16,9	83,1	0,0	0,0

(continued)

Table 2. (*continued*)

CY - Cyprus	27,5	72,5	1,5	−1,5
LV - Latvia	6,4	93,6	−1,6	1,6
LT - Lithuania	20,7	79,3	0,5	−0,5
LU - Luxembourg	13,5	86,5	−0,6	0,6
HU - Hungary	17,1	82,9	0,0	0,0
MT - Malta	15,0	85,0	−0,3	0,3
NL - Netherlands	13,9	86,1	−0,5	0,5
AT - Austria	14,5	85,5	−0,4	0,4
PL - Poland	11,7	88,3	−0,8	0,8
PT - Portugal	19,0	81,0	0,3	−0,3
RO - Romania	27,0	73,0	1,5	−1,5
SI - Slovenia	9,7	90,3	−1,1	1,1
SK - Slovakia	13,2	86,8	−0,6	0,6
FI - Finland	14,1	85,9	−0,5	0,5
SE - Sweden	24,5	75,5	1,1	−1,1

Source: Authors according to Eurostat (2021)

Results presented in Table 2 show that in 2020 the deviation of women's employment in the ICT sector of the EU-27 from the EU-27 average ranges from 2.4 σ in Denmark to -1.6 σ in Latvia. The deviation of employed men in the ICT sector from the EU-27 average is in the same range, but in the opposite direction, in Latvia, 1.6 σ to -2.4 σ in Denmark.

Although statistically, there is no significant gap between EU-27 countries in the employment of women with ICT education in Denmark, women's employment is almost twice as high as the average, precisely 2.4 σ, and the employment of men is lower than the EU −27 average by 2.4 σ. The employment of women with ICT education in Latvia is 2.67 times lower than the EU-27 average (−1.6 σ), and it is more than five times lower than that of women in Denmark. From these results arises the need and guidance for further examination: what are the significance and the effects of explanatory variables that contribute to widening the gender gap, whether the result is in favour of women or men, as shown by the differences in Denmark in favour of women and Latvia in benefit men (Fig. 4).

When observing the discrepancies between men and women in ICT sector employment in a specific EU-27 country, it is noticeable that men employees considerably positively deviate from the EU-27 average, and women negatively in Latvia, Slovenia,

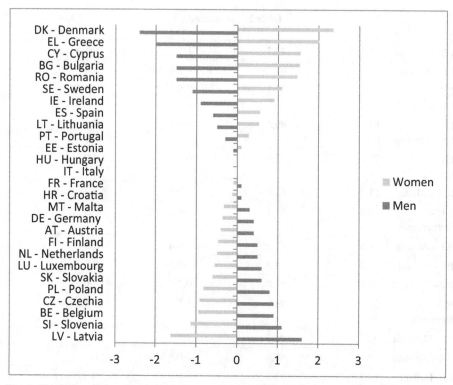

Fig. 4. Deviation of the share of women and men employed in the ICT sector from the EU-27 average, 2020 in σ. Source: Authors according to Eurostat (2021)

Belgium and Czechia. Women ICT employees in the ICT sector deviate positively from the EU-27 average (while man ICT employees notably negatively deviate) in Denmark, Greece, Cyprus, Bulgaria, Romania, Sweden, and Ireland. Although the share of women ICT specialists is significantly lower than men, the analysis of deviations of countries from the EU-27 average shows that in a larger number of countries, women deviate more positively from the average, i.e. their employment is higher than that of men. Women's employment in the ICT sector is EU-27 average in nine countries. In Estonia, Hungary, Italy, France and Croatia, there is no deviation from the EU-27 average, or it is insignificant.

However, the results confirm that statistically speaking, there is no large deviation of the EU-27 from the EU-27 average, which was approved by Chebyshev's Theorem [59, 60], according to which for any numerical data set, at least 75% of the data lie within two standard deviations of the mean, that is, in the interval with endpoints $\mu \pm 2\sigma$. Specifically, according to the results presented, 26 EU-27 countries or 96% of countries, are within $\mu \pm 2\sigma$, and all countries are within $\mu \pm 2.4\,\sigma$.

In contrast to the results presented in a research paper by Pisker, Radman-Funarić, Sudarić [53] in 2019, the largest positive and largest negative deviation of the share of women employed in the ICT sector is present in Central and Eastern European countries, while in other countries it is closer to the EU-27 average, in 2020, this deviation does not follow such an observation, respectively a similar grouping of countries cannot be performed.

To avoid the dispersion of data from other countries, Table 3 shows the percentages of female employment in 2019 and 2020. The standard deviation and arithmetic mean were calculated from 2011 to 2019 for each country separately. Behind this column is

Table 3. Z values of the change in the percentage of women employed in ICT by country.

	2019	2020	SD	MEAN	Z	
Belgium	13.4	10.9	2.09	11.79	-1.19	F
Bulgaria	29.2	27.4	5.82	28.41	-0.31	
Czechia	8.0	11.1	2.77	8.98	1.12	R
Denmark	18.6	32.9	1.55	16.57	9.25	R
Germany	13.8	14.8	0.23	13.54	4.41	R
Estonia	17.9	18.1	7.30	22.84	0.03	
Ireland	22.0	23.2	3.94	28.9	0.30	
Greece	27.4	30.6	5.94	30.54	0.54	
Spain	22.3	20.9	2.68	20.61	-0.52	
France	22.3	16.6	3.23	14.47	-1.77	F
Croatia	16.4	16.4	6.05	17.28	0.00	
Italy	16.0	16.9	3.31	21.03	0.27	
Cyprus	26.9	27.5	6.19	31.04	0.10	
Latvia	24.8	6.4	8.27	22.67	-2.22	F
Lithuania	15.7	20.7	4.18	16.82	1.20	
Luxembourg	23.6	13.5	4.35	13.98	-2.32	F
Hungary	13.7	17.1	1.86	13.48	1.83	R
Malta	17.5	15.0	3.29	18.43	-0.76	
Netherlands	12.2	13.9	2.72	13.11	0.62	
Austria	25.0	14.5	4.53	15.14	-2.32	F
Poland	10.2	11.7	2.27	12.1	0.66	
Portugal	15.6	19.0	3.51	19.97	0.97	
Romania	26.1	27.0	2.01	27.93	0.45	
Slovenia	20.0	9.7	5.56	11.27	-1.85	F
Slovakia	13.4	13.2	3.73	14.54	-0.05	
Finland	14.2	14.1	6.74	24.32	-0.01	
Sweden	25.3	24.5	1.68	24.96	-0.48	

the Z value of the change in the percentage of employed women in the ICT sector from 2019 to the pandemic of 2020. In the last column, countries where the percentage of women employed in the ICT sector has fallen by more than one standard deviation, are marked in red and with the letter F, while countries with the percentage of women employed in the ICT sector are marked in green and with the letter R. grew by more than one standard deviation.

5   Conclusion

The COVID-19 pandemic overall and specifically, when we discuss gender issues, needs to be understood in a Chinese origin word for the term crisis *Wéijī* being composed of two parts: *Wéi* meaning danger and *jī* meaning opportunity. From experience and emerging data presented, it is possible to project that the impacts of the COVID-19 global recession will result in a prolonged dip in women's income and overall labour force participation, as an opposite phenomenon to the overall increase in demand for ICT specialist employment will inevitably grow and speed up.

The COVID-19 pandemic response, therefore, respecting UNs recommendation [52, 61] need to address the following issues to disable further women ICT employment representation degradation: relevant institutions are to collect sex-disaggregated data to ensure that the pandemic does not disproportionately burden women; gender expertise in national, regional and global level response teams and task forces are to be ensured; social protection plans and emergency economic schemes are to perceive gender perspective and take into account unpaid workload performed by women; potentiate specific constraints for women entrepreneurs and women in the informal sector. Additionally, it is also necessary to assure role model social transfers (coaching and mentoring) and ensure women's leadership and participation in COVID-19 pandemic response plans in the short and long term.

The observations and findings given in this paper are as follows:

1. analysis conducted shows that women ICT specialist employment in 2020 in overall ICT specialist employment has fallen compared to 2019 by 0.1 percentage points.
2. Latvia has recorded the most significant decline with a drop of 18.4 percentage points, while the most significant increase is present in Denmark by 14.3 percentage points. When we presented the change concerning the variations of individual countries, the results were similar. In this case, Latvia (2.22) is in third place behind Luxembourg (2.32) and Austria (2.32), although these results are very similar. On the other hand, Denmark's highest growth was observed, regardless of the methodology (9.25).
3. in 2020, the deviation of women's employment in the ICT sector of the EU-27 from the EU-27 average ranges from 2.4 σ in Denmark to -1.6 σ in Latvia.
4. With negative trends in women's ICT sector employment, positive one is present in men's employment and vice-versa.
5. The results presented confirm that statistically speaking, there is no large deviation of the EU-27 from the EU-27 average.

The pandemic of COVID-19 severely influenced global society in all its aspects. Socio-economic responses different national countries deployed in their effort to alleviate shocks and disturbances emerged were applied in the form of a first aid model, with crisis management often tapping into the dark. Although it has been shown how women country leaders were more successful and effective in suppression of pandemic consequences [26] While it might be too simplifying to explain such extreme differences between Latvia and Denmark in our research, it certainly is a supportive fact towards EIGE data with the case of men prime minister in position in Latvia and female in Denmark. Additional evidence supporting this thesis comes from trust in government differences between these two countries according to OECD 2020 data, where Latvia scores 30.7 per cent while Denmark scores 71.6 per cent [62].

Although Finland, Sweden, Denmark, Estonia and the Netherlands are EU-27 leaders in overall women's digital scores, Romania, Bulgaria, Poland, Hungary, and Italy are at the bottom of the scale according to DESI 2021 [4]. ICT specialist lead potential lies in different parts of EU-27. The EU policymakers must prepare to tailor fitted national implementation frames to boost up the women ICT specialists' interest, acceptance, and retention.

Unfortunately, the data used are not always the result of the same methodology, which differs between countries. It is also evident that there are some strange oscillations in the effects of individual countries in the period from 2011 to 2020. Still, on the other hand, it is the only reliable source that aggregates data from individual countries.

Future research should explore structural and cultural barriers to woman's ICT education and employment through qualitative approach assessment.

References

1. McKinsey and Company: McKinsley Global Surveys 2021: A year in review. McKinsey & Company, New York (2021)
2. European Commission: 2030 Digital Compass: the European way for the Digital Decade. European Commission, Brussels (2021)
3. European Commission: Path to the Digital Decade. https://eur-lex.europa.eu/resource.html?uri=cellar:6785f365-1627-11ec-b4fe-01aa75ed71a1.0001.02/DOC_1&format=PDF (2021). Accessed 31 Mar 2022
4. European Commission: Women in Digital Scoreboard 2021. https://digital-strategy.ec.europa.eu/en/news/women-digital-scoreboard-2021 (2021). Accessed 31 Mar 2022
5. Castells, M.: The Information Age: Economy, Society and Culture (3 volumes). Blackwell, Oxford **1997**, 1998 (1996)
6. Mauss, M.: The gift: The Form and Reason for Exchange in Archaic Societies, Routledge (2002)
7. OECD: Guide to Measuring Information Society. OECD, Paris (2011)
8. Barton, J.: Preparing Workers for the Expanding Digital Economy. Investing in America's Workforce, p. 251 (2018)
9. Davaki, K.: The underlying causes of the digital gender gap and possible solutions for enhanced inclusion of women and girls (2018)
10. Hafkin, N.J.: Cinderella or Cyberella?: Empowering Women in the Knowledge Society. Kumarian Press (2006)
11. Bimber, B.: Measuring the gender gap on the Internet. Soc. Sci. Q. **81**(3), 868–876 (2000)
12. Bandias, S., Sharma, R.: The workplace implications of ageism for women in the Australian ICT sector. Int. J. Bus. Humanit. Technol **6**, 7–17 (2016)

13. Martin, A.E., Phillips, K.W.: Blind to bias: The benefits of gender-blindness for STEM stereotyping. J. Exp. Soc. Psychol. **82**, 294–306 (2019)
14. Moore, K., Griffiths, M., Richardson, H., Adam, A.: Gendered futures? Women, the ICT workplace and stories of the future. Gend. Work. Organ. **15**, 523–542 (2008)
15. Huyer, S., Sikoska, T.: Overcoming the gender digital divide: understanding ICTs and their potential for the empowerment of women, INSTRAW Santo Domingo (2003)
16. Pisker, B., Radman-Funaric, M., Ramanathan, H.: Global issues in gender inequality: a comparative study. In: 9 International Scientific Symposium Region Entrepreneurship Development. Leko Simic, M., Crnkovic, B. - Osijek: Josip Juraj Strossmayer University of Osijek, Faculty of Economics in Osijek, 1246–1260 (2020)
17. Pisker, B., Radman-Funarić, M., Kreševljak, I.: The glass ceiling patterns: gap evidence. In: International Scientific Symposium: Economy of eastern Croatia - Vision and Growth, pp. 1047–1061 (2019)
18. OECD: Bridging the Digital Gender Divide Include, Upskill, Innovate. OECD (2018)
19. Frieze, C., Quesenberry, J.L.: Cracking the Digital Ceiling: Women in Computing Around the World. Cambridge University Press (2019)
20. Berger, P.L., Luckmann T.: The Social Construction of Reality: A Treatise in the Sociology of Knowledge. Anchor (1966)
21. Crenshaw, K.: Demarginalizing the intersection of race and sex: a black feminist critique of antidiscrimination doctrine, feminist theory and antiracist politics. In: u. Chi. Legal f., p. 139 (1989)
22. Hofstede, G.: Culture's Consequences: Comparing Values, Behaviours, Institutions and Organizations Across Nations. Sage publications (2001)
23. United Nations: Goal 5: Achieve Gender Equality end Empower all Women and Girls. United Nations, New York (2021)
24. Nefesh-Clarke, L., Orser, B., Thomas, M.: COVID-19 Response Strategies, Addressing Digital Gender Divides (2020)
25. European Commission: A Union of Equality: Gender Equality Strategy 2020–2025. https://eur-lex.europa.eu/legal-content/EN/TXT/?uri=COM%3A2020%3A152%3AFIN (2020). Accessed 15 Jan 2022
26. European Institute for Gender Equality: Gender Equality and the Socio-economic Impact of the COVID-19 Pandemic. Publications Office of the European Union, Luxembourg (2021)
27. Adam, A.: Gender, Ethics and Information Technology. Springer (2005)
28. Publications Office of the European Union: Women and men in ICT: a chance for better work-life balance. European Institute for Gender Equality, Luxembourg (2018)
29. Ashcraft, C., Eger, E., Friend, M.: Girls in IT: The Facts. Boulder, CO: National Centre for Women & Information Technology (NCWIT). Retrieved July 2013 (2012)
30. Girón, A., Correa, E.: Post-crisis gender gaps: women workers and employment precariousness. J. Econ. Issues **50**, 471–477 (2016)
31. Tsiganou, J.: The impact of crisis on gender inequality: the Greek case. In: Social Inequalities in Europe Conference, Athens, Greece, 20 June 2014 (2014)
32. Patterson, L., Benuyenah, V.: The real losers during times of economic crisis: evidence of the Korean gender pay gap. Int. J. Manpower **42**, 1238–1256 (2021)
33. Kaya, S.A., Bahçe, E.M.: Estimating the impact of the 2008–09 economic crisis on work time in Turkey. Feminist Economics **19**(3), 181–207 (2013)
34. Jaba, E., Pârțachi, I., Chistrugă, B., Balan, C.B.: Gender employment gap in EU before and after the crisis. Procedia Econ. Fin. **20**, 326–333 (2015)
35. Bishu, S.G., Guy, M.E., Heckler, N.: Seeing gender and its consequences. J. Public Aff. Educ. **25**, 145–162 (2019)

36. Dahlmann, N., Elsner, M., Jeschke, S., Natho, N., Schroder, C.: Gender gap in technological disciplines: Societal causes and consequences. In: 2008 IEEE International Symposium on Technology and Society (2008)
37. Morchio, I., Moser, C.: The gender pay gap: Micro sources and macro consequences (2021)
38. Ferrant, G., Kolev, A.: Does gender discrimination in social institutions matter for long-term growth?: Cross-country evidence (2016)
39. Vitores, A., Gil-Juárez, A.: The trouble with 'women in computing': a critical examination of the deployment of research on the gender gap in computer science. J. Gend. Stud. **25**, 666–680 (2016)
40. Castaño Collado, C., Webster, J.: Understanding women's presence in ICT: the life course perspective. Int. J. Gender Sci. Technol. **3**, 364–386 (2011)
41. Simonsen, M., Corneliussen, H.G.: Can Statistics Tell Stories About Women in ICT? Vestlandsforsking- Western Norway Research Institute (2019)
42. Grogan, K.: How the entire scientific community can confront gender bias in the workplace. Nature Ecol. Evol. **3**, 11 (2018)
43. Galpin, V.: Women in computing around the world. ACM SIGCSE Bull. **34**, 94–100 (2002)
44. Lagesen, V.A.: A cyberfeminist utopia? Perceptions of gender and computer science among Malaysian women computer science students and faculty. Sci. Technol. Human Values **33**, 5–27 (2008)
45. Mellström, U.: The intersection of gender, race and cultural boundaries, or why is computer science in Malaysia dominated by women? Soc. Stud. Sci. **39**, 885–907 (2009)
46. Hickel, J.: What does degrowth mean? A few points of clarification. Globalizations **18**, 1105–1111 (2021)
47. Mariscal Avilés, J., Mayne, G., Aneja, U., Sorgner, A.: Bridging the gender digital gap. Economics 13, 2019-9 (2019). Walter de Gruyter GmbH, Berlin, Germany
48. Kerras, H., Sánchez-Navarro, J.L., López-Becerra, E.I., de Miguel Gómez, M.D.: The impact of the gender digital divide on sustainable development: Comparative analysis between the European Union and the Maghreb. Sustainability **12**(8), 3347 (2020)
49. Kostoska, O., Kocarev, L.: A novel ICT framework for sustainable development goals. Sustainability **11**, 1961 (2019)
50. Saidu, A., Tukur, A., Adamu, S.: Promoting sustainable development through ICT in developing countries. Eur. J. Comput. Sci. Inform. Technol. **2**, 24–29 (2014)
51. Hilty, L.M., Hercheui, M.D.: ICT and sustainable development. In: What kind of information society? Governance, virtuality, surveillance, sustainability, resilience, pp. 227–235. Springer (2010)
52. United Nations: Policy Brief: The Impact of COVID-19 on Women. United Nations, New York (2020)
53. Pisker, B., Radman-Funarić, M., Sudarić, Ž: Women in ICT: the case of croatia within European union. In: Jallouli, R., Bach Tobji, M.A., Mcheick, H., Piho, G. (eds.) ICDEc 2021. LNBIP, vol. 431, pp. 3–15. Springer, Cham (2021). https://doi.org/10.1007/978-3-030-929 09-1_1
54. United Nations: Impact of the COVID-19 Pandemic on Trade in Digital Economy. United Nations, New York (2021)
55. Šošić, I.: Primjenjena statistika. Školska knjiga, Zagreb (2006)
56. Radman-Funarić, M.: UVOD U GOSPODARSKU STATISTIKU Tko kaže da lažem? u potpisu–Statistika (2018)
57. Everitt, B.S., Skrondal, A.: The Cambridge Dictionary of Statistics. University Press, Cambridge (2010)
58. Eurostat: Employed Persons with ICT Education by Sex. Eurostat, Brussel (2021)
59. Bienaymé, I.-J.: Considérations à l'appui de la découverte de Laplace sur la loi de probabilité dans la méthode des moindres carrés. Imprimerie de Mallet-Bachelier (1853)

60. Tchebichef, P.: Des valeurs moyennes. Journal de Mathématiques Pures et Appliquées **2**(12), 177–184 (1867)
61. United Nations: Shared Responsibility, Global Solidarity: Responding to Socio-economic Impacts of COVID-19. United Nations, New York (2020)
62. OECD: Trust in Government. https://data.oecd.org/gga/trust-in-government.htm (2021). Accessed 31 Mar 2022

3D Printing During the Covid-19 Pandemic in Lebanon

Strategic Cooperative Behavior to Reduce the Global Shortage of Personal and Protective Equipment (PPEs)

Racquel Antoun-Nakhle⬤, Rim Haidar(✉)⬤, and Nizar Hariri⬤

Faculté de sciences économiques, Observatoire Universitaire de La Réalité Socio-Economique, Université Saint-Joseph, Beirut, Lebanon
{racquel.nakhle,nizar.hariri}@usj.edu.lb, rimhaidar@hotmail.com

Abstract. The COVID 19 pandemic has caused an unprecedented health and economic crisis which was characterized by a rapid shortage of Personal Protective Equipment (PPEs). Over the last few decades, academics and practitioners have argued that 'public health' should be considered as a Global Public Good (GPG), with a particular emphasis on the control of infectious diseases. The provision of GPGs today—nationally and internationally—involves multiple authorities and actors of varying power at different jurisdictional levels. Strategic behavior and noncooperative and cooperative game theory plays a major role in the success or failure of GPG provision. During the Covid-19 pandemic, the PPEs shortage was alleviated by the involvement of the 3D Printing community which implemented several initiatives. Indeed, health care providers, 3D printing organisations, designers and engineers cooperated to supply PPEs. Software designers released their PPEs digital files, and by choosing freeware, they contributed to the production of the GPG. In this paper, we argue that the success of the 3D printing community in establishing a culture of shared knowledge and data to increase the supply of medical PPEs was made possible thanks to the availability of technology (including 3D Printing and scanning, Artificial Intelligence, and nanomedicine). A game theory model will be used to illustrate the cooperative strategic behaviour of various players involved in this process, and the lessons learned are instrumental for public health policies as well as for intellectual property laws.

Keywords: 3D printing · Covid-19 · PPE · Global public good · CDC · Game theory

1 Introduction

In the fall of 2019, a novel coronavirus (Severe Acute Respiratory Syndrome-Cov-2 virus) COVID-19 was first detected in Wuhan, in China, then it quickly spread across the globe. The World Health Organization (WHO) declared Covid-19 a pandemic in March 2020. The pandemic has increased demand for global public health (Li et al. 2020).

© The Author(s), under exclusive license to Springer Nature Switzerland AG 2022
M. A. Bach Tobji et al. (Eds.): ICDEc 2022, LNBIP 461, pp. 33–52, 2022.
https://doi.org/10.1007/978-3-031-17037-9_3

The spread of communicable disease illustrates the direct effects of globalization on health. An important response to the increasing global consciousness associated with globalization is the concept of global public goods. It offers the potential both to improve the health effects of globalization itself and to provide broader benefits to health worldwide (Woodward et al. 2002).

The "global public goods' concept seeks to identify services which, when provided globally, confer greater benefits than when provided at the national level, through their cross-border effects (Woodward et al. 2002).

Controlling an infectious disease like COVID-19 involves a far wider range of actors: not simply individual countries and their governments, but other countries with their respective governments, as well as non-governmental institutions, public–private partnerships, charitable organizations, which sometimes act alone and other times in coalitions and networks (Buchholz and Sandler 2020).

In part, the challenge is that different countries have different production capabilities; indeed, no country has the domestic capabilities to produce all the equipment it needs alone. That's why GPGs' contributors should coordinate the global production and distribution of medical equipment. We must consider, then, contributors' strategic behavior, which necessitates a game-theoretic foundation to understanding the provision of GPGs (Kaul et al. 1999).

The COVID 19 pandemic has caused an unprecedented health and economic crisis. With limited resources and urgent needs for medical supplies, healthcare support or treatments, the global health crisis called for innovative solutions, when various emerging medical technologies (including 3D Printing and scanning, Artificial Intelligence, nanomedicine) were shared and used to overcome the global supply shortages. In this context, 3D printing played a crucial role, since even individual consumers could contribute to the production efforts, if they have access to the appropriate 3D technology. Indeed, many emerging platforms (Siemens, HP, etc.) have openly shared their knowledge, and to some extent their corporate exclusive properties, to help developing countries and vulnerable populations overcoming the supply-shortages of medical equipment (Tsikala Vafea et al. 2020).

More generally, 3D printing and 3D scanning are surely eroding the dichotomy between physical and virtual worlds, blurring the traditional distinctions between tangible and intangible goods (for example between authentic piece of arts and mere copies) or even or between production and consumption (Antoun-Nakhle et al. 2020). Yet, following the outburst of the Covid-19 pandemic, industrial implications of 3D technologies in the health sector seemed to be disrupting the dividing line between private and public goods (Bricongne et al. 2021). Indeed, in the context of the global health crisis, and considering the global effort to fight the pandemic, the global supply of Personal Protective Equipment (or Medical PPEs, such as surgical masks or medical gloves, etc.) was largely dependent on three-dimensional printing and sharing of industrial designs.

On one hand, piracy is usually considered as one of the major problems in digital production, increasingly challenging intellectual property laws and regulations (Li et al. 2021), yet extensive use of 3D printing has remarkably helped decreasing the global shortages in PPE and supporting national public health systems, without conflicting with intellectual property rights (Narayan et al. 2022). Many national States have imposed confinement measures and normalized the daily use of PPE on their citizens, since private protective practices are deemed to be public goods, and various platforms have emerged in this context, offering an open and a free access to PPE code files, thus transforming a corporate software in a freeware that enables any user around the world to effectively produce affordable and equitable safety kits.

The success of the 3D printing community in establishing a culture of shared knowledge and data to increase the supply of Medical PPE was made possible through the available technology involved in this process, and the lessons learned are instru-mental for public health policies as well as for intellectual property laws.

Some examples from Lebanon, a country with a failing State and failing public health sector, will be used to illustrate the above.

This paper is structured as follow: First we introduce the conceptual framework: Communicable Diseases Control (CDC) as Global Public Good (GPG); characterization and provision process of GPGs. Second, we focus on Personal Protective Equipment (PPE) as an input for producing CDC and the role of 3D printing technology in providing PPEs during the pandemic Third follows a discussion on the cooperative strategic behavior of PPEs Community; the choices of various players involved in this process are illustrated by a game theory model. The final section concludes.

2   Communicable Disease Control as Global Public Good

In the twenty first century, disease events are no longer exclusive domestic concerns of national authorities (Aginam 2017). Since securing one country's health requires securing the health of others. Globalization has highlighted the global interconnectedness of health. Globalization of travel, changes in technology and the liberalization of trade affect health and global immunity, as well as the ability of Communicable Diseases (CD) to travel faster and further than ever before (Smith and MacKellar 2007).

An important response to the increasing global consciousness associated with globalization is the concept of Global Public Goods (GPG). It offers the potential both to improve the health effects of globalization itself and to provide broader benefits to health worldwide (Woodward et al. 2002).

The theoretical foundations of GPGs concept are rooted in the microeconomic theory of national public goods. The theory was pioneered by Samuelson (1954, 1955) and Musgrave (1959). Although the notion of GPGs did not capture the attention of economists and other social scientists until Kindleberger (1986).

A public good is a good or a service that is nonexcludable and nonrivalrous in consumption: once provided it is available to all, and consumption by one person does not prevent others from consuming it. The "global public goods' concept seeks to identify services which, when provided globally, confer greater benefits than when provided at the national level, through their cross-border effects (Woodward et al. 2002).

Public goods differ from private goods in several important respects, but a very central difference is the degree to which they generate spillover effects, or externalities, when consumed. Goods, whether public or private, can be colloquially but accurately described as products, programs, activities, or services. The presence of externalities may lead to government intervention either to encourage the potential for positive spillover effects or to discourage the negative (WHO Report 2002).

Global public goods (GPGs) share the properties of traditional public goods, but also spill across the borders of different countries and have 'global or near global' consequences as a result: for instance, addressing climate change, avoiding financial crises, managing refugee flows, maintaining world peace, and many others (Buchholz and Sandler 2020).

GPGs must meet two criteria. The first is that their benefits have strong qualities of publicness (nonrivalry and nonexcludability). The second criterion is that their benefits are quasi universal in terms of countries (covering more than one group of countries), people (accruing to all population groups), and generations (extending to both current and future generations). This property makes humanity as a whole the beneficiary of GPGs (Kaul et al. 1999).

The four properties of GPGs are benefit nonrivalry, benefit non-excludability, spillover range, and aggregator technology. The latter refers to the way overall contributions are combined to create a public good (Sandler et al. 2002).

The provision of public goods today—nationally and internationally—involves multiple authorities and actors of varying power at different jurisdictional levels. Global public goods' provision is the sum of national public goods plus international cooperation—and it becomes clear that what is required is a multi-country, multilevel, and often multisector and multi-actor process (Kaul et al. 1999).

Over the last few decades, academics and practitioners have argued that 'public health' should also be considered as a GPG, with a particular emphasis on the control of infectious diseases (Kaul et al. 1999).

International collaboration is required in preventing the cross border spread of communicable disease. The international agencies work with counties to stimulate global supply through concerted action at the national level. In contributing to the global good, countries also stand to benefit themselves, often considerably. Hence, its contribution to the global good is no more or less than its contribution to the national good (WHO Report 2002).

Controlling an infectious disease like COVID-19 is not a monolithic activity, but involves many different tasks, such as creating a vaccine or producing personal protective equipment (PPE). The knowledge of how to produce medical equipment depends on the stock of knowledge that is developed in each individual country (Brown and Susskind 2020).

The challenge is that different countries have different production capabilities; indeed, no country has the domestic capabilities to produce all the equipment it needs alone.

By their nature, GPGs often require that a large number of countries coordinate actions; thus, we must consider countries' strategic behavior, which necessitates a game-theoretic foundation to understanding the provision of GPGs (Kaul et al. 1999).

According to Sandler's (Sandler et al. 2002) classification of GPGs regarding their "aggregation technology", the vaccine's discovery is a best-shot GPG: whether or not a vaccine is found strongly depends on the particular countries that contribute the most to its discovery. Preventing the virus' spread, for example, is a weakest-link GPG: as long as there is a single country that fails to control the disease within its own borders, it is possible that the virus spreads beyond its borders and around the world.

Provision of CDC requires a "weakest link" approach. Once eradication has been achieved, all countries benefit (non-excludability benefit) and they do not have to compete for their share of the benefits (nonrivalry). Eradication programs are excludable by definition, the supply and provision of CDC rely on collective, local, national, and international levels (WHO Report 2002).

Disease surveillance, for instance, is a threshold GPG: only once a critical number of countries or regions have tracking systems in place is it possible for the global community to understand the epidemiology of the virus. Thinking of these goods as GPGs is revealing because it shows why countries must cooperate not just in developing vaccines and treatments but also in coordinating the global production and distribution of medical equipment: testing kits, ventilators and related technologies, PPE, cleaning materials (Brown and Susskind 2020).

The eradication of infectious diseases on a global scale provides benefits from which no country could be excluded, and from which all countries will benefit without depriving the others. Therefore, Communicable Disease Control (CDC) could be considered as Global Public Goods (GPG). No one in a population can be excluded from benefiting from a reduction in risk of infectious disease when its incidence is reduced, and one person benefiting from this reduction of risk does not prevent anyone else from benefiting from it as well. The CDC within one country reduces the probability of their transmission to other countries. The benefits of CDCs are thus non-rival: one person's lower risk of contracting a disease does not limit the chances of others in lowering the risk too (Smith 2003).

CDC requires a wide range of inputs, some are essential to produce CDC others only make its attainment easier, cheaper or faster, affecting its economic viability or political feasibility. However, some inputs are public goods and other are private goods. Indeed, its production requires excludable inputs (private goods), such as vaccines, PPEs, Condoms, as well as non-excludable inputs such as knowledge of preventive interventions and best practice in treatment. In this sense CDC may be "partially excludable". No one can be excluded from benefiting from a lower risk, but some can benefit more than others (Smith et al. 2004).

Because countries may be contributors or noncontributors to a particular GPG, coalition formation and behavior play a role, as do strategic interactions between a contributor coalition and other countries. For GPGs, unlike public goods, there are layers of actors -individual citizens, each country, and countries collectives – whose interactions are relevant. GPGs generally involve countries or institutions as the agents, while public goods involve individuals as agents (Kaul et al. 1999).

The knowledge associated with producing and distributing the medical equipment effectively is a 'summation' GPG, where countries are able to re-use and build upon the expertise of others. The WHO, for instance, is trying to support this objective through the COVID-19 Technology Access Pool (C-TAP) and the Access to COVID-19 Tools Accelerator (ACT), both of which attempt to make available the data, knowledge, and intellectual property required to produce a variety of health technologies (from diagnostic equipment to vaccines) (Brown and Susskind 2020).

3   PPEs as Inputs for CDC Production

3.1   Description of the PPEs Market Structure

Personal Protective Equipment or Medical PPEs include medical masks (respirators and surgical masks), eye protection (face shield, goggles), coveralls, gowns, shoe covers, aprons and gloves.

PPE is used as a shield between the health professionals and germs and must be used by the hospital staff during the pandemic. PPEs are one of the measures for the improvement of occupational health and safety. PPEs can generally be described as non-pharmaceutical barriers against the virus dissemination (Tsikala Vaefa et al. 2020).

Before the crisis, the global PPE market accounted for around 8 billion USD. China and the USA produce the majority of every PPE category (around 60% of global production) except for gloves, which are mostly manufactured in Malaysia (65% of global production) and Thailand (20% of global production) (Mordor intelligence, Asian Development Bank 2020).

The biggest exporter worldwide was China: 41% of total exports of coveralls, aprons, and gowns; 44% of total exports of masks and 59% of total exports of eye protection; USA exported mainly across North and Latin America and Germany served almost exclusively European countries (ITC Trade map, OECD 2019).

3.2   Shortage in PPE Market Due to Covid-19 Pandemic

Despite the high level of concentration in global PPE production, there is significant interdependence of trade: every country depends on another for at least one PPE type.

The Covid 19 pandemic has caused a surge of demand for medical supplies and spare parts, which has put pressure on the manufacturing sector (UK Aid Report 2020).

The Covid 19 pandemic has illustrated the vulnerability of conventional global supply chain. Medical equipment businesses were relying on overseas production in developing countries to minimize costs. As a result, there is an unprecedented shortage of PPE for healthcare workers, lack of ventilators and spare parts for patients. Countries that are affected have imposed bans on the export of PPE and other product critical for health, The biggest PPE exporters have themselves been severely hit by Covid 19 pushing governments to impose export restrictions impacting the whole world (Salmi et al. 2020).

Before Covid 19, PPEs were essentially produced for health system customers. Nowadays PPEs sales concern medical and non-medical consumers. Covid 19 triggered a surge in global PPE production: medical mask manufacturing spiked by as much as 1200%. Around half of this increased production was delivered by incumbents and the other half came from new markets entrants (UK Aid Report 2020).

During the pandemic, PPE unit prices dramatically increased. In order to enhance national autonomy, governments actively encouraged local manufacturers to increase capacity through mobilizing funds to support PPE production (USA, China, Morocco, etc.) or through waiving customs duties and VAT on imports (European Union) (UK Aid Report 2020).

Increasing manufacturing capacity has put the PPE supply chain under pressure, especially with regard to raw materials: for example: respirators and surgical masks production suffered from shortage in melt-blown non-mover ingredient, gloves production from shortage in nitrile (UK Aid Report 2020).

The PPE shortage in 2020 led to worldwide shortages and rocketing prices. Supply chains were not organized for delivery and consumption on a huge scale. When the need for PPE surged simultaneously in many countries in early 2020, prices climbed to record highs and the lack of organized markets prompted some buyers to turn to black market (Bricongne et al. 2021).

3.3 3D Printing Contribution to Tackle Shortage in PPE Supply

The mismatch between supply and demand eased thanks to local producers that had an incentive to extend or shift their production, imports from countries that could afford to be net exporters and to alternative producers who sprang up using more sophisticated production methods such as 3D printing (Bricongne et al. 2021).

3D printing has demonstrated its competitive advantage in this emergency situation: a resilient advanced manufacturing network enabled by a distribution of 3D printing factories has great potential. These factories could be co-located at hospitals and transportation hubs to quickly serve the needs of the medical profession (Choong et al. 2020).

Three-Dimensional printing or AM is a technology that turns digital files into solid objects. Once the file is designed with the use of either a software program like Autocad or Tinkercad or a 3D scanner, the model is sliced into layers and the printer fabricates the object by printing layer by layer (Choong et al. 2020).

Over the past decade, 3D printing has been increasingly implemented in the medical industry. For example: surgical implants, tools and templates for operators. Major advantages of 3D Printing are its ability to offer mass customization, to produce free form parts on demand and to cater to lot size indifference and other patient specific design.

Three-dimensional printing is a quickly emerging field that can help in the design of medical equipment and can more readily supply needed materials at reduced costs. Utilization of 3D printing technology would increase access to these supplies and create more personalized equipment that can better protect medical personnel. As a result, 3D Printing communities and companies operated to ease the breakdown in the medical supply chain (Tsikala Vafea et al. 2020).

In the current Covid-19 pandemic 3D Printing has been increasingly used to print spare parts for medical devices and protective gear, due to the unavailability of supplies (Salmi et al. 2020).

Key benefits of 3D Printing over conventional manufacturing are faster production, digital storage and traceability of part files, reduction in delivery time and ability to produce components regardless to the complexity of part geometry. 3D printing enables the manufacturer to make any kind of product on demand, flexibly and at the point of need, as long as it meets the printer and material specifications. Traditional industries, on the other hand, exploit economies of scale to amortize fixed costs, but are more specialized and need more time to adapt their supply chains. 3D printers can manufacture items locally and close to the market, even if borders are closed and global value chains disrupted (Bricongne et al. 2021).

Products manufactured using 3D Printers in the Covid19 pandemic are:

1- Face mask: used by frontline workers, hospital staff and individual people; pandemic demand exceeds 10 billion. Face masks need to be fitted appropriately in order to adequately prevent air and small droplets from entering around the edges of the mask. 3D laser scanning allows measurement of exact facial parameters, enabling the production of personalized masks (Salmi et al. 2020).

2- Face shield used by frontline workers and some individuals; pandemic demand exceeded 1 billion. Using open-source data, face shields can also be produced with biodegradable material, allowing at-home, on-demand production (Salmi et al. 2020).

3. Nasal swab for every person to be tested; pandemic demand exceeded 100 million. Three-dimensional printing technology can assist in the production of nasopharyngeal test swabs. The assistance of 3D printing in production of these materials would allow for widespread population testing. With increased access to testing, policy regarding carrier tracing and isolation to prevent the spread of the virus could be more conservative and effective (Salmi et al. 2020).

4. Venturivalve for hospital demand pandemic demand exceeded 10 million. 3D printing has also been implemented to produce venturi valves (key components of the respiratory support equipment). These valves were difficult to produce given their design being subject to copyright and patent covers (Salmi et al. 2020).

3.4 Crowdsourcing: The Role of E-Platforms in Spreading Knowledge

To maintain a high level of confidence in 3D Printing technology, it is important to ensure the technological suitability and accountability of new approved designs and certified materials to harness the benefits of this technology. Federal agencies and government authorities have implemented regulations and drawn up guidelines that manufacturers of 3D printed medical devices must comply with (Choong et al. 2020).

In response to the European Commission's call for support in the fight against Covid-19 Pandemic, a range of initiatives and online-platforms have been set up to bring together the 3D Printing community in a technology-driver, cross-border, fast and effective pandemic control strategy (Strulack-Wójcikiewicz and Bohdan 2017).

Researchers and clinicians from all over the world were bought together to crowd-source their innovative ideas, and resources to quickly develop the treatment guidelines and research strategies. "Crowdsourcing" was used to collect and analyze data and produce PPEs by sharing open designs for 3D printing. Crowdsourcing classically means involving a large number of people who work collectively to solve a problem or complete a task with some objectives; it's an activity of broadcasting a task to a large and undefined crowd rather than to a designated organization, team, or individual. For instance, Isinnova and FabLab in Italy printed valves for a hospital in Brescia, in Spain a non-profit e-platform, "3DCovid19.tech", was set by a group of 800 experts in 3d Printing to provide more than 11 hospitals in PPEs (Strulack-Wójcikiewicz and Bohdan 2017).

Many platforms have been created globally to coordinate support in the fight against pandemic: e "CAR3D", implemented by a European consortium with the support of EIT Health/European institutions and the CEN (European Committee for Standardization, echoing the norms issue), the platform aims to design, develop and validate reusable masks and other PPEs that comply with all the European Union quality and safety requirements and specifications making that design available for replication around Europe. The platform links between PPE designers, producers and raw materials suppliers.

AMN platform (Additive Manufacturing Network) was created by Siemens to support efficient design and 3d printing of medical PPEs (CAR 3D Platform).

Many businesses and individuals engaged in 3D Printing globally, including such giants as "Hewlett-Packard" (manufacturer of 3D printers), "Materialise" (Belgian provider of 3D printing services) have published free 3D Printing models of accessories for the fight against the pandemic on their websites. As a response to the emerging crisis situation, science and innovation communities have made a fundamental contribution to set the PPE market by raising digital supply (Li et al. 2020).

The health sector in Lebanon could be a perfect illustration of these global trends, since the severe pre-covid financial crisis in 2019 has led to a failure of the public health sector. Lebanon has suffered from significant shortages of personal protective equipment (PPEs) during the Covid-19 pandemic (Khoury et al. 2020), which has led to a surge in the prices of masks, gloves, safety glasses and shoes, respirators, vests, and full body suits. Despite the latter, health workers, frontliners and citizens have managed to protect themselves thanks to the efforts of the industrial, educational and health sectors in using three-dimensional technology to produce personal protective equipment (PPEs) (IDAL 2020).

As a matter of fact, Lebanon has benefitted from the prototypes suitable for 3D printing which were produced by other countries such as the Czech Republic that has developed the certified "PRUSA" face shields designed by Prusa research (Prusa Research 2020). Indeed, recognizing that health is a global responsibility, developers and designers of 3D printed PPEs have made all the files required for production, assembly, and sterilization available online. In fact, knowledge spillovers have played a major role in producing 3D printed PPEs (Bouncken and Barwinski 2021) and even in perfecting some prototypes designed abroad by a country it inspired.

In a nutshell, following the international trend of 3D printing PPEs, private Lebanese initiatives based on three-dimensional printing implemented by the industrial, educational and the health sectors have contributed to reduce the shortage in PPEs within the Lebanese health sector. These initiatives have benefitted from the international knowledge spillovers and prove that the Lebanese population could rely on 3D printing as a potential for future production since it a workforce highly skilled in design and creative economy.

The table below (Table 1) summarize some of the most promising initiatives to produce PPEs in Lebanon during Covid-19 pandemic.

Table 1. Lebanese initiatives in producing PPEs during Covid-19 pandemic

Implementing organization/persons in Lebanon	Output	Description of the initiative
Lebanese American University *Lebanese American University (LAU) in collaboration with the LAU Mobile Clinic and the LAU Coronavirus Telecare*	3D printed "PRUSA" face shields	• *LAU's initiative consisted in producing face shields to protect frontliners using 3D printing technology* • *LAU has chosen to produce the PRUSA model face shields designed and certified by Prusa research in Czech Republic (*Prusa Research 2020*). since it was fast to produce (*Novak and Loy 2020*) and raw materials required for production were available in Lebanon (*LAU news 2020*)* • *Nevertheless, the 3D printers available ate the LAU's Engineering Lab and Research center were not suitable for mass production, which has led to their use at their maximal capacity of printing 40 min per face shield*

(continued)

Table 1. (*continued*)

Implementing organization/persons in Lebanon	Output	Description of the initiative
Berytech	3D printed "Proto Shield" inspired by the PRUSA shield Potential production of, face masks and spare parts for existing health care machines	• *The Digital Fabrication Lab (Fab Lab) team at Berytech, a Lebanese ecosystem for entrepreneurs, has designed and produced the "Proto Shield", which design and prototype were inspired by the Prusa face shield* (Prusa Research 2020) • *The cost of production of one Proto shield is USD 1.2 per a 40 cm × 30 cm face shield, and the machine used is the laser cutter which takes 3.38 min to cut a 0.5 mm PETG sheet* (Berytech website 2021) • *Furthermore, the Fab Lab has the capacity to prototype, among other things, face masks and spare parts for existing health care machines which can be 3D printed using the machines available at the Fab Lab 1* (FAb Lab website 2021) *such as the CNC Milling Machine – Shopbot, the Desktop CNC Router – Blue Elephant, the Laser Cutter – Epilog Fusion M2, the 3D Printer – DELTA WASP 40 70 and many others. Using these machines costs USD 7 to USD 30 per day per user and the usage daily time limit varies between 2 to 4 h per user* • *Fab Lab is in contact with "Helpful Engineer", a global network gathering more than 5,000 volunteering researchers, engineers, and doctors around the world* • *Berytech's Fab Lab has also close contacts with many 3D printed PPEs initiatives in the Arab region* (IDAL 2020)

(*continued*)

Table 1. (*continued*)

Implementing organization/persons in Lebanon	Output	Description of the initiative
American University of Beirut (AUB)	3D printed AUB N95 Mask and the AUB COVID Non-invasive Ventilation Mask	• *The Covid19FabLab of the American University of Beirut has gathered the expertise of engineers and prototype designers to develop two models of face masks, these are the AUB N95 Mask and the AUB COVID Non-invasive Ventilation Mask using three-dimensional printing technology* (Covid19FabLab website 2020) • *Moreover, the design files of the two masks are made available online* • *Firstly, the Covid19FabLab team has been inspired by N95 masks which were available online and certified, then they have amended the prototype to ensure the comfort of health workers and citizens that wear such masks during long working hours while at the same time ensuring a filtration of 95 percent. Other factors were taken into consideration such as reusability and the biocompatibility of materials used during the production process*
The laboratory of the Beirut Eye & ENT hospital	Face masks made of diving masks	• *Ziad Khoueir and Henry Fakhoury, two doctors working at the Beirut Eye & ENT hospital got inspired by an initiative initiated in Italy* (Assaf 2020) *which consisted in transforming diving masks sold by Decathlon into face masks allowing breathing without intubation* • *This initiative modified the Decathlon masks by adding 3D printed adapters* (Vicini et al. 2021; Profili et al. 2021) • *To modify the initial diving mask into a protective mask, the snorkel of the diving mask is removed and replaced by a connector to which a filter is connected* • *To be able to connect the mask to the filter, the doctors contacted the "Raidy Printing Group". The latter used 3D printing to produce specific valves from a computer model provided by a German research group*

(*continued*)

Table 1. (*continued*)

Implementing organization/persons in Lebanon	Output	Description of the initiative
Edgar Meksass (architect)	Reusable face masks	• *Edgar Meksass, a Lebanese architect, was also inspired by a Swedish mask model to design and produce a medically certified face mask that covers all the face (IDAL 2020)* • *The architect's 3D printers produced 155 reusable masks per day and were sold on a Lebanese local platform, beiruting.com* • *A single mask can be produced within only 48 min*
Paul Abi Nasr (industrialist) and Henry Fakhoury (MD)	Protection gears combining improved filtration and reducing aerosolization and respiratory dead space barrier	• *Paul Abi Nasr, Lebanese industrialist, CEO of Polytextile group, and Henry Fakhoury mentioned above have joined forces to produce protection gears combining improved filtration and reducing aerosolization and respiratory dead space barrier* • *The developed protection gears reduce the need to combine several PPEs such as N95 mask, face shields and protective glasses* • *The masks were offered to the "Rafic Hariri University Hospital", Beirut greatest public hospital*

4 Discussion

Ensuring Sufficient Provision of PPEs: Matching Contributors' Behavior

The global scale of the Covid-19 pandemic coupled with travel restrictions and a halt in international commerce led to an early depletion of PPE reserves with global demand exceeding production capacity worldwide. In consequence, many health workers, and especially frontliners, were left unprotected from the pandemic (Burki 2020), which led to further transmission of the virus.

In response to the WHO's call to address shortage in PPEs, the community's efforts focused on supplying PPEs to hospitals, health workers and citizens. The latter was possible thanks to community's involvement and to online 3D printing cooperative platforms such as Materialise OnSite and Shapeways.

3DPrinting technology relies on 3 inputs: the 3D printer, the raw materials, and the digital files. The latter are problematic as companies typically aim to protect their designs and ensure their intellectual property (Teixeira and Ferreira 2019). Digital files are club goods, excludable but non-rival. Nevertheless, open-source, platforms, designers, and even some companies have started sharing their designs, rendering collaborative development possible (Budinoff et al. 2021). For instance, PRUSA research published its 3D printing models for the "PRUSA PRO" shield on their website and inspired the

Lebanese American University to produce face shields and protect frontliners using 3D printing technology (LAU News 2020). Hence, club goods have turned into free public goods which are non-excludable and non-rival.

This said, how can the shift in the companies' behavior during the Covid-19 pandemic be explained? Economic agents are rational (Smith 1791). Indeed, the pandemic has generated negative externalities on the "rational" individuals' health and wealth, and the alleviation of these negative externalities has become a necessity that would give back the rational agents their health and wealth. PPEs may prevent the transmission of the virus, which means that producing PPEs contributes could contribute to alleviate the effects of the pandemic, and even lead to its end. Therefore, it was imperative that CDCs become GPGs.

Software designers have started to make the digital files and designs required for manufacturing PPEs using three-dimensional printing technology publicly available, aiming to reduce the negative externalities caused by the pandemic on an international scale. By choosing freeware, designers contributed to the production of the GPG.

The Covid-19 pandemic has therefore led to a shift in the normal repartition of produced public and private goods in a market. As a matter of fact, markets generally relatively under-produce public goods (Anomaly 2015) in comparison to what is socially optimal since private actors are not able to capture the full social benefit of producing them (Moon et al. 2017). The designer's choice is triggered by 3DP technology: free designs will stop pandemic if production of PPEs will be in-Time. Their contribution in releasing one input will be efficient if 3DP community manages to use this factor to set the PPE equilibrium market.

Many platforms have been created globally to coordinate and support efficient design and 3D printing of medical components needed by medical staff. Consequently, digital, open-source, and collaborative marketplaces were put in place to provide solutions for healthcare professionals. Forums and collaborative hubs for inventors and manufacturers were also created.

Researchers and clinicians from all over the world were bought together to crowd-source their innovative ideas, and resources to quickly develop the treatment guidelines and research strategies. "Crowdsourcing" was used to collect and analyze data and produce PPEs by sharing open designs for 3D printing. Crowdsourcing classically means involving a large number of people who work collectively to solve a problem or complete a task with some objectives; it's an activity of broadcasting a task to a large and undefined crowd rather than to a designated organization, team, or individual (Strulack-Wójcikiewicz and Bohdan 2017).

Hence, as a response to the emerging crisis, science and innovation communities have made a fundamental contribution to set the PPE market by raising digital supply. The main input in the production process was open-source data for digital files: Perfect Knowledge.

This is what A. Smith called invisible hand for setting the imbalance between supply and demand. In this paper, we believe the 3D printing e-platforms have played the role of a "hand", made visible thanks to the open-source knowledge they provided to suppliers, in remediating to the imbalance between supply and demand of PPEs in Lebanon and worldwide.

5 Methodology

The provision of GPGs today—nationally and internationally—involves multiple authorities and actors of varying power at different jurisdictional levels. Strategic behavior
and, thus, noncooperative and cooperative game theory plays a major role in the success
or failure of GPG provision. PPEs shortage was alleviated by the involvement of the
3DPrinting community. Indeed, a number of initiatives of different scales have been
quickly set up: health care providers, 3D printing organisations, designers and engineers united their efforts to supply PPEs. Software designers released PPEs digital files,
choosing freeware, designers contributed to the production of the GPG (Buchholz and
Sandler 2021).

We envisage the model below, inspired by the game theory, to highlight the
cooperative strategic behavior of the 3DP Community in producing PPEs.

In a sequential-move game, one player (the first mover) takes an action before another
player (the second mover). Then, the second mover observes the action taken by the first
one before deciding what action it should take. We consider a sequential-move game in
which software designers represent the first mover and 3DP community represent the
second mover.

To analyze this sequential-move game, we use a game tree[1] (Kreps and Wilson 1982),
which shows the different strategies[2] that each player can follow in the game and the
order in which those strategies get chosen. The Fig. 1 below shows the game tree for the
PPE market players' game.

The order of moves flows from left to right. Because "Software Owners" move first,
they are in the leftmost position. For each of owners' possible action, the tree shows the
possible decisions for "3DP community".

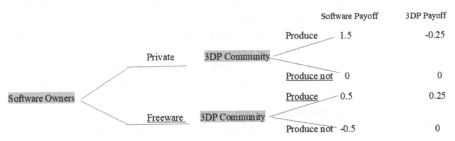

Fig. 1. Game tree of the PPE market players' game

As stated above, the designers move first and can choose among two strategies:
release the digital files as an open-source and making them public goods or to keep the
data and sell the digital files as private goods.

The 3DP Community moves next (having observed the Owners' move), also having
two options: whether to be able to produce PPEs In-Time to tackle the PPEs shortage

---

[1] A diagram that shows the different strategies that each player can follow in a game and the
order in which those strategies get chosen.

[2] A plan of the actions that a player in a game will take under every conceivable circumstance
that the player might face.

and contribute to ending the pandemic or to be unable to produce In-Time, thus not contributing to end the pandemic.

Designers evaluate their payoffs[3] in a rational way. Indeed, selling digital files as private goods will raise their profit to 0.5, but releasing them as public goods will make them lose (−0.5) in profit. Nevertheless, reaching their goal in contributing to end the pandemic In-Time would raise their profit to 1. Finally, if they are unable to slow the pandemic's growth, they will have 0 as profit.

If Designers choose to sell their files as private goods, and the 3DP Community chooses to produce than the pandemic will stop and their payoff will be 1.5; they earn 0.5 from selling files and 1 for achieving their goal.

If Designers choose to sell their files as private goods, and the 3DP Community chooses to produce not than the pandemic won't stop and their payoff will be 0; they couldn't sell the files, neither achieve their goal.

If Designers choose freeware, and the 3DP Community chooses to produce than the pandemic will stop and their payoff will be 0.5; they lose 0.5 for releasing freeware and earn 1 for achieving their goal.

If Designers choose freeware, and the 3DP Community chooses not to produce than the pandemic won't stop and their payoff will be −0.5; they lose 0.5 for releasing freeware but couldn't stop pandemic.

In the light of the owners' move, the 3DP Community also evaluate their payoffs in a rational way as follows: getting the digital file as Private Good will cost them − 0.5 in cost. Producing PPEs means supporting a production cost of 0.25 (cost of raw materials, energy and efforts) Succeeding in producing PPEs in-time will contribute to end the pandemic and their profit will be 0.5. Not being able to produce the PPEs In-time to slow the pandemic growth and their profit be 0.

N.B: The players: Software Designers and the 3DP Community get different payoffs when reaching the same purpose in stopping the pandemic. This difference is explained regarding their economic global position. Software Designers correspond to large corporate enterprises in rich countries their contribution to stop the spread of the worldwide disease would be considered as a proof of their social responsibility that affects their reputation. The 3DP Community are local producers and technicians, their contribution is purely altruistic.

This said, what is the plausible outcome of the game?

In order to apply backward induction[4] in this game, we must find the 3DP Community's optimal choice: Produce or Not. (In Fig. 1, 3DP Community's optimal choices are underlined):

If Software Designers chooses "private good", 3DP Community's best choice is Not to produce. Indeed, 3DP Community's will have to choose between producing or not: Producing means supporting the cost of the digital file (−0.5) and the cost of production (−0.25) to stop the pandemic and win (+0.5), the payoff of this choice is (−0.25); benefits-costs = $0.5 - (0.5 + 0.25) = -0.25$; Not Producing means no cost and no

---

[3] The payoffs in the game are the amount that each player can expect to get under different combinations of strategy choices by the players.

[4] A procedure for solving a sequential-move game by starting at the end of the game tree and finding the optimal decision for the player at each decision point.

contribution to stop the pandemic: benefits and costs are null, the payoff of this choice is 0. The Community's best choice is Produce Not (0 is greater than −0.25).

If Software Designers chooses to consider the digital files as freeware, released for free, 3DP Community's best choice is produce In-Time. Indeed, 3DP Community's will have to choose between producing or not: Producing means supporting the unique cost of production (−0.25), the digital file is free, stopping the pandemic and wining (+0.5), the payoff of this choice is (+0.25); benefits-costs = 0.5–0.25 = +0.25; Not Producing means no cost and no contribution to stop the pandemic: benefits and costs are null, the payoff of this choice is 0. The Community's best choice is to produce (0.25 is greater than 0).

As we work backward in the tree, we assume that Software Designers anticipates that 3DP Community will choose its best response to each action they might take.

We can then determine which of Software Designers' two strategies gives them the highest profit, by identifying the profit that they get from each option it might choose, given that 3DP Community responds optimally:

If Software Designers chooses "private good", then given 3DP Community's optimal reaction, Software Owners' profit will be 0.

If Software Designers chooses "Freeware", then given 3DP Community's optimal reaction, Software Owners' profit will be 0.5 (1–0.5).

Thus, Software Designers attains the highest profit when they chose: "Freeware".

Assuming that 3DP Community will always make their best (payoff-maximizing) response, Software Designers can maximize their own payoff by choosing "Freeware", as 3DP Community's best response will be producing In-Time. At this equilibrium, Software Owners' profit will be 0.5 and 3DP Community's profit is 0.25.

Concluding Remark

GPGs must meet two criteria: The first is that their benefits have strong qualities of publicness (nonrivalry and non-excludability). These features place them in the general category of public goods. The second criterion is that their benefits are quasi universal in terms of countries, people, and generations. This property makes humanity as a whole the beneficiary of GPGs (Kaul et al. 1999).

Global public goods' provision requires a multi-country, multilevel, and often multisector and multi-actor process. Provision of CDC requires a "weakest link" approach. Once eradication has been achieved, all countries benefit (non-excludability) and they do not have to compete for their share of the benefits (nonrivalry). Eradication programs are excludable by definition, the supply and provision of CDC rely on collective action on local, national; and international levels (WHO Report 2002).

The global scale of the Covid-19 pandemic coupled with travel restrictions and a halt in international commerce quickly generated an early depletion of PPE reserves with global demand exceeding production capacity worldwide. In consequence, many health workers, and especially frontliners, were left unprotected from the pandemic (Burki 2020).

As we saw in this paper, three-dimensional printing has contributed to remediate to the PPEs shortage. The latter was motivated by the strategic cooperative behavior of soft-ware designers that have started to make the digital files and designs required for producing PPEs using 3D printing technology open source, thus producing GPGs. Hence, by establishing a culture of shared knowledge and data, the 3D printing community was able to increase the supply of PPEs. In the game theory model we used, we illustrated the Strategic cooperative behavior of Software Designers and the 3DP community in-volved in this process.

In contrast, the Covid-19 vaccines remained private properties of pharmaceutical com-panies and labs (Big Pharma) protecting their patents (Newey 2020), and all the public debates over a patent waiver for vaccines have not yet succeeded in reaching the highest political spheres, despite the proposal that was submitted to the World Trade Organi-zation by a large group of developing countries in May 2021.[5]

As a matter of fact, vaccination could be considered as the perfect illustration of what economists call a "Global Public Good". Yet the "vaccine nationalism" has not only reflected major competition (and conflicts) between Chinese, Russian, European, and American regulations and industries (Boseley 2020), but it has also marked a turning point in the global efforts deployed to contain the spread of the pandemic, with a global tendency to privatize a common good. Thus, vaccination campaigns all over the world seemed to contradict the open access approach that was reflected in the three-dimen-sional share and use of PPE, since the former was organized by market-driven (and to some extent neoliberal) health policies shaped by economic nationalism and protection-ist values, while in the latter was mainly driven by wavering the patent on exclusive ownerships of industrial designs.

References

Aginam, O.: Between isolationism and mutual vulnerability: a south-north perspective on global governance of epidemics in an age of globalization. In: Kirton, J.J. (ed.) Global Health, pp. 463–478. Routledge (2017). https://doi.org/10.4324/9781315254227-34

Anomaly, J.: Public goods and government action. Polit. Philos. Econ. **14**(2), 109–128 (2015)

Berytech website: https://berytech.org/profiles/face-shield/ (2021)

Boseley, S.: US and UK 'lead push against global patent pool for COVID-19 drugs'. The Guardian 17 (2020)

Bouncken, R., Barwinski, R.: Shared digital identity and rich knowledge ties in global 3D printing—A drizzle in the clouds? Glob. Strategy J. **11**(1), 81–108 (2021)

Bricongne, J.C. et al.: How 3D printing could tackle PPE shortages during a future pandemic. LSE COVID-19 Blog (2021)

Brown, G., Susskind, D.: International cooperation during the COVID-19 pandemic. Oxford Rev. Econ. Policy **36**(Supplement_1), S64–S76 (2020)

Buchholz, W., Sandler, T.: Global public goods: a survey. J. Econ. Lit. **59**(2), 488–545 (2021)

---

[5] Proposal 21–4307, submitted the 25 May 2021 to the Council for Trade-Related Aspects of Intellectual Property Rights of the WTO, "WAIVER FROM CERTAIN PROVISIONS OF THE TRIPS AGREEMENT FOR THE PREVENTION, CONTAINMENT AND TREATMENT OF COVID-19", at the request of the delega-tions of the African Group, the Plurinational State of Bolivia, Egypt, Eswatini, Fiji, India, Indonesia, Kenya, the LDC Group, Maldives, Mozambique, Mongolia, Na-mibia, Pakistan, South Africa, Vanuatu, the Bolivarian Republic of Venezuela and Zimbabwe. Available online: https://docs.wto.org/dol2fe/Pages/SS/directdoc.aspx?filename=q:/IP/C/W669R1.pdf&Open=True.

Budinoff, H.D., Bushra, J., Shafae, M.: Community-driven PPE production using additive manufacturing during the COVID-19 pandemic: survey and lessons learned. J. Manuf. Syst. **60**,
799–810 (2021)

Burki, T.: Global shortage of personal protective equipment. The Lancet Infect. Dis. **20**(7), 785–
786 (2020)

Choong, Y.Y.C., et al.: The global rise of 3D printing during the COVID-19 pandemic. Nat. Rev.
Mater. **5**(9), 637–639 (2020)

Covid19FabLab   website: https://www.aub.edu.lb/msfea/Covid19FabLab/Pages/default.aspx
(2020)

Fab Lab – Berytech. https://berytech.org/fablab/machines/ (2021)

IDAL: Innovation triggered by the COVID-19 crisis: lebanese success stories. https://lebanonup
dates.com/covid-19-measures/innovation-triggered-by-the-covid-19-crisis-lebanese-success-
stories/ (2020)

ITC Trade map, OECD: https://www.trademap.org/Index.aspx?AspxAutoDetectCookieSupp
ort=1 (2019)

Kaul, I., Grunberg, I., Stern, M.A.: Defining global public goods. In: Kaul, I., Grunberg, I., Stern,
M. (eds.) Global public goods: international cooperation in the 21st century, pp. 2–19. Oxford
University PressNew York (1999). https://doi.org/10.1093/0195130529.003.0001

Khoury, P., Azar, E., Hitti, E.: COVID-19 response in Lebanon: current experience and challenges
in a low-resource setting. JAMA **324**(6), 548–549 (2020)

Kindleberger, C.P.: International public goods without international government. Am. Econ. Rev.
76(1), 1–13 (1986)

Kreps, D.M., Wilson, R.: Sequential equilibria. Econometrica **50**(4), 863 (1982). https://doi.org/
10.2307/1912767

LAU news: https://news.lau.edu.lb/2020/soe-designs-and-3d-prints-face-shields.php (2020)

Li, S., et al.: Open design and 3D printing of face shields: the case study of a UK-China initiative.
Strateg. Des. Res. J. **13**(3), 511–524 (2020)

Moon, S., Røttingen, J.A., Frenk, J.: Global public goods for health: weaknesses and opportunities
in the global health system. Health Econ. Policy Law **12**(2), 195–205 (2017)

Musgrave, R.A.: The Theory of Public Finance: A Study in Public Economy. McGraw-Hill, New
York (1959)

Newey, S.: WHO patent pool for potential COVID-19 products is 'nonsense,' pharma leaders
claim. The Telegraph (2020)

Novak, J.I., Loy, J.: A quantitative analysis of 3D printed face shields and masks during COVID-19.
Emerald Open Research **2**, 42 (2020)

Profili, J., Dubois, E.L., Karakitsos, D., Hof, L.A.: Overview of the user experience for snorke-
ling mask designs during the COVID-19 pandemic. In: Healthcare, vol. 9, no. 2, p. 204.
Multidisciplinary Digital Publishing Institute (2021)

Prusa Research: Prusa Face Shield.2020. https://www.prusaprinters.org/prints/25857-prusa-face-
shield

Salmi, M., Akmal, J., Pei, E., Wolff, J., Jaribion, A., Khajavi, S.: 3D Printing in COVID-19:
productivity estimation of the most promising open source solutions in emergency situations.
Appl. Sci. **10**(11), 4004 (2020)

Samuelson, P.A.: The pure theory of public expenditure. The Rev. Econ. Stat. **36**, 387–389 (1954).
https://doi.org/10.2307/1925895

Samuelson, P.A.: Diagrammatic exposition of a theory of public expenditure. The Rev. Econ. Stat.
37(4), 350–356 (1955). https://doi.org/10.2307/1925849

Sandler, T., Arce, D.G.: A conceptual framework for understanding global and transnational public
goods for health. Fiscal Stud. **23**(2), 195–222 (2005)

Smith, A.: An Inquiry Into the Nature and Causes of the Wealth of Nations: By Adam Smith, vol.
4. JJ Tourneisen and JL Legrand (1791)

Smith, R.D., MacKellar, L.: Global public goods and the global health agenda: problems, priorities and potential. Globalization and Health **3**(1), 1–7 (2007)

Smith, R., Woodward, D., Acharya, A., Beaglehole, R., Drager, N.: Communicable disease control: a 'Global Public Good' perspective. Health Policy Plann. **19**(5), 271–278 (2004)

Strulak-Wójcikiewicz, R., Bohdan, A.: The concept of an e-platform cooperation model in the field of 3D printing during the COVID-19 pandemic. Procedia Comput. Sci. **192**, 4083–4092 (2021)

Teixeira, A.A., Ferreira, C.: Intellectual property rights and the competitiveness of academic spin-offs. J. Innov. Knowl. **4**(3), 154–161 (2019)

Tsikala Vafea, M., Atalla, E., Georgakas, J., Shehadeh, F., Mylona, E.K., Kalligeros, M., Mylonakis, E.: Emerging technologies for use in the study, diagnosis, and treatment of patients with COVID-19. Cell. Mol. Bioeng. **13**(4), 249–257 (2020)

UK Aid Report: https://www.google.com/search?q=UK+Aid+Report%2C+2020&oq=UK+Aid+Report%2C+2020&aqs=chrome..69i57j69i60.741j0j7&sourceid=chrome&ie=UTF-8 (2020)

Vicini, C., et al.: Overview of different modified full-face snorkelling masks for intraoperative protection. Acta Otorhinolaryngologica Italica **40**(5), 317 (2020)

World Health Organization: Global public goods for health: the report of Working Group 2 of the Commission on Macroeconomics and Health. World Health Organization (2002)

Woodward, D., Drager, N., Beaglehole, R., Lipson, D.: Globalization, global public goods and health. In: Trade in health services: global, regional and country perspectives, pp. 3–11 (2002)

Li, X., Liao, C., Xie, Y.: Digital piracy, creative productivity, and customer care effort: evidence from the digital publishing industry. Mark. Sci. **40**(4), 685–707 (2021)

Narayan, J., Jhunjhunwala, S., Dwivedy, S.K.: 3D printing during COVID-19: challenges and possible solutions. In: Sandhu, K., Singh, S., Prakash, C., Sharma, N.R., Subburaj, K. (eds.) Emerging Applications of 3D Printing During CoVID 19 Pandemic, pp. 179–192. Springer Singapore, Singapore (2022). https://doi.org/10.1007/978-981-33-6703-6_10

Asian Development Bank (ADB): ADB to Provide ˜ Million to Support Strained Supply Chains in Fight Against COVID-Š. News Release. March. https://www.adb.org/news/adb-provide-millionsupport-strained-supply-chains-fight-againstcovid-Š (2020)

Assaf, C.: Des masques de plongée reconvertis pour l'usage médical. L'Orient Le Jour. https://www.lorientlejour.com/article/1212924/des-masques-de-plongee-reconvertis-pour-lusage-medical.html (2020)

Antoun-Nakhle, R., Hariri, N., Haidar, R.: Pricing digital arts and culture through PWYW strategies: a reconsideration of the Ricardian theory of value. In: Tobji, M.A.B., Jallouli, R., Samet, A., Touzani, M., Strat, V.A., Pocatilu, P. (eds.) Digital Economy. Emerging Technologies and Business Innovation: 5th International Conference on Digital Economy, ICDEc 2020, Bucharest, Romania, June 11–13, 2020, Proceedings, pp. 166–176. Springer International Publishing, Cham (2020). https://doi.org/10.1007/978-3-030-64642-4_14

Digital Business Models for Education and Healthcare

Success Factors for the Use of Open Educational Resources - A Quantitative Survey with Students

Carla Reinken$^{(\boxtimes)}$ (iD) and Annette Kalinovich

Osnabrück University, Osnabrück, Germany
`carla.reinken@uni-osnabrueck.de`

Abstract. Digitalization is increasingly establishing numerous electronic teaching and learning innovations. Educational content is more often provided cooperatively, and interest in Open Educational Resources (OER) is growing. In terms of learning content and educational resources, the global development of the Open Education movement plays a key role. OER have gained increased attention in recent years due to their potential to reduce educational demographic, economic, and geographic boundaries and promote lifelong as well as personalized learning. For a successful implementation and use of OER, it is essential to identify conditions and success factors for stakeholders. These success factors will be assessed by means of a quantitative survey with students as the main user group. The aim is to identify factors from the perspective of learners that contribute to a willingness to use OER and increase acceptance. In addition, user-oriented recommendations for action will be derived by involving the students. For this purpose, 131 students from different German universities were asked by means of a quantitative online survey.

Keywords: Success factors · Open educational resources · Higher education · Digitalization

1 Introduction

Digitization is increasingly establishing numerous electronic teaching and learning innovations today [1]. Educational content is being provided cooperatively more and more often. One of the most recent developments in teaching is the implementation of unrestricted and free access to scientific content via the Internet [1]. This educational innovation is called "Open Educational Resources (OER)" or "Open Courseware (OCW)". In this context, OER are supposed to allow a new, extended and precise access to information and resources and thus establish a sustainable and digital learning infrastructure [2]. On a global level, numerous initiatives with different approaches and models have taken steps towards the establishment, integration and dissemination of OER. This has led to an increase in the number of OER-related programs, projects and the popularity of OER in recent years [3]. The goal of OER initiatives is to provide free access to high-quality educational resources on a global scale. From large institutional or institutionally funded initiatives to diverse small-scale activities, the number of projects and programs

M. A. Bach Tobji et al. (Eds.): ICDEc 2022, LNBIP 461, pp. 55–69, 2022.
https://doi.org/10.1007/978-3-031-17037-9_4

related to OER has grown rapidly in the last few years [4]. Accordingly, university education is also affected by the progressive digital networking of the education sector [5]. These cross-university educational resources are likely to reduce demographic, economic, and geographic educational boundaries within and between universities [4]. In order to achieve the greatest possible efficiency of these digital, freely and openly accessible teaching and learning resources, it is of utmost importance to create optimal conditions in this regard [6]. In order to ensure the success of OER, it is essential to identify conditions that can have an influence on the usage behavior as well as success factors from the stakeholders involved. Therefore, this research explores success factors based on which students, as the main user group, would agree to use cross-university teaching resources. Thus, the following research question arises: *Which success factors are identified by students that lead to a higher degree of inclination to use OER?*

To answer this question, this paper is divided into two multimethod sections: On the one hand, a literature review is conducted and on the other hand, a mixed-method survey with a quantitative focus is used. In order to identify theoretical foundations as well as preliminary success factors within the OER concept, a literature search was first conducted. A mainly quantitative survey method is used to identify, verify, or even refute factors related to student intentions to use OER [7]. Hypotheses are derived from the research question, which are tested by a questionnaire for students. An explorative, qualitative question is placed before the quantitative questionnaire in order to ask unbiased about personal success factors in relation to OER. Otherwise, the questionnaire consists exclusively of closed questions. In addition, independent variables are elaborated, which can have an influence on the dependent variable, consequently on the stated degree of inclination towards the use of freely available educational resources. The aim is to ascertain the most important success factors for the use of OER from the perspective of students in order to achieve a high user acceptance when these factors are taken into account.

2   Open Educational Resources

In the course of digitalization, modified forms of learning and teaching are increasingly developing that can enable the right to education not only within universities, but now on an international and inter-university level [8]. Inter-university teaching is increasingly exported beyond the internal boundaries of institutions or even individuals. This content is often distributed openly, collaboratively, and free of charge over the Internet [9]. These are referred to as Open Educational Resources or Open Courseware [9]. The most recent definition of OER from UNESCO is "Open Educational Resources (OER) are learning, teaching and research materials in any format and medium that reside in the public domain or are under copyright that have been released under an open license, that permit no-cost access, re-use, re-purpose, adaptation and redistribution by others" [10]. Open Educational Resources are contents that integrate learning and reference materials [9]. These can include complete open courses, course materials, content modules, textbooks, journals, videos, images, or even tests [11]. The relevance of OER is steadily increasing and is of great interest worldwide [4]. According to OER Atlas 2017, OER-based events have increased fivefold compared to 2015, while the number of OER projects has nearly tripled and the range of services has increased by 70% [2]. In general, OER have come to be seen as an invaluable educational resource for institutions and faculty in every region [12].

A key element that separates OER from other learning and teaching resources is openness. The emphasis on open licensing is essential in this respect, as it provides the legal basis for the implementation of OER by defining precise conditions for access to information [13]. In 2001, Professor Lawrence Lessing at Harvard University developed an open license approach that has become globally established in recent years [14]. The non-profit organization Creative Common (CC) is the result of his licensing framework [14]. It includes legal mechanisms to ensure that creators of materials can both acknowledge and share their content simultaneously [1]. It also allows commercial activities to be restricted and prevents or allows content to be adapted and modified by users of OER [14]. Openly licensed educational resources are often accessed via software systems called repositories [15]. These digital systems serve the continuous collection, administration and storage of Open Educational Resources and thus act as a kind of library [16]. Repositories should include a well-maintained and effective indexing system for the origin and use of content and pedagogical approaches. Consequently, useful feedback and comments should be integrated, as well as indicators of high quality content [15].

The cultural shift towards a sustainable digital learning environment within different repositories could lead to a stronger emergence of social learning tools and an increase in group-based learning in the future [1]. The core potentials of OER are seen as legal certainty, quality optimization, cooperative knowledge development, and flexible content sharing [17]. In relation to the most important stakeholder group, the learners, these factors can lead to different synergies. Qualitative resources available at any time can initially increase the performance of learners. This is mainly possible by removing restrictions on the use of digital materials [14]. Especially since the cost of accessing openly licensed materials is greatly reduced compared to traditional resources [18]. By definition, OER may be shared, are adaptable and reusable. This ensures a shift away from passive learning and absorption, allowing learners to take a more active role in the learning process [2]. By means of the more flexible and cooperative handling of OER, an increase in efficiency and quality can be realized in the mid-term [9]. Through the growing number of resources and the regular evaluation of OER, a constructive and timely feedback culture can be established, which often seems to be missing in other learning arrangements [13]. At best, deficits, suggestions for improvement, and enhancements to content can be addressed, which can improve content quality [17].

3   Formation of Hypotheses

Through a literature review, the most important factors that seem to have an influence on OER could be filtered [19]. There is a consensus that influencing factors regarding OER can be of political, technical, legal, economic, social or didactic nature. In order to be able to formulate relevant hypotheses related to the individual factors, predictors were identified. The hypothesis model in Fig. 1 shows the influencing factors and predictors, as well as the assignment to the respective hypothesis.

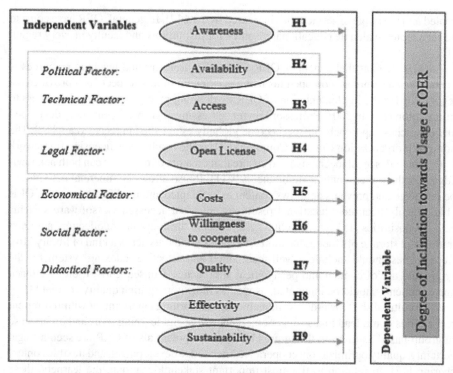

Fig. 1. Hypothesis model

Awareness Factor. The first question to be answered at this point is whether the participants are already familiar with the OER concept. Because in order to be able to integrate OER in the educational context, a development of awareness about free and digital educational resources can be relevant [20]. Without explicit knowledge about the definition, the open licensing, multimedia publication, and accompanying opportunities of OER, individuals may not be incentivized to incorporate them into their daily study routine [21]. Extensive awareness of OER would favor the likelihood of use from a student perspective. *H1: Extensive awareness about OER correlates positively with the degree of inclination towards OER use.*

Political Factor. It also needs to be stated whether students are aware of the availability of open learning objects, repositories as well as other digital locations of OER in order to use them profitably. In addition, the question arises whether an OER environment is provided on the university side [22]. It can be assumed that an active and cooperative provision of OER on the part of the institutions and lecturers would promote a use of OER through the increased availability [23]. *H2: The factor of availability of OER has an impact on the degree of inclination towards the use of OER.*

Technical Factor. Technical factors may also be a prerequisite for the adoption of OER. Here, the question of uncomplicated accessibility and usability of different formats arises [1]. The key element of OER lies in the idea of editability and reusability of learning objects [4]. Therefore, the urgency is to achieve technical functionality and interoperability between data, software, hardware and services [15]. *H3: Open access to cross-university teaching resources correlates positively with the degree of inclination towards the use of OER.*

Legal Factor. Copyright aspects must also be considered in the context of intellectual property. The generally representative open licensing approach and the fundamental rights of Creative Common integrated in it could therefore play an important role in the use of OER [4]. First, the question arises whether students are generally aware of copyright issues about OER [8]. If so, different terms and conditions, as well as basic rights integrated into them, may address different needs in university learning, and thus have an impact on students' decision to use OER [24]. Some standardized licenses allow the user to only reproduce the materials used, while others even grant adaptations and edits. Thus, individual conditions can be crucial [14]. *H4: An awareness of open licenses correlates positively with the degree of inclination towards the use of OER.*

Economic Factor. The decision to use open resources can also be influenced by economic factors. OER are, in theory, openly available to learners. The term "open"refers primarily to free access, meaning freedom of use, but not necessarily to freedom of costs [25]. In most cases, however, OER are freely available at no cost. Thus, the question arises whether OER would be preferred to traditional educational resources in the future due to cost savings [26]. Furthermore, accompanying costs may arise from the use of information and communication infrastructures to process and share materials [27]. This could be a barrier to long-term use of OER. Thus, the next hypothesis to be answered by this study is as follows: *H5: Costs are related to the degree of inclination towards the use of OER.*

Social Factor. Learning is a social process based on continuous communication and collaboration as well as review and revision of study results [4]. In this context, students act not only as active users, but also as creators of open teaching and learning resources. Therefore, in order to establish a dynamic OER network, it is essential to sensitize users to the culture of sharing and collaboration. Thus, the next hypothesis emerges: *H6: The willingness to cooperate is related to the degree of inclination towards the use of OER.*

Didactical Factors. In particular, the didactic factor of quality is most frequently discussed in the literature. The dynamic use of OER results in a higher permeability of content. This often leads to uncertainty about the trustworthiness, objectivity, or even accuracy of the information source, compared to traditional educational materials [1]. A negative perception of quality would imply a negative correlation to the adaptation of OER. To ensure that students do not lose interest in educational resources, quality assurance is important on both a subject-content and a learning-context level [1]. One way of quality management are review methods through internal quality assessment processes, open peer review models or even external user evaluations, which need to be continuously monitored and improved [9]. The perception of the quality of OER on the part of students should therefore also be tested in the form of a hypothesis. *H7: The more positive the perceived quality of OER is, the higher the degree of inclination towards the use of OER.*

Furthermore, not only the content relevance of cross-university resources is of fundamental importance, but also goal-oriented and effective results in the use it-self [28]. Due to the openness aspect, digital resources allow students to realize potentials in the direction of self-directed and long-lasting learning, which in turn can result in an improvement of student performance [28]. Based on this, the question is whether the use of OER increases performance by increasing effectiveness. *H8: The higher the perceived effectivity in learning by using OER, the more likely the degree of inclination towards the use of OER.*

The final question refers to the sustainability of OER, which can influence the decision to use it. This last point targets the security of existing OER in repositories and the increasing number of available OER. *H9: A positive perception about the future stock of OER and their sustainability, increases the degree of inclination towards the use of OER.*

4   Research Method

4.1 Research Design and Sample

In the context of OER, open exchange implies that knowledge content should be made freely available on non-commercial terms wherever possible. Consequently, the question arises how such a project can be sustainably established or maintained. For this reason, the research object aims to identify success factors that must be ensured in order to successfully implement OER and make it sustainably attractive for students. For this purpose, a survey with students was conducted in order to analyze these success factors. An online questionnaire is selected as a measuring instrument. The questionnaire is used to identify underlying potential factors that can significantly influence students' intention to use OER. In order to collect these factors, a mixed-method approach is adopted, as the questionnaire consists of open and closed questions. However, the main focus will be on the quantitative analysis. To transfer the formulated items within a standardized online questionnaire, the free online survey application LimeSurvey was used. Within the questionnaire, different items are formulated in terms of different task types. The open question is answered in a bullet-point manner using short-answer tasks, without any predefined answer alternatives, while closed questions are designed in a multidimensional manner. The closed questions are answered by predefined statements. They are evaluated by means of a 5-point Likert scale (see Table 1).

It is a verbally defined rating scale of the evaluation, whereby an ascending ordinal scaled subdivision from a strong disagreement "Strongly Disagree" to a strong agreement "Strongly Agree" is selected [29]. This corresponds to a bipolar scale polarity, ranging from a negative pole to a positive pole [30]. This prevents a forced attitude and ensures the adoption of a neutral middle position as well as a refutation of the predefined hypotheses.

At the beginning of the questionnaire, a few demographic data are collected (gender, age group), as well as information about the course of study, intended degree and name of the university. Afterwards, the awareness of OER is asked and a general OER term definition is given in order to enable a common understanding of the term. Next, an exploratory open-ended question is asked about the use of OER. This qualitative question

Table 1. Sample excerpt from the online questionnaire – closed question

	Strongly Disagree	Disagree	Neither Disagree Nor Agree	Agree	Strongly Agree
In my opinion, OER should run technically flawlessly on all end devices.	◯	◯	◯	◯	◯
In my opinion, the use of OER should not require any additional software or hardware.	◯	◯	◯	◯	◯

asks, "What factors do you consider important in increasing your personal intention to use OER?" This question is intended to be answered in a bullet point manner and to provide information about initial assessments of success factors in the use of OER.

The open question was evaluated by a qualitative content analysis according to Mayring [31]. For this purpose, all relevant free text answers were paraphrased at the beginning [31]. This is followed by an initial abstraction of the paraphrases by means of a generalization, in order to enable a step-by-step reduction and subsumption of sub-categories based on this [31]. The first reduction was carried out by shortening semantically identical paraphrases. In a second reduction, identical paraphrases were grouped, which were then formed into categories. Thereby, subcategories are inductively formed from the given statements in order to be able to include as much content as possible in the analysis. These were then aggregated and finally differentiated into main categories. In this context, care was taken to form the categories as precisely, disjunctively and comprehensively as possible [32]. The purpose of qualitative content analysis is to gather new insights that go beyond presumed hypotheses.

In the next step, predefined hypotheses (see Sect. 3) are verified or falsified by means of closed questions. The hypotheses include political, technical, copyright, financial, social and also didactic aspects that can have a positive as well as negative influence on participants.

In order to further determine the relevant conditions for the use of Open Educational Resources by students, statistical elaborations are made regarding predefined items. Univariate characteristic values were determined by means of SPSS, whereby frequencies and mean values were calculated [32]. Furthermore, a bivariate correlation analysis and significance testing was performed using cross-tabulations and correlations, as well as a linear regression analysis [32]. To check the structure of predefined variables, factor analysis and reliability analysis were conducted. At the end three further questions follow, which manifest an identification of different preferences over previous items and allow a prognosis about a future integration of OER in the everyday study life. There is also the possibility to add further comments in a free text field in order to include factors that were not covered by the answers to the given questions.

During the conception of the questions, as well as the measurement of the variables, attention is paid to quantitative and qualitative quality criteria, e.g. intersubjectivity, in order to obtain exact and error-free values [32]. To guarantee an objective and independent analysis and interpretation of the data, the reliability and reproducibility as well as the validity of the measurement, some pretests were carried out before the survey started [32]. Ten participants took part in the pretest.

After the pretest, the survey was distributed to enrolled students. There were no restrictions for the semester or the field of study, so a heterogeneous cross-section of the student body can be represented. The sample composition can be seen in Table 2.

Table 2. Sample composition

Gender	Age (Years)	Degree	Subject area	Educational institution
48 Male	5 17–20	54 Bachelor	9 Engineering	66 Osnabrück University
81 Female	119 20–29	58 Master	46 Business and Economics	10 Goethe University Frankfurt
2 Others	7 30–39	11 State examination without teaching degree	19 Liberal Arts	8 Leibniz University Hannover
		4 State examination with teaching degree	14 Arts, Music	4 Osnabrück University of Applied Sciences
		3 Doctorate	12 Social Sciences	3 University of Münster
		1 Others	12 Education	3 University of Koblenz-Landau
			8 Mathematics and sciences	3 Georg-August-University Göttingen
			3 Media Studies	34 Others
			1 Human medicine/health sciences	

(*continued*)

Table 2. (*continued*)

Gender	Age (Years)	Degree	Subject area	Educational institution
			1 Agricultural, forestry, nutritional sciences, sports	
			6 Others	

The adjusted population consists of a total of 131 students who participated in the survey. The most common age in this sample is between 20 and 29 years old at 91%. In this survey, 81 females, 48 males, and 2 diverse participated. In addition, 41% of the respondents reported being in the Bachelor's degree program, while 44% were already in the Master's degree program. In addition, another 9% are in the teaching field, 3% are pursuing a non-teaching state exam, and 3% are doctoral students. Half of all respondents are studying at the Osnabrück Univeristy, another 8% are enrolled at Goethe University Frankfurt am Main and 6% at Leibniz University Hannover. The remaining participants reported studying at another 18 educational institutions in Germany.

5   Results

5.1   Results of the Qualitative Content Analysis

The following section will now present the results of the open-ended question regarding students' use of OER. Based on the question: What factors do you consider important for the use of OER?, a categorization of success factors in the use of Open Educational Resources is made, which are summarized in the following figure (Fig. 2).

Technical. Technical factors in particular appear to be highly relevant in the decision to use OER. Approximately 40.8% of all respondents (out of 131 responses) state that wide-ranging access to OER is decisive for the use of OER. This should always be open (6.2%), unrestricted (6.2%), independent of location (5.4%), unlimited in time (4.6%) and digital (13.1%). In addition, access should be both possible without any registration (2.3%) and compatible with different end devices (3.1%). Furthermore, 36.9% of the respondents indicate that OER formats should be offered with a high ease of use. This includes enabling a clear (6.2%), compact (0.8%), simple and understandable (13.8%), as well as intuitive (1.5%) usability of open resources. Furthermore, they should be easy, uncomplicated and quickly accessible. This offers the transition to the next technical aspect, the usability of OER. According to 4.6% of the participants, OER should offer a simple, location-independent, offline download option. Here, it is occasionally stated that a good Internet connection, mobility and flexibility should be ensured in order to make optimal use of OER. Processing and further use of OER should be unrestricted, without loan periods or limited terms, and should therefore be included.

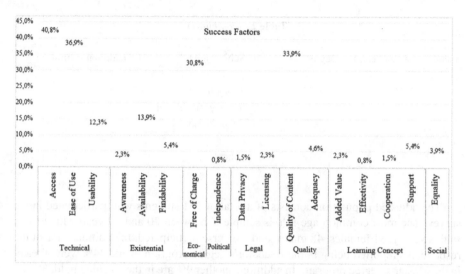

Fig. 2. Success factors for the use of OER

Existential. Regarding the awareness of OER, 2.3% of the participants indicate that information and knowledge about OER and its availability would be beneficial. An explicit mention of availability as a usage criterion of OER happens in 13.9% of the participants. Open Educational Resources should be multimedia (3.9%), extensive (5.4%) and widely available across internal boundaries (2.3%). One respondent also mentioned that there should be an availability of complementary programs for the use of OER. Two other respondents added that digital resources should also be offered in different languages. Once the open resources are made available, they should also be findable, according to 5.4% of the respondents. In particular, catalogs should be easy to find using helpful search algorithms.

Economical. It is also evident in the students' open responses that OER should be free of charge. Although by definition OER should be free and thus free of charge, almost 1/3 of the respondents again emphasize the actual freedom of charge.

Political. Furthermore, one respondent mentions the necessary independence of OER providers from economic actors.

Legal. Legal factors also seem to play a role for four respondents. Among other things, data privacy aspects are mentioned and appropriate or open licensing is considered important.

Quality. For one third of the students, the quality of OER plays an important role. 6.9% of the respondents list quality in general, with 5.38 further percent differentiating this according to quality of content. The following content quality requirements are listed: comprehensibility (3.9%), quality (2.3%), completeness (1.5%), correctness (3.1%), actuality (1.5%), and reliability (2.3%) of the digital resources. In addition, the adherence to quality standards is considered relevant by 9.2% of the respondents. For the security, trustworthiness and traceability of the information within the digital resources, serious source information and scientific standards are important to students when using OER. The adequacy of resources in terms of subject specification is also mentioned by 4.6% of participants. Here, a diverse and subject-related scope of resources should be available, at best with the coordination to the own curriculum.

Learning Concept. With regard to the use of OER, further aspects are also emphasized which, in summary, can serve long-term learning. On the one hand, there should be an added value in the targeted use of OER and on the other hand, an effective, cooperative and supportive behavior is desired by other individuals. This includes a networked and scientific exchange, as well as support (5.4%) by means of learning support through feedback, discussions, as well as through further information and advice on how OER can be used.

Social. In addition, one respondent mentioned equality in the use of OER, which was specified by four other participants through public domain use.

5.2 Results of the Statistical Analysis

In this section, the results of the study survey are comparatively presented and interpreted. The main focus here is on verifying or even refuting the predefined hypotheses.

H1: Extensive awareness about OER correlates positively with the degree of inclination towards OER use. First, it should be clarified whether the concept of Open Educational Resources is generally known. Thus, 67.2% of the respondents stated that they were not aware of OER, while 32.8% were. Among the participants with an existing knowledge of OER, the level of awareness was also asked. Among them, the majority shows low (12.2%) and very low (7.6%) knowledge. Consequently, the sample has only limited knowledge about OER, which is at least limited to hearsay. The linear regression performed confirms that high awareness of OER increases students' likelihood of using OER by 1.848 units (B = 1.848; $p \leq 0.05$). Accordingly, the hypothesis presented here can be confirmed.

H2: The factor of availability of OER has an impact on the degree of inclination towards the use of OER. This hypothesis considers the provision of OER on the part of the educational institution and lecturers, thus also the existence of repositories. It can be seen that 13.9% of the respondents perceive aspects of availability as important in the open-ended questions, summarizing that it should be free, multimedia, extensive, widely available and enabled in different languages. However, the descriptive evaluation shows that about half of the participants have no knowledge of whether there is any institutional provision or use or creation of OER on the university side and on the lecturing side. In contrast, Pearson's correlation analysis indicates that a high availability of OER is significantly positively correlated with a future probability of use ($r = 0.330$). This is also confirmed by the statistical regression, because an increase in availability by one unit increases the intention to use by 0.298 units ($\beta = 0.298$; $p \leq 0.05$). Accordingly, this hypothesis can also be confirmed.

H3: *Open access to cross-university teaching resources correlates positively with the degree of inclination towards the use of OER.* In the descriptive analysis, the majority of subjects indicate that accessibility to OER should not require additional software and hardware. Also, OER should run technically flawlessly on all devices and be displayed correctly on different end devices. Furthermore, the need for sufficient technical means for editing, modifying, and publishing OER is more likely to be agreed upon. If access to OER is technically accessible, students are more likely to use them. Unrestricted access is frequently associated with an intention to use ($\chi^2 = 25.232$; $p \leq 0.001$). According to Pearson's correlation test, this variable also shows significance ($r = 0.365$). Consequently, unrestricted access is frequently associated with a positive intention to use and the hypothesis can be confirmed.

H4: *An awareness of open licenses correlates positively with the degree of inclination towards the use of OER.* An open mention of licensing aspects turns out to be relatively low. Only three respondents stated that this is an important factor for the use of OER, with a further six respondents identifying general licensing rights as an obstacle. The variable regarding open licensing shows no significance within statistical tests, neither in the intercorrelation matrix nor in the bivariate regression. Thus, the fourth hypothesis has to be rejected overall. This result may be explained by the fact that aspects of licensing are more likely to be considered from the producer's point of view.

H5: *Costs are related to the degree of inclination towards the use of OER.* Especially the sustainability of the cost-free provision of OER seems to play an important role. The cost factor (sustainability) is a significant predictor for the implementation of the OER concept. On the one hand, this has a positive association ($\chi 2 = 21.714$; $p \leq 0.001$) and a positive correlation ($r = 0.391$) towards the future use of OER. Thus, an increased provision of explicitly long-term free Open Educational Resources in the future, as well as free complementary tools, are associated with the use of OER by students. This hypothesis can be considered as confirmed.

H6: *The willingness to cooperate is related to the degree of inclination towards the use of OER.* A high will to cooperate is associated with the future use of OER by more than half of the respondents ($\chi 2 = 22.355$; $p \leq 0.001$). This is accompanied by a positive correlation of the correlation analysis ($r = 0.184$). Consequently, a trending but small positive correlation is statistically detected. It is also evident from the descriptive frequency analysis that the culture of sharing educational materials with fellow students is perceived to be quite relevant and sharing educational content is generally considered to be an important component of education. Overall, the hypothesis can be rather confirmed as a positive statistical relationship was found.

H7: *The more positive the perceived quality of OER is, the higher the degree of inclination towards the use of OER.* The open survey shows a considerable relevance, while statistical methods do not prove this, thus the qualitative factor cannot be clearly verified. Ensuring the quality of the content of open content, as well as the continuous maintenance and updating of digital resources, and the creation of reliable quality standards are, despite this, essential measures for the success of OER.

H8: *The higher the perceived effectivity in learning by using OER, the more likely the degree of inclination towards the use of OER.* It was checked whether OER should facilitate students' knowledge acquisition, support them in achieving learning objectives, or promote independent learning and problem-solving skills. In all cases, the rather and completely agreement is at least 75 and at most 95 percent in total. These affirmative attitudes toward the factor of effectiveness of OER are confirmed statistically. Thus, 84 participants rather or completely agree with these items, while next to them they indicate a future use as likely. This association is found to be significant in the course of cross-tabulation ($\chi^2 = 24.29$; $p \leq 0.001$) and proved by means of a positive correlation ($r = 0.282$). Consequently, effectively creating better study performance by means of supportive and facilitative activities is related to successful use of OER. As a result, the hypothesis is more likely to be accepted.

H9: A positive perception about the future stock of OER and their sustainability, increases the degree of inclination towards the use of OER. During the structural review of the present items, no meaningful category is selected by means of the factor and reliability analysis and therefore the associated items are not statistically reviewed further. Accordingly, the ninth hypothesis cannot be interpreted. Nevertheless, the results of the descriptive frequency analysis are of interest here, because they provide a tendency outlook on the future stock of OER and therefore serve as a forecasting tool.

6 Discussion

The focus of the work is to survey the conditions of use of digital educational resources for an increased intention to use on the part of students. Here, the focus was on specific requirements that can generate successful and accessible usage intention. As a result, a student survey was conducted, from which key success factors were derived and recommendations for action are given below.

Steps must be initiated to achieve a higher level of awareness regarding OER. In this context, students must be provided with comprehensive information on the possible uses of OER, so marketing efforts and promotion of OER are necessary. For this purpose, higher education institutions should promote and facilitate info-events, as well as awareness-raising activities. Students would benefit from this, as well as lecturers who could promote the creation and use of OER in their teaching. In order to successfully establish OER on a broad basis, measures must be implemented in the future to ensure inclusive and equal access to high-quality resources. This refers primarily to technical accessibility (barrier-free) and the provision of OER free of charge. Building on this, steps must be taken in the future to ensure reliable quality assessment, assurance and control from a professional point of view. On this point, lecturers as creators of OER are particularly affected and should follow uniform quality guidelines. Higher education institutions are responsible for such guidelines and should work with lecturers to develop criteria and benchmarks. Once OER are at a solid level, measures should continue to be taken to increase awareness or knowledge of the added value and potential uses of OER and associated popularity on the part of students. The introduction of an OER policy could be an important framework in this regard, providing guidance to higher education institutions and educators. Through the establishment of supportive frameworks and the possibility of performance recognition, incentives and an increased commitment to the use and simultaneous production of OER can be achieved in the long term. An official listing of OER locations would also be beneficial to make it easier for students to find materials or official repositories. Furthermore, the realization of a long-term free usability of OER is an indispensable necessity; therefore, financing systems must be created in the future that fulfill this requirement for students.

If these measures are implemented extensively and restrictions are minimized, the use of Open Educational Resources can be increased in the daily study routine. The adaptation prospects of Open Educational Resources in the everyday university life of the students are evaluated as critical in this work. Although an increased willingness to use OER on the part of the students can be noted, a low willingness to participate with regard to cooperation and the creation of open resources is found. Moreover, students present abundant technical and qualitative terms of use that must be met in the future on the part of OER providers. In this course it becomes clear that on the way to the implementation of the OER concept some steps must be introduced, in order to be able to exhaust far-reaching potentials in this respect. Nevertheless, these findings can be built upon in further research so that the establishment of OER at higher education institutions can be promoted.

References

1. Bergamin, P., Filk, C.: Open Educational Resources (OER). Ein didaktischer Kulturwechsel. Offene Bildungsinhalte (OER), Teilen von Wissen oder Gratisbildungskultur, pp. 25–38 (2009)
2. Neumann, J., Muuß-Merholz, J.: OER Atlas 2017: Open Educational Resources - Deutschsprachige Angebote und Projekte im Überblick. Hochschulbibliothekszentrum des Landes Nordrhein-Westfalen (hbz), Zentralstelle für Lernen und Lehren im 21. Jahrhundert e.V. Verlag, Köln, Hamburg (2017)
3. Niegemann, H., Weinberger, A. (eds.): Handbuch Bildungstechnologie: Konzeption und Einsatz digitaler Lernumgebungen. Springer Berlin Heidelberg, Berlin, Heidelberg (2020)
4. Yuan, L., MacNeill, S., Kraan, W.G.: Open Educational Resources-Opportunities and challenges for higher education (2008)
5. Müller, H.M.: Neue kultur der auswertung von wissen. In: Bergaming, P., Pfander, G. (eds.) Offene Bildungsinhalte (OER): Teilen von Wissen oder Gratisbildungskultur? pp. 39–71. hep, der Bildungsverlag, Bern (2009)
6. Braßler, M., Holdschlag, A., van den Berk, I.: Nachhaltige Zukunftsperspektiven. Erstellung von Open Educational Resources (OER) in der Hochschullehre (2017)
7. Wilde, T., Hess, T.: Forschungsmethoden der Wirtschaftsinformatik. Wirtschaftsinformatik **49**(4), 280–287 (2007)
8. OECD: Giving Knowledge for Free: The Emergence of Open Educational Resources. Center for Educational Research and Innovation. OECD Verlag, Paris (2007)
9. Hylén, J.: Open Educational Resources: Opportunities and Challenges, pp. 1–10. OECD Verlag, Paris (2006)
10. UNESCO: UNSECO-Empfehlung zu Open Educational Resources (OER), Records of the General Conference, 40th session, Paris, November 2019, Resolutions (2019)
11. Hewlett Foundation: White Paper: Open Educational Resources - Breaking the Lockbox on Education. Retrieved from http://www.hewlett.org/library/hewlett-foundation-publication/whitepaper-open-educational-resources (2013)
12. Katsusuke, S., Mitsuyo, K., Hiroyuki, S., Yasuhiro, T., Rieko, I., Naoshi, H.: A survey of the awareness, offering, and adoption of OERs and MOOCs in Japan. Open Praxis **9**(2), 195–206 (2017)

13. Malina, B., Neumann, J.: Was sind Open Educational Resources? und andere häufig gestellte Fragen zu OER. Deutsche UNESCO-Kommission eV, Bonn (2013)
14. Butcher, N.: A basic guide to open educational resources (OER). Commonwealth of Learning (COL) (2015). https://doi.org/10.56059/11599/36
15. Downes, S.: Models for sustainable open educational resources. Interdisc. J. E-Learn. Learn. Objects 3(1), 29–44 (2007)
16. UNESCO: UNESCO Forum on the Impact of Open Courseware for Higher Education in Developing Countries. Final Report, p. 27. UNESCO, Paris (2002)
17. Koschorreck, J.: Open Educational Resources (OER): Der DIE-Wissensbaustein für die Praxis, pp. 1–7 (2018)
18. Erdsiek-Rave, U., John-Ohnesorg, M.: Schöne neue Welt?: Open Educational Resources an Schulen. Friedrich-Ebert-Stiftung, Abt. Studienförderung (2014)
19. Weller, M.: The Battle For Open How openness won and why it doesn't feel like victory. Ubiquity Press (2014). https://doi.org/10.5334/bam
20. Shigeta, K., Koizumi, M., Sakai, H., Tsuji, Y., Inaba, R., Hiraoka, N.: A survey of the awareness, offering, and adoption of OERs and MOOCs in Japan. Open Praxis 9(2), 195–206 (2017)
21. Ikahihifo, T.K., Spring, K.J., Rosecrans, J., Watson, J.: Assessing the savings from open educational resources on student academic goals. Int. Rev. Res. Open Distrib. Learn. 18(7), 126–140 (2017)
22. Bremer, C., Ebner, M., Hofhues, S., Köhler, T. Lißner, A. Lorenz, A., Schmidt, M.: Open Educational Resources und ihre Rolle an Hochschulen Rahmenbedingungen fur die Erzeugung, Bereitstellung und Nutzung. In: Digitale Medien und Interdisziplinaritat, pp. 291–294. Waxmann Verlag GmbH, Münster (2015)
23. Orr, D., Rimini, M., Damme, D.: Educational Resources: A Catalyst for Innovation. Educational Research and Innovation. OECD Publishing, Paris (2015)
24. Allen, I.E., Seaman, J.: Opening the Curriculum: Open Educational Resources in US Higher Education, pp. 1–49. Babson Survey Research Group (2014)
25. Kreutzer, T.: Open Educational Resources (OER), Open-Content und Urheberrecht. iRights.Law (2013)
26. Deimann, M., Neumann, J., Muuß-Merholz, J.: Whitepaper Open Educational Resources (OER) an Hochschulen in Deutschland: Bestandsaufnahme und Potenziale 2015. 1. Auflage, open-educational-ressources.de, Transferstelle für OER, Hagen, Hamburg, Köln (2015)
27. Butcher, N., Malina, B., Neumann, J.: Was sind Open Educational Resources? Und andere häufig gestellte Fragen zu OER. UNESCO, Dt. UNESCO-Komm., Bonn (2013)
28. Reinmann, G., Ebner, M., Schön, S.: Hochschuldidaktik im Zeichen von Heterogenität und Vielfalt: Doppelfestschrift für Peter Baumgartner und Rolf Schulmeister. BoD-Books on Demand (2013)
29. Bühner, M.: Einführung in die Test-und Fragebogenkonstruktion. Pearson Deutschland GmbH (2011)
30. Moosbrugger, H., Kelava, A.: Testtheorie und Fragebogenkonstruktion, 2nd edn. Springer Verlag, Berlin Heidelberg (2012)
31. Mayring, P.: Qualitative Inhaltsanalyse: Grundlagen und Techniken. Beltz Verlag, Weinheim Basel (2015)
32. Raithel, J.: Quantitative Forschung: Ein Praxiskurs: VS Verlag für Sozialwissenschaften. Springer, Wiesbaden (2008)

AI-Based Business Models in Healthcare: An Empirical Study of Clinical Decision Support Systems

Marija Radić[1]([⊠]) [iD], Claudia Vienken[1], Laurin Nikschat[1], Thore Dietrich[1], Holger Koenig[1], Lorenz Laderick[1], and Dubravko Radić[1,2]

[1] Fraunhofer Center for International Management and Knowledge Economy (IMW), Leipzig, Germany
marija.radic@imw.fraunhofer.de
[2] Leipzig University, Leipzig, Germany

Abstract. *Objectives:* By 2025, 90 percent of all care providers worldwide are expected to adopt cognitive AI help as evidence-driven care for their patients. Among all AI applications, clinical decision support systems (CDSS) are most likely to improve patient outcomes in the next 5–10 years. The objective of this paper is to analyze the business models of AI-based CDSS on the market to allow for generic statements on the design and state of the art of such business models. The study thereby aims at maximizing the utility of this technology by providing a basis for future business model considerations in this area.

Methods: Based on a comprehensive market analysis for AI-based solutions in the healthcare domain, we identify a sample of 36 commercially available CDSS and analyze their business models using the theoretical business model concept by Gassmann et al. [10].

Results: As a result, we identify generic attributes and alternate conditions of CDSS business models on the market in the respective key business model elements value proposition, value creation and value capture.

Conclusions: Based on the results, we develop a business model framework for AI-based CDSS that gives a first overview of the design of business models in this new technology field. Our findings contribute to closing a gap in the scientific literature and provide as a basis for future business model considerations.

Keywords: Clinical decision support systems · Artificial intelligence · Business models · Digital health

1 Introduction

The market potential of AI-supported systems in healthcare is very high and is projected to grow by on average 70% to over USD 6 billion in 2022 [1]. Clinical applications that predict diseases, personalize treatment, prevent adverse events or manage outcomes account for 50% of all revenues. By 2025, a democratization of AI is expected with more than 90% of care providers worldwide adopting cognitive AI help for their patients

M. A. Bach Tobji et al. (Eds.): ICDEc 2022, LNBIP 461, pp. 70–79, 2022.
https://doi.org/10.1007/978-3-031-17037-9_5

[2]. According to a study by emerj [3], there is expert consensus that among all AI applications decision support systems are most likely to improve patient outcomes in the next five to ten years with hospitals and healthcare facilities being the primary target groups. In summary, the market is highly attractive due to a large market potential for providers, a high market growth but at the same time a currently rather low market penetration rate. In light of the market's infancy, the current lack of transparency on offerings in the market as well as lack of scientific literature on business models is not surprising. The high potential of clinical decision support systems is already becoming apparent. In a study from 2019, 157 dermatologists from twelve university hospitals in Germany competed against a computer to detect skin tumors. The computer diagnosed more accurately than humans in 136 cases [4]. Most research studies, however, focus on the role of artificial intelligence for business processes in the healthcare industry or deal with the clinical and financial benefits of Clinical Decision Support Systems (CDSS) [5, 6].

The objective of the present study is to shed more light on the topic of AI-based CDSS business models. To the best of our knowledge, there is currently no database available, which provides comprehensive information on commercially available AI-based healthcare solutions. For this aim, we develop an AI-in-Healthcare market monitor to get an insight into the vibrant market. For the current study, we identify 36 AI-based decision support systems and analyze their business models using publicly available information. In the following, we describe the methods used and present the results of the business model analysis. The paper closes with a conclusion and discussion of our results.

2 Methods

The basis for our study is a comprehensive market analysis for AI solutions in the healthcare domain. Through desktop research, relevant companies, research institutes and startups, which are active in the field of AI in healthcare, were first identified based on articles, blogs, newsletters, and further sources and then saved as structured profiles in an internal company database. Currently, the database contains information on more than 1400 providers classified in startups (21%), established companies (51%) and research institutions (28%). For each provider, the database contains general information such as the provider's name, location, funding information and acquisitions as well as specific information on offered products and initiatives, indications, technologies, target groups and medical applications. To the best of our knowledge, currently no comparable database exists.

This database was the foundation for our research on business models for AI-based CDSS. Given the wide variety of systems, there is no generally accepted definition for a CDSS [6]. Systems come in different varieties and differ primarily in their level of intelligence and support. This makes them difficult to characterize formally. In the context of this paper, three criteria were applied to determine the sample of analyzed providers: First, we follow the definition, which refers to "CDSS as digital systems that provide the decision maker with the right information at the right time to support healthcare professionals in making clinical decisions" [6]. Second, only companies and startups that describe their product as an AI-based CDSS were selected from the database. Research projects were excluded from the analysis since the focus of the paper is to address existing business models in the market. In addition, only systems targeting physicians as end users were included. This leaves us with overall 33 companies and startups with 36 different CDSS systems.

2.1 Business Model Analysis Approach

Clinical decision support system providers will only be successful in the market if they commercialize the economic value of the technology used [7]. This requires the definition and development of a well-defined underlying business model for these systems. The term 'business model' is not conclusively defined in the scientific literature. Therefore, several concepts have been developed to operationalize the business model as a theoretical concept [8]. However, at the most basic economic level, a business model describes the logical approach of how an organization earns profit [9]. Gassmann, Frankenberger and Csik [10] build on this definition and define a theoretical concept – the Business Model Triangle - to describe the term business model based on the four dimensions target customer, value proposition, value creation and value capture [10] (Fig. 1).

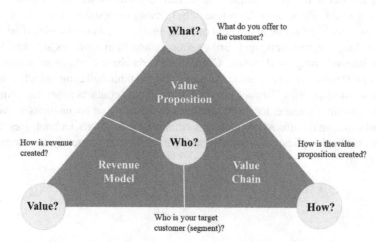

Fig. 1. The business model triangle by Gassmann, Frankenberger, and Csik [10].

Following this concept, the definition of relevant target customer segments is necessary to carefully develop the business model's value proposition. The value proposition describes all products or services a company offers to create value for its customers. The business model element value creation considers all relevant processes, activities, resources, and capabilities necessary to deliver the business' value proposition. Cost structures and revenue mechanisms are displayed in the business model element defined as value capture.

In the following, this Business Model Triangle is used to illustrate and analyze underlying business models of selected CDSS on the market. Hence, the dimensions value proposition, value creation and value capture are used to structure the business model elements for CDSS. Given the definition of CDSS used in this paper, the target group is restricted to physicians. The business model dimension target group is therefore fixed and not explicitly considered in the following business model analysis.

We conducted a morphological analysis based on information available in the company database and respective publicly accessible company websites. For the analysis, sources in English or German language were considered. Morphological analyses are commonly used to analyze multidimensional concepts such as business models [11, 12]. As a structured approach, this analysis allows to identify relevant business model attributes for products or services in a specific context [13]. Hence, the information collected on the CDSS business models is used to identify generic elements for each of the three business model dimensions. The findings are presented in a morphological box. In this representation, the identified generic business model attributes are defined as alternate conditions for CDSS business models [11].

3 Business Model Analysis

Overall, we examine 33 companies with 36 different CDSS systems. The descriptive statistics shows that most of the companies are from the United States (49%) and Europe (42%). Based on the SME definition of the European Commission [14], about half of the companies are small companies with 10 to 50 employees (49%). One third are large companies with more than 250 employees (33%), followed by microenterprises with a share of 12% and medium-sized companies with 6% (Fig. 2).

An examination of the founding year reveals that 49% of the companies are less than 10 years old and can thus be defined as startups [15]. The remaining companies are predominantly established companies that are at least 10 years old (Fig. 3).

Number of employees

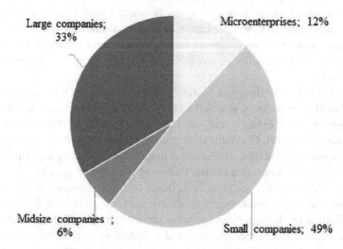

Fig. 2. Company size by number of employees.

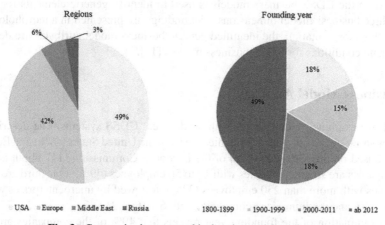

Fig. 3. Companies by geographical region and founding year.

4 Results

The results of the CDSS business model analysis and the characteristics of the respective business model elements value proposition, value creation and value capture are shown in the CDSS business model framework (Fig. 4).

Figure 4 shows a systematic presentation of the 36 different products. This is done by dividing the offerings into three business model elements and which target group was addressed. With their common categories of the main characteristics. These are assigned to categories which mentioned most frequently, with a list of the main properties. This

Business Model Elements	Attributes	Alternate Conditions					
Value Proposition	level of care	prevention	diagnosis	therapy recommendation		therapy support	
	indication	oncology	cardiology	radiology	pneumology	pharmacology	other indications
	impact	efficiency improvement / cost savings				patient engagement	
Value Creation	database	clinical trials	knowledge database	clinical guidelines		expert knowledge	monitoring of vital data
	methods	machine learning	data analytics	statistical methods		clinical pathway	imaging
	interfaces	electronic health records		clinical information system		mobile applications for physicians or patients	
Value Capture	pricing model	full licence		partial license	single purchase options		
	additional services	laboratory service					
Target Group	physicians						

Fig. 4. CDSS business model framework.

toll gives a brief overview of what is actually offered by the 36 products before continuing with the further analysis.

4.1 Value Proposition

The business model analysis shows that the *value proposition* of clinical decision support systems is mainly composed of three different attributes. These attributes can be divided into level of care and indication addressed as well as impact. We defined the levels of care based on the five pillars of health care, which consist of prevention, diagnosis, therapy, rehabilitation, and care [16]. Overall, four different levels of care were identified that are in focus of the analyzed CDSS, with many (N = 23) of them operating on at least two levels simultaneously. The four levels of care represent prevention, diagnosis, therapy recommendation and therapy support. Diagnosis and therapy recommendation are the most frequent care levels, with a share of 58% each, followed by therapy support with a share of 44%. Only six of the CDSS (17%) are used for prevention purposes. A statistically significant correlation was identified between the care levels of diagnosis and therapy support (p = 0,023).

83% of all CDSS' value propositions include statements concerning efficiency improvements or cost savings on their website. Furthermore, almost 60% of the systems described an improvement in the treatment pathway through the clinic with more compliance (patient engagement).

With respect to indications, 18 different indications were identified, with several CDSS covering multiple indications (17 out of 36 CDSS). The predominant indication is oncology with 14 CDSS, followed by cardiology and radiology with shares of 22% and 19% of the products, and pneumology and pharmacology with a share of 17% and 14% of all products.

A statistically significant correlation was only found between oncology and radiology (p = 0,049). In summary, the value proposition analysis for the CDSS shows that most systems focus on supporting the medical practitioner with diagnosis and therapy recommendation for indications in the field of oncology, cardiology and radiology thus leaving many green field opportunities for researchers and companies. The primary communicated impact of these systems is efficiency improvement for medical practitioners and patient engagement in the therapy process.

4.2 Value Creation

Our business model analysis shows that the CDSS' *value creation* can be stratified along the lines of databases, methods and interfaces that can be used to enhance the decision support process. With regards to the underlying data, the largest share of CDSS considers clinical trials for the decision support process, whereas 14 systems are linked to a knowledge database such as cancer registries or drug databases. In addition, some CDSS take expert knowledge (e.g., curatorship of experts and their knowledge) into account. Furthermore, monitoring of vital data or the consideration of clinical guidelines are relevant databases for clinical decision support processes.

Concerning methods, the analyzed CDSS mostly state to use machine learning (52%), data analytics (50%) or statistical methods (50%) for decision support. In addition, 18 systems refer to clinical pathways for the decision support process. Imaging is used as a method by 11 systems. Interfaces used by CDSS are electronic health records (58%), clinical information systems (27%) or mobile applications for physicians or patients (25%). The AI Pathway Companion from Siemens Healthineers [17], for example, is a tool to support medical decision-making. It uses artificial intelligence to incorporate all relevant disease-specific and patient-related data into the decision-making process. This also includes the interface to the patient file. The goal is to establish a patient-specific therapy pathway. The value creation analysis for the CDSS shows that the decision support is mainly based on machine learning or statistical methods. These methods frequently consider clinical guidelines and pathways or additional patient data to obtain a valid result.

4.3 Value Capture

The business model analysis in the element *value capture* shows that two pricing models predominate. The systems use a software licensing model in most of the cases (64%), 6 systems offer single purchase options for e.g., additional hardware such as connectors on their website. Moreover, the systems do not use a uniform licensing model. The models differ in their designs between e.g., subscription licenses - from a monthly to an annual subscription – to a feature license, which limits the features an end user can use. When offering such a licensing model, 39% of the systems offer a modular system. Selected CDSS also offer additional services such as a laboratory services e.g., for blood sample analysis (11%). These systems, for example, apply AI-methods to genomics on results from separately analyzed patient samples or offer a service for the physician to analyze patient samples within 4 weeks. These services additionally support the decision process.

5 Conclusion

Based on the analysis, we develop a business model framework for AI-based CDSS. The framework contains generic attributes and their alternate conditions for CDSS business models and gives a first overview on the design of business models in this new technology field. The analysis shows that these systems currently focus mainly on the leading causes of death i.e., heart diseases and cancer [18]. The support of these systems focuses on varying levels of care such as prevention, diagnosis, therapy recommendation using machine learning and statistical methods. The majority of analyzed CDSS use licensing as a pricing model, which is of little surprise since these are classical software products.

Only a few CDSS additionally offer laboratory services within the scope of decision support. These include the processing of e.g., tissue or blood samples to create genetic maps or compare them with existing databases. Most of the manufacturers promise an improved treatment pathway and patient process and advertise potential efficiency gains.

AI technologies are taking off in healthcare today for different reasons: First, there is mounting pressure to reduce health care costs and improve outcomes in developed countries. Second, there has been an explosion in the availability of health care data. Third, advances in hard- and software make it possible to harness that data in new, powerful ways. As AI-based innovations take off, they will allow providers to diagnose disease earlier with greater accuracy—and ultimately manage it more effectively. Such advances will be critical drivers that help deliver value-based healthcare i.e. the best patient outcomes at the lowest possible cost [19]. Critical for the implementation of value-based healthcare are economically sustainable business models for AI-based solutions. Due to the infancy of the market, little is known about AI-based business models so far. The objective of this paper is thus to analyze the business models for AI-based clinical decision support systems, which are expected to enter the markets with greatest likelihood first.

6 Discussion

Our analysis is based on an AI in Healthcare market monitor which currently contains profiles of more than 1400 companies and their products for AI healthcare applications. The focus of the study was on CDSS products which are already available on the market. For the empirical study, a sample of 36 commercially available CDSS were identified and analyzed using the theoretical business model concept of Gassmann, Frankenberger, and Csik [10].

The business model analysis reveals that AI-based clinical decision support systems have both similarities and differences with respect to the design of their business models. We thus derive a business model framework that provides an overview of possible business model characteristics in the field of AI-based CDSS.

The importance of AI-based CDSS in patient care is undisputed. Still these systems are rarely used in everyday clinical practice. Not least because several ethical and legal issues remain to be resolved [20]. For this reason, a uniform and rapid legal basis and security for providers and users of such systems would be urgently required at an international level to improve patient care and further advance the development of new innovative business models. This would ensure a high level of acceptance among physicians and patients alike, which is an important prerequisite for such innovations in practice [21]. Our study has several limitations, which are related to the availability of information regarding the examined CDSS business models. The analysis is mainly based on information available on publicly accessible company websites. Furthermore, only systems marketed on websites in German or English language are included. Hence, this restriction is likely to exclude additional relevant systems on the market or business model aspects, which are not transparently communicated on the respective company websites. The desktop research approach further limits the validity of statements related to the business models. Moreover, the identification and definition of attributes in the respective business model elements was necessary to allow for a comparison of the individual systems. These designations may not be able to describe all systems in detail and should be considered as a selection of relevant characteristics. While this paper certainly contributes to the literature on AI-based business models in healthcare, future analyses will be required to extend the sample of analysis and the definition of respective business model elements.

Acknowledgements. This work was supported as a Fraunhofer Lighthouse Project.

References

1. Frost and Sullivan: AI Market for Healthcare IT: Revenue forecasts by end-user segment, Global, 2017–2022 (2018)
2. Report Linker: Global AI in Healthcare Market Report for 2016–2027. https://www.report linker.com/p05251483/Global-AI-in-Healthcare-Market-Report-for.html. Last Accessed 25 Jun 2021
3. Emerj: Machine Learning in Healthcare: Expert Consensus from 50+ Executives. https://emerj.com/ai-market-research/machine-learning-in-healthcare-executive-consensus/. Last Accessed 28 June 2021
4. Brinker, T.J., et al.: Deep learning outperformend 136 of 157 dermatologists in head-to-head dermoscopic melanoma image classification task. Eur. J. Cancer **113**, 47–54 (2019)
5. Winter, J.: Innovativer einsatz künstlicher intelligenz bei bildgebenden verfahren im klinischen alltag. In: Pfannstiel, M.A., Kassel, K., Rasche, C. (eds.) Innovationen und Innovationsmanagement im Gesundheitswesen, pp. 701–714. Springer, Wiesbaden (2020). https://doi.org/10.1007/978-3-658-28643-9_37
6. Steinwendner, J.: Klinische Entscheidungsunterstützungssysteme: von der Datenrepräsentation zur künstlichen Intelligenz. In: Pfannstiel, M.A., Kassel, K., Rasche, C. (eds.) Innovationen und Innovationsmanagement im Gesundheitswesen, pp. 683–699. Springer, Wiesbaden (2020). https://doi.org/10.1007/978-3-658-28643-9_36
7. Chesbrough, H.: Business model innovation: opportunities and barriers. Long Range Plan. **43**, 354–363 (2010)
8. Zott, C., Amit, R., Massa, L.: The business model: recent developments and future research. J. Manag. **37**(4), 1019–1042 (2011)
9. Osterwalder, A., Pigneur, Y.: Business Model Generation: A Handbook for Visionaries, Game Changers, and Challengers. John Wiley & Sons, New Jersey (2010)
10. Gassmann, O., Frankenberger, K., Csik, M.: The Business Model Navigator: 55 Models that will Revolutionise your Business. FT Press, Upper Saddle River, NJ (2014)

11. Täuscher, K., Hilbig, R., Abdelkafi, N.: Geschäftsmodellelemente mehrseitiger plattformen. In: Schallmo, D., Rusnjak, A., Anzengruber, J., Werani, T., Jünger, M. (eds.) Digitale Transformation von Geschäftsmodellen. SBMI, pp. 179–211. Springer, Wiesbaden (2017). https://doi.org/10.1007/978-3-658-12388-8_7

12. Lüdeke-Freund, F., Gold, S., Bocken, N.M.P.: A Review and typology of circular economy business model patterns. J. Ind. Ecol. **23**(1), 36–61 (2018)

13. Ritchey, T.: Problem structuring using computer-aided morphological analysis. J. Oper. Res. Soc. **57**, 792–801 (2006)

14. European Commission: SME definition. https://ec.europa.eu/growth/smes/sme-definition_en. Last Accessed 18 Jun 2021

15. Kollmann, T., Jung, P.B., Kleine-Stegemann, L., Ataee, J., de Cruppe, K.: Deutscher Startup Monitor 2020. https://deutscherstartupmonitor.de/wp-content/uploads/2020/09/dsm_2020.pdf. Last Accessed 24 Jun 2021

16. Zinke, G., Frederking, A., Krumm, S., Schaat, S., Schürholz, M.: Anwendung künstlicher intelligenz in der medizin. https://www.digitale-technologien.de/DT/Redaktion/DE/Downloads/Publikation/SSW_Policy_Paper_KI_Medizin.pdf?__blob=publicationFile&v=6. Last Accessed 28 Jun 2021

17. AI-Pathway Companion. https://www.siemens-healthineers.com/de-ch/digital-health-solutions/digital-solutions-overview/clinical-decision-support/ai-pathway-companion. Last Accessed 23 Apr 2022

18. Centers for Disease Control and Prevention: Number of deaths for leading causes of death. https://www.cdc.gov/nchs/fastats/leading-causes-of-death.htm. Last Accessed 28 Jun 2021

19. Boston Consulting Group: Chasing Value as AI Transforms Health Care. https://www.bcg.com/de-de/publications/2019/chasing-value-as-ai-transforms-health-care. Last Accessed 28 Jun 2021

20. Gerke, S., Minssen, T., Cohen, G.: Ethical and legal challenges of artificial intelligence-driven healthcare. In: Bohr, A., Memarzadeh, K. (eds.) Artificial Intelligence in Healthcare. Academic Press (2020)

21. Schmidt-Logenthiran, T., Stephan, M.: Digitalisierung im Krankenhaus: Nutzerakzeptanz als Voraussetzung für Digitale Innovationen. Springer Fachmedien Wiesbaden GmbH, ein Teil von Springer Nature (2020)

Implementing an Agile Change Process to Improve Digital Transformation in Higher Education Teaching

Jonas Kötter[1]([envelope])[iD] and Agnes Mainka[2][iD]

[1] Department of Business Administration, Organization and Business Informatics,
University of Osnabrück, Osnabrück, Germany
`jonas.koetter@uni-osnabrueck.de`
[2] Department of Computer Science, University of Osnabrück, Osnabrück, Germany
`agnes.mainka@uni-osnabrueck.de`

Abstract. Due to the pandemic, teaching formats had to be transformed from analog to digital within a very short time. Many teachers and students had not enough time to meet these changes in an organized way. In this study, we examine, how an agile change process can be designed in the university sector according to the change management guidelines. First, the implementation of the agile change process according to Scrum will be described. Then, the requirements for an agile process model based on the students' viewpoint will be evaluated at a German University. In total, 1300 students participated in an online survey with open and closed questions from 5/15/2020 till 5/22/2020 at the University of Osnabrück. We distinguish between novice (first and second semester) and advanced (third and higher semester) students. A total of 779 statements from open questions were available for further evaluation. The content analysis results in 48 items and eight dimensions. These items represent requirements from students' viewpoint. The dimension communication offers the greatest potential for improvement in digital teaching. In future contributions, activities should be developed to implement the collected requirements in an agile framework with relevant recommendations for action.

Keywords: Agile development · Change management · E-learning · HEI

1 Introduction

The way of teaching at universities was fundamentally changed due to the lockdown during the pandemic in the spring of 2020 in Germany [10]. In the very short term, face-to-face courses were transformed to digital formats to enable students to continue their studies under pandemic conditions. This results in

---

Supported by the University of Osnabrück.

worldwide growing importance of e-learning [33,37]. In the short-term development of digital teaching formats, classic as well as agile and thus more flexible and adaptable development methods could be identified [6]. However, the development of digital teaching formats with agile methods was already known before the pandemic [15]. In the long run, we will see which digital formats will remain at universities after the pandemic and how they will perform. There is growing evidence that blended learning will continue, even students and lectures come back to their physical learning spaces [37,45]. It is necessary to collect empirical data to integrate experiences of digital teaching into the university's strategy, culture and structure. This information and the involvement of all stakeholders in the strategic development process can contribute to making the universities fit for the future [5].

The aim of the paper is, on the one hand, to demonstrate a possible agile development process in the university context. On the other hand, to elaborate requirements for an agile process model based on the students' viewpoint. The identified requirements will also be prioritized based on student preferences using the MoSCoW principle (*must have*, *should have*, *could have*, and *won't have*) [11]. Accordingly, the following research questions will be answered:

RQ1: How to design an agile change management process in the university sector?

RQ2: Is Scrum a feasible process development model in a higher education e-learning environment?

RQ3: Which requirements apply in the field of e-learning by students?

RQ4: Which differences exist in e-learning requirements between first-year and advanced students?

To answer the research questions, first, the topics change management and agile development in higher education institutions (HEI) are introduced concerning the current literature in section two. Based on this, we describe the agile change process according to Voigt et al. which follows Kotter's change management process model (**RQ1**), [21,39]. The research methodology and the target population of the survey are described in section three. The students' requirements base on a systematic literature analysis on relevant applications of Scrum in the university context (**RQ2**) and a university wide survey. The results are presented in section four. The identified requirements, including a comparison of novice students and students in higher semesters (**RQ3**), are transferred to an agile model by using a prioritization principle (MoSCow). In section five follows the discussion of the identified requirements from the literature review and the survey regarding the integration into an agile development process (**RQ4**). In the conclusion, the main results, limitations of this work, and future research areas are presented.

2 Literature Review

Due to the continuing pandemic, most of the university lectures had to be transformed from mainly physical to digital formats [6]. The lectures were under pressure to offer immediately e-learning possibilities for their students. There was no time for a long-term change process. Cheema and Bils et al. explicitly indicate that the time frame for decisions is relevant in this context [5,10]. Thus, a short period harms decision-making within a change process.

In a study by a German university, around 230 lectures of this university should state their biggest challenges within digital teaching [18]. About 27% indicated that they felt the transformation was too fast. About 21% indicated that the workload was too high and about 19% criticized a lack of contact with students. Krüger describes in his work, that the length of the time-horizon depends on each individual situation. However, strategic change takes more time than, for example, a liquidity bottleneck that can be resolved in the short term [22]. A current trend shows that e-learning becomes more and more important for universities, not only due to the worldwide pandemic. This is shown, for example, in changing demographic variables of students or the possibility of digital access from outside the university [31]. In the future, HEI need to create a process as part of strategic change that includes digital teaching and e-learning.

There are a variety of definitions for e-learning. Some authors define e-learning as, for example, exclusive access to resources [27,34]. Other authors such as Kumar, Wotto, and Bèlanger [23] define e-learning as the supported learning that is characterized by digital electronic tools and media. In a systematic literature review, Sangra identified four definition clusters (technology, system-oriented, communication, and educational paradigm) and concluded that a holistic e-learning definition should be viewed from different angles and should consist of the four clusters [34]. In this work, e-learning is understood as a way of learning, which is characterized by the use of digital technologies, provides access to resources, and has a special focus on communication or interaction.

2.1 Change Management

The term change management can be understood as a continuous process of renewal to align the capabilities and structure of an organization. The objectives of change management are based on both internal and external customers of the company and the constantly changing requirements of the company [29]. The process of change and the associated changes are omnipresent in current organizations, which can also be foreseen further in the future [2]. R. T. By concludes that the speed at which change is occurring has never been faster than it is nowadays [9]. Furthermore, he emphasizes that there is often a lack of a valid framework for implementing and executing change.

Like Kotter, many authors in the field of change management argue that change and the associated changes never begin because change never ends [42]. Therefore, many organizations try to adapt to the constant evolution of their environment by creating a learning organizational culture or trying to work in an agile manner according to Scrum or Just in Time [2]. Increased agility and the associated aspects of, for example, flexible adaptation to changes, flexible processes, or shortened development times are just some of the advantages that characterize agile change management [38]. Agile methods originate from software development projects, but they are suitable as well for larger change projects in which participatory implementation plays a major role [24]. Voigt et al. provide a systematic literature review of agile methods applied in the university sector [39]. Scrum, as well as JiTT (Just in Time Teaching), were identified as adaptable agile development methods [39]. According to this investigation, we categorized the agile development processes of e-learning into the six phases of change management by Kotter [21]. In the first phase, a strong *leadership coalition* of e-learning experts is to be formed. In a second step, the e-learning vision should be developed (*conceptualize vision*), which can consist, for example, of different requirements, specifications, or sub-tasks. During this step, the IT and didactic support should also contribute their expertise to provide instructional methods. In addition, space, time, and financial constraints should be considered at this step in the conceptual design. After the conception, in the third phase (*communicate vision*) benefits of the new e-learning strategy are highlighted and the developed core elements are communicated to the stakeholders. The following step (*enable others in terms of the vision*) is to enable work solutions with the provided technology that are efficient as possible for the students. In the next phase (*make short-term success visible*) teachers create tasks that are realized immediately. In addition, support helps lecturers by testing the learning platform. In the sixth and final phase within the agile process model, the lecturer should learn from occurred mistakes (*consolidate improvements*).

2.2   Agile Development in Higher Education Institutions

Scrum follows the basic principles of change management with the positive effect of increased motivation of the participants [24]. It was first developed in the 1990s and it continues to be adapted. A *Scrum Guide* defines specific rules for handling the agile model. Scrum can be understood as a framework that can be used to generate adaptive solutions to problems of a complex nature. With the help of iterative cycles and an incremental approach, knowledge is generated from experience [35]. Thus, this agile model is ideally suited for learning from the experiences made in digital teaching. Scrum is composed of stakeholders (e.g. *Scrum Team*), *Scrum Events*, and *Scrum Artefacts*. We adapted the agile model of Scrum to the context of HEI e-learning development (Fig. 1).

According to the Scrum framework, different stakeholders (*Scrum Team*) work together in agile development. This team consists, for example, of developers, the *Product Owners*, and a *Scrum Master*. There are no hierarchies within this heterogeneous team. Outside of this team, there may be other stakeholders with which the project team can collaborate.

Introducing *Scrum* as an agile development process model at a university at first the *Scrum Team* have to be identified. At a University the first step in introducing the agile development process (*Scrum*) to define a *Scrum Team*. In the framework of Schwaber and Sutherland [35], the *Scrum Team* should be a group of about ten participants to implement the requirements into *Increments* in a targeted manner. Due to the university-wide transformation to digital teaching, the lecturers with staff from different subject areas or institutes should each be

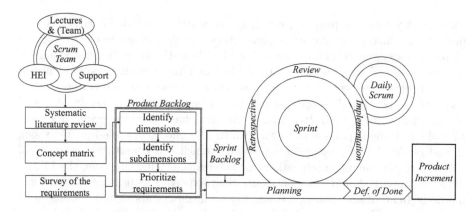

Fig. 1. Agile process

understood as an agile *Scrum Team*. This team is responsible for the individual implementation and thus also for the success. According to Voigt et al., the management of the HEI has no direct role in the implementation of an agile process model [39]. The IT and didactic support of the institutions should assist the lecturers and the team. At a university usually more than ten lectures or staff members create digital teaching units. Therefore, it is necessary to form further subdivisions. These may be naturally formed according to their institutes or subject areas whereas interdisciplinary networks of team members may additionally increase productivity. In general, smaller teams can react faster, communicate more efficiently, and are more productive [35].

In the next step, a *Product Backlog* with requirements has to be established. Additionally, we introduce three steps for the identification process of these requirements. Based on a systematic literature review we examined methods to identify and prioritize requirements from students' viewpoints. Next, the requirements are clustered and illustrated within a concept matrix. Based on this matrix the requirements from the students' viewpoint are collected through a survey. These requirements form the *Product Backlog*. Content analysis is needed to identify the dimensions and sub-dimensions of the requirements. Finally, the requirements are prioritized for the implementation process. Primarily, high-priority requirements are documented in the *Sprint Backlog*. The outstanding process steps in the Scrum framework as illustrated in figure one will be explained according to the results in Sect. 5 (discussion) to demonstrate how to realize the requirements.

3   Method

This paper aims to demonstrate an agile process model for HEI e-learning development based on students' requirements. The investigation starts with a systematic literature analysis according to Webster and Watson to identify already derived requirements within the Scrum framework [41]. The process of validation and exclusion of the literature is described in the results. In addition, a concept matrix helps to categorize the identified literature into different fields of application (Table 1) [41].

In the next step, the research design for the student survey is described which builds the basis for the product backlog. It is based on a university-wide qualitative and quantitative standardized survey. The survey was carried out from 5/15/2020 to 5/22/2020 during a national lock-down (two months after the beginning of the summer semester 2020). The population includes all students at the university. In total, 1300 students participated in the study anonymously. The online questionnaire was implemented with the research tool Lime Survey hosted at the university. After the data was collected and reviewed, a total of 779 data sets were available for content analysis which was performed according to Mayring [26]. Missing, incomplete (no information on semesters) and duplicate data sets were excluded for further analysis [14]. Within the framework of the content analysis, a multi-stage procedure was used to inductively reduce the qualitative data material till the identification of dimensions and items [26]. The responses were cross-coded by two researchers to further increase objectivity. The target population includes a total of 326 novice students (first and second semester) and 453 students from higher semesters. In the literature, no census of the classification of novice and experienced students can be identified. We define first-year students as students who are in their first or second semester. As part of the standardized qualitative and quantitative survey, all students were asked the same question: *What did you miss most about the digital semester?* Students were able to answer at their discretion without space restrictions and in an anonymous form.

4   Results

In the following, the results of the identification process of the requirements are presented. First, a systematic literature analysis was conducted to identify requirements from already published work (figure two). For this purpose, search terms with different synonyms were used for the query. The search was performed in both English and German. A total of 22 contributions were identified in Web of Science, ERIC, Scopus, and ScienceDirect with the search string: (universit* OR hei) AND ("e-learning" OR "digital learning" OR "digital format*") AND scrum. In the first step of the systematic review, two unavailable, two duplicate, and one article in another language were excluded. After reading the abstract, one article was deleted due to a different focus. In the third step, after reading the full text, another contribution was excluded, because no requirements could be identified. A summary of the results from the systematic literature review is illustrated in the concept matrix in table one according to Webster and Watson [41]. In addition to the identified articles, this also presents the field of application of the used *Scrum Frameworks* (Fig. 2).

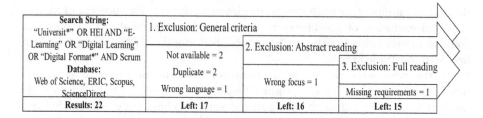

Search String: "Universit*" OR HEI AND "E-Learning" OR "Digital Learning" OR "Digital Format*" AND Scrum **Database:** Web of Science, ERIC, Scopus, ScienceDirect	1. Exclusion: General criteria		
	Not available = 2	2. Exclusion: Abstract reading	
	Duplicate = 2	Wrong focus = 1	3. Exclusion: Full reading
	Wrong language = 1		Missing requirements = 1
Results: 22	**Left: 17**	**Left: 16**	**Left: 15**

Fig. 2. Systematic literature review

Table 1. Scrum framework concept matrix

Field of application	Literature														
	1	2	3	4	5	6	7	8	9	10	11	12	13	14	15
	[17]	[19]	[7]	[30]	[13]	[4]	[16]	[43]	[3]	[32]	[20]	[25]	[8]	[36]	[12]
Development	x	x		x	x		x	x				x	x		x
Learning		x			x									x	
Assessment									x	x	x				

The 15 identified and analyzed articles can be categorized into three fields of application: *development, learning,* and *assessment.* In the category *development,* the Scrum Framework is described from two different perspectives: On the one hand, for the development of digital teaching materials and on the other hand, as a process model for the agile development of software. In addition to software development, the Scrum Framework was applied for 3D modeling. The category *learning* includes knowledge enhancement, e.g. by explaining Scrum to the students in a playful way with the help of "Minecraft". Also, other gamification possibilities, like a virtual avatar, are used to get to understand the Scrum framework and processes. The category *assessment* contains the critical examination of the studies. These articles describe how to evaluate according to the *Scrum Framework,* e.g. with the purpose to identify competence gaps of students. One article confirms a research gap of a university-wide survey of requirements. In all 15 articles, it was possible to identify technically formulated requirements such as requirements for data, security, quality, navigability, sound, photos, and videos. In three of the 15 articles, the requirements are divided into functional and non-functional requirements [12,13,36].

Looking at the empirical data, the 779 analyzed answers from the survey include a diverse range of mentioned items by the students. Most students indicate one (n = 779), two (n = 368), or three (n = 138) items. More than three items are listed by 39 students. For the evaluation, the items are grouped in eight dimensions as shown in Table 2 and 3. Items are counted by the number of mentions. One student may mention more than one item in one dimension. The results need to be investigated carefully due to the lock-down situation which has resulted in a need for ad-hoc online learning solutions and with the view of social isolation.

To prioritize the identified items for further use in Scrum, the MoSCoW principle will be used at this point, introduced by Dai Clegg in 1994 [11]. It demonstrates how to prioritize requirements into *must have*(m), *should have*(s), *could have*(c), and *won't have*(w). *Must have* defines the most relevant requirements, which are to be converted absolutely. The *should have* requirements also have a high priority. *Could have* requirements are desirable but do not have a high priority. The *won't have* requirements do not have to be implemented directly and can be saved for further *Sprints* [1]. The classification of the requirements was conducted by the researchers based on the number of identified mentions. It would be possible to conduct diverse student groups to assist in this step as well. Overall, about 67% were categorized as *must have* requirements, about 29% as *should have* requirements, about three percent as *could have* requirements, and less than one percent as *won't have* requirements.

Within the dimension 1. technical issues the students mention problems having a stable internet connection (n = 13) or the availability of soft- and hardware, e.g. a webcam (n = 3). Others mention that they are not satisfied with the university online learning and meeting platform (n = 3). By 2. limited availability the students count canceled group activities like making music and doing sports (each n = 9). This was due to the lock-down in Germany. Excursions and practical training were also canceled (n = 13). Ten students mention that in some cases lectures were not offered at all due to the ad hoc switch to online learning. Further, the students missed 3. places during online learning. The learning environment, the library, and the university canteen are mentioned more often by students at higher semesters (n = 45, n = 37, n = 34 vs. n = 29, n = 23, n = 13). The academic atmosphere was missed by both groups of students. A further problem for the students was the missing 4. structure. Daily routines (n = 47) and leisure time (n = 33) are mentioned the most. Concerning the dimension 5. study the students refer to unavailable or unplanned exams (n = 58) and a lack of information (n = 27). Lectures reliability (n = 15) and overview (n = 14) are mentioned in conjunction with missing information and communication. Many students criticize the teaching format (n = 148) of the offered 6. lectures. Particularly, students in higher semesters were unsatisfied (n = 98). Students in their first year had more problems regarding the high workload (n = 26). The dimension with the highest mentions is 7. communication. As general (n = 576) everything was counted related to getting in touch with other persons. The high ratio of mentions allows us to take a more differentiated view of this dimension which will be discussed in the next section. The results show that interaction with students (n = 189, n = 198) and lectures (n = 98, n = 102) is highly mentioned by both student groups, as well as face-to-face meeting (n = 98, n = 115). The last identified dimension is 8. personal, which is related to feelings, behavior, or literacy. Seven students describe that they do not feel accepted by their environment as a student with a high workload because they are sitting at home. Especially, advanced students (n = 6) had to struggle with this. Keeping one's own motivation high was a problem for both student groups (each n = 7).

Looking at the differences between first-year and advanced students in e-learning requirements (**RQ4**) some differences could be identified. Advanced students know that lectures can offer diverse teaching formats and therefore ask for it in the digital environment (teaching format, n = 98). Students in their first year have more problems relating to the high workload (n = 26). Both student groups have in common that they are looking for a daily structure with routines and free time. The students are looking for a daily structure and regular access to new materials or new lecture videos. Most students wish to have more contact with other students and lecturers. 128 students miss knowledge sharing at the campus and in seminars.

5   Discussion

We introduced in this paper how requirements from students' points of view could be evaluated and prioritized. With this we can describe in the following section an iteration cycle and discuss our findings. Additionally, recommendations for action are presented for the first *must have* requirement. The most frequently identified requirement of students in the first and third semester is located in dimension eight (item 8.1). Students would like to have more personal contact with other students (*missing contacts*). Although this is the most important *must have* requirement, it should not be implemented because the social distancing due to the COVID-19-Pandemic still exists. Therefore, the second most important *must have* requirement should be addressed at this point: Students would like to have more interaction with other students (dimension = 8. communication). Both items 8.1 (*missing contacts*) and 7.1 (*interaction with students*) focus on contact with other students, so a change in one item can change the other item (target harmony).

Within Scrum the *Definition of Done* needs to be clear for each requirement before the *Sprint* starts. After the requirement for the *Sprint Backlog* has been defined, the *Planning* and *Implementation* phase follows (see Fig. 1). According to Voigt et al., in this phase, the lectures and the team have to implement midterm products, and the IT- and Didactic-Support should provide and test tools or platforms [39]. Most of the requirements were identified in the dimension of interaction, so the recommendations for action should have a high level of interaction. A low level of interaction for example would be realized by using shared application systems such as GoogleCods, TitanPad, discussion forums, or e-mail. Higher levels of interaction could be reached in online self-assessment tasks. The tasks set can be conducted in group work. In addition, learning communities could be implemented which communicate via collaboration software [40]. These possibilities of increasing interaction using gamification could be confirmed in the systematic literature review in the articles [4,7], and [36]. The most common interaction typology [44] according to Moor (*"Three Types of Interactions"*) [28] includes three domains, one of which is learner to learner interaction. Studies that have addressed the learner perspective have identified several factors that influence student interaction, such as the group work used, the environment in which the course is conducted, and the community in which the course

Table 2. Part 1: Identified dimensions of digital learning requirements

d	Items	n	a	p
1. technical issues	1. general	4	11	s
	2. internet connection	3	10	s
	3. availability (hard- and software)	2	1	c
	4. satisfaction with the online learning and meeting platform	2	1	c
2. limited availability	1. excursions and practical training	7	6	s
	2. lectures	3	7	s
	3. university sport	3	6	c
	4. music groups	3	6	c
3. places	1. learning environment	29	45	s
	2. university canteen	23	37	s
	3. library	13	34	s
	4. academic atmosphere	14	18	s
4. structure	1. daily routines	22	25	s
	2. leisure time	15	18	s
	3. variety in daily routine	6	10	s
	4. separation of living, work, and leisure	8	7	s
	5. time	2	7	c
5. study	1. exams	20	38	s
	2. general information	7	20	s
	3. lectures reliability	8	7	s
	4. lectures overview	5	9	s
6. lectures	1. teaching format	50	98	m
	2. workload	26	15	s
	3. teaching format and materials	10	15	s
	4. communication	7	13	s
	5. knowledge sharing	4	12	s
	6. teaching format and materials overview	3	1	c
	7. teaching format and materials reliability	2	1	c
7. communication	1. interaction with students	189	198	m
	2. face-to-face	98	115	m
	3. interaction with instructors	98	102	m
	4. knowledge sharing	62	66	m
	5. interaction with students for knowledge sharing	51	52	m
	6. interaction with instructors for knowledge sharing	23	31	s
	7. interaction with students for knowledge sharing face-to-face	23	22	s
	8. interaction with instructors for knowledge sharing face-to-face	15	18	s
	9. interaction with university services	2	2	c

d = Dimensions, n = Novice Students (first and second semester)

a = Advanced Students (third and higher semester), p = Prioritization

takes place [44]. York and Richardson concluded that it is not clear which is the best recommendation for action to increase interaction. In total, the researchers

Table 3. Part 2: Identified dimensions of digital learning requirements

d	Items	n	a	p
8. personal	1. missing contacts	266	310	m
	2. exercise	5	16	s
	3. student's motivation	7	7	s
	4. instructor's digital literacy	2	7	c
	5. finance	6	3	c
	6. environmental recognition of the current situation	1	6	c
	7. instructor's motivation	4	2	c
	8. being anonymous	1	2	c
	9. student's digital literacy	1	1	c
	10. mental load	1	1	c
	11. nothing	2	7	w

d = Dimensions, n = Novice Students (first and second semester)
a = Advanced Students (third and higher semester), p = Prioritization

proposed eleven categories in their article to increase interaction. One possible action could be the creation of a community. Students should first get to know each other, establish a trustful relationship with rules and encourage interaction [44]. Considering the IT- and Didactic-Support, the lectures and teams should regularly review the progress of the *Sprint* in *Daily Scrum Meetings* and flexibly adjust in case of deviations from the defined target [35]. After a learning community has been established, the next phases (*Review* and *Retrospective*) follow. According to Voigt et al., lectures and the team should evaluate the conducted activities and learn from the mistakes [39]. During the *Sprint Review*, the most important results are compiled by the lecturers and the team. The *Sprint Backlog* objectives are compared with the achieved results [35]. In the *Retrospective* phase, the lectures and the team review how to work more efficiently in the future. Useful improvements can be included in the *Product Backlog* and can be prioritized again [35]. Finally, the first iteration cycle ends with the realization of the first requirement (*Definition of Done*). After the first cycle, the *Increment* represents the learning community, which needs to be constantly developed in an agile way. Regular requirement analyses can be used to reduce the barriers in a target-oriented process.

6 Conclusion

The current article demonstrates a successful agile change management process in the field of e-learning at a university. In summary, an agile process model was explained, which is aligned based on the classic phases of change management (**RQ1**). According to the systematic literature review, Scrum was already used in other areas in the context of HEI, such as gamification, or for the purpose to identify competence gaps of students (**RQ2**). However, this is the first university-wide study that deals with the inquiry of requirements according to Scrum. A total of eight dimensions (1. technical issues, 2. limited availability, 3. places, 4. structure, 5. study, 6. lectures, 7. communication, 8. personal) with 48 items could be identified for both novice students and advanced students (**RQ3**). Furthermore, we only identified minimal differences in the requirements between students in the initial study phase and students in higher semesters (**RQ4**).

The research focus of this work is on the requirements and not on the implementation. In subsequent studies, the phases (*Implementation, Review,* and *Retrospective*) should be further evaluated to design a comprehensive approach. The current results are limited to one university at the time of investigation during the nationwide lock-down. To be able to analyze a change in requirements in the long term, it is important to implement additional studies to identify the effects of the current pandemic and to improve e-learning for the future.

References

1. Ahmad, K.S., Ahmad, N., Tahir, H., Khan, S.: Fuzzy_MoSCoW: a fuzzy based MoSCoW method for the prioritization of software requirements. In: International Conference on Intelligent Computing, Instrumentation and Control Technologies (ICICICT), pp. 433–437. IEEE (2017)
2. Appelbaum, S.H., Habashy, S., Malo, J.L., Shafiq, H.: Back to the future: revisiting Kotter's 1996 change model. J. Manag. Dev. **31**(8), 764–782 (2012)
3. Babič, F., Gašpar, V., Šatala, P.: New trends in mobile technologies education in Slovakia: an empirical study. In: 16th International Conference on Emerging eLearning Technologies and Applications (ICETA), pp. 37–42. IEEE (2018)
4. Naik, N., Jenkins, P., Newell, D.: Learning agile scrum methodology using the groupware tool trello® Through collaborative working. In: Barolli, L., Hussain, F.K., Ikeda, M. (eds.) CISIS 2019. AISC, vol. 993, pp. 343–355. Springer, Cham (2020). https://doi.org/10.1007/978-3-030-22354-0_31
5. Bils, A., et al.: Corona-semester 2020 - ad-hoc-Maßnahmen evaluieren und nachhaltig verankern, pp. 1–17. Hochschulforum Digitalisierung (2020)
6. Blömer, L., Voigt, C., Hoppe, U.: Corona-Pandemie als Treiber digitaler Hochschullehre. In: Zender, R., et al. (eds.) DELFI 2020 - Die 18. Fachtagung Bildungstechnologien der Gesellschaft für Informatik e.V, pp. 343–348. Gesellschaft für Informatik e.V. (2020)
7. Bourdeau, S., Coulon, T., Petit, M.C.: Simulation-based training via a "readymade" virtual world platform: teaching and learning with minecraft education. IT Prof. **23**(2), 33–39 (2021)
8. Brenner, B., Hummel, V.: A seamless convergence of the digital and physical factory aiming in personalized Product Emergence Process (PPEP) for smart products within ESB Logistics Learning Factory at Reutlingen University, vol. 54, pp. 227–232. Elsevier (2016)
9. By, R.T.: Organisational change management: a critical review. J. Chang. Manag. **5**(4), 369–380 (2005)
10. Cheema, M.S.: Covid-19 revolutionising higher education: An educator's viewpoint of the challenges, benefits and the way forward. Life Sci. Med. Biomed. **4**(9), 1–6 (2020)

11. Clegg, D., Barker, R.: Case Method Fast-track: A RAD Approach. Addison-Wesley Longman Publishing Co., Inc. (1994)
12. Da Silva, D.A., et al.: Health care transformation: an academic application system case study. IFAC-PapersOnLine **51**(27), 413–418 (2018)
13. Diaz, J., Saldana, C., Avila, C.: Virtual world as a resource for hybrid education. Int. J. Emerg. Technol. Learn. (iJET) **15**(15), 94–109 (2020)
14. Döring, N., Bortz, J.: Datenaufbereitung. In: Döring, N., Bortz, J. (eds.) Forschungsmethoden und Evaluation in den Sozial- und Humanwissenschaften. S, pp. 579–595. Springer, Heidelberg (2016). https://doi.org/10.1007/978-3-642-41089-5_11
15. Gale, T.C., Chatterjee, A., Mellor, N.E., Allan, R.J.: Health worker focused distributed simulation for improving capability of health systems in Liberia. Simul. Healthc. **11**(2), 75–81 (2016)
16. Gaspar, J., et al.: A mobile serious game about the pandemic (COVID-19 - did you know?): Design and evaluation study. JMIR Serious Games **8**(4) (2020). https://doi.org/10.2196/25226
17. Hadi, S.H., et al.: Developing augmented reality-based learning media and users' intention to use it for teaching accounting ethics. Educ. Inf. Technol. **27**, 1–28 (2021). https://doi.org/10.1007/s10639-021-10531-1
18. Hamborg, K., Mainka, A., Kukharenka, N., Koetter, J.: Befragung der Lehrenden zum digitalen Sommersemester 2020. Universitäty Osnabrück (2020)
19. Herrmann, I., Münster, S., Tietz, V., Uhlemann, R.: Teaching media design by using scrum. a qualitative study within a media informatics elective course. In: 14th International Conference on Cognition and Exploratory Learning in Digital Age (CELDA 2017). International Association for Development of the Information Society (IADIS) (2017)
20. Konert, J., Bohr, C., Bellhäuser, H., Rensing, C.: Peerla - assistant for individual learning goals and self-regulation competency improvement in online learning scenarios. In: IEEE 16th International Conference on Advanced Learning Technologies (ICALT), pp. 52–56. IEEE (2016)
21. Kotter, J.P.: Leading Change. Harvard Business School Press (1996)
22. Krüger, W.: Strategische erneuerung: probleme und prozesse. 5. Auage. In: Krüger, W., Bach, N. (eds.) Excellence in Change. PSS, pp. 33–61. Gabler Verlag, Wiesbaden (2014). https://doi.org/10.1007/978-3-8349-4717-8_2
23. Kumar Basak, S., Wotto, M., Belanger, P.: E-learning, m-learning and d-learning: conceptual definition and comparative analysis. E-Learn. Digit. Media **15**(4), 191–216 (2018)
24. Lauer, T.: Change Management: Fundamentals and Success Factors. Springer, Heidelberg (2020). https://doi.org/10.1007/978-3-662-62187-5
25. Maurer, P., Raida, A.C., Lücker, E., Münster, S.: Visual media as a tool to acquire soft skills - cross-disciplinary teaching-learning project SUFUvet. In: Workshop Gemeinschaften in Neuen Medien (GeNeMe) 2016, pp. 196–208. TUDpress (2016)
26. Mayring, P.: Qualitative inhaltsanalyse. In: Mey, G., Mruck, K. (eds.) Handbuch Qualitative Forschung in der Psychologie. Band 2: Designs und Verfahren, 2. Auflage, pp. 495–511. Springer, Wiesbaden (2020). https://doi.org/10.1007/978-3-658-26887-9_52
27. Moore, J.L., Dickson-Deane, C., Galyen, K.: E-learning, online learning, and distance learning environments: are they the same? Internet High. Educ. **14**(2), 129–135 (2011)
28. Moore, M.: Three types of interaction. Am. J. Dist. Educ. **3**(2), 1–7 (1989)

29. Moran, J.W., Brightman, B.K.: Leading organizational change. Career Dev. Int. **6**(2), 111–119 (2001)
30. Oersen, C., Wyngaard, R., Nkabinde, L.: An immersive mobile application for improved learning and virtual tour experience: a nature reserve perspective. In: ITU Kaleidoscope: Industry-Driven Digital Transformation (ITU K), pp. 1–8. IEEE (2020)
31. Park, S.Y.: An analysis of the technology acceptance model in understanding university students' behavioral intention to use e-learning. J. Educ. Technol. Soc. **12**(3), 150–162 (2009)
32. Porubän, J., Bačiková, M.: Live it projects at a university in large-scale. In: International Conference on Emerging eLearning Technologies and Applications (ICETA), pp. 275–281. IEEE (2016)
33. Salmon, G.: Flying not flapping: a strategic framework for e-learning and pedagogical innovation in higher education institutions. ALT-J **13**(3), 201–218 (2005)
34. Sangrà, A., Vlachopoulos, D., Cabrera, N.: Building an inclusive definition of e-learning: an approach to the conceptual framework. Int. Rev. Res. Open Distrib. Learn. **13**(2), 145–159 (2012)
35. Schwaber, K., Sutherland, J.: The Scrum Guide. Scrum Alliance (2020)
36. Scott, E., Rodríguez, G., Soria, A., Campo, M.: Experiences in software engineering education: using scrum, agile coaching, and virtual reality. In: Overcoming Challenges in Software Engineering Education: Delivering Non-Technical Knowledge and Skills, pp. 250–276. IGI Global (2014)
37. Singh, H.: Building effective blended learning programs. In: Challenges and Opportunities for the Global Implementation of E-Learning Frameworks, pp. 15–23. IGI Global (2021)
38. Stoica, M., Mircea, M., Ghilic-Micu, B.: Software development: agile vs. traditional. Inform. Econ. **17**(4) (2013)
39. Voigt, C., Blömer, L., Kötter, J., Hoppe, U.: Agile change to digital teaching during and after corona pandemic for flipped classroom courses - an overview of tasks and responsibilities. J. E-Learn. Res. **1**(1), 1–14 (2021)
40. Wannemacher, K., Jungermann, I., Scholz, J., Tercanli, H., von Villiez, A.: Digitale Lernszenarien im Hochschulbereich. Arbeitspapier Nr. 15 (2016)
41. Webster, J., Watson, R.T.: Analyzing the past to prepare for the future: writing a literature review. MIS Q. **26**(2), xiii–xxiii (2002)
42. Weick, K.E., Quinn, R.E.: Organizational change and development. Annu. Rev. Psychol. **50**(1), 361–386 (1999)
43. Wong, K., Patzelt, M., Poulette, B., Hathaway, R.: Experiences in simulating a software product team for a MOOC. In: Proceedings of the Western Canadian Conference on Computing Education, pp. 1–6 (2019)
44. York, C.S., Richardson, J.C.: Interpersonal interaction in online learning: experienced online instructors' perceptions of influencing factors. J. Asynchronous Learn. Netw. **16**(4), 83–98 (2012)
45. Zawacki-Richter, O.: The current state and impact of Covid-19 on digital higher education in Germany. Hum. Behav. Emerg. Technol. **3**(1), 218–226 (2021)

A Maturity Model for Open Educational Resources in Higher Education Institutions – Development and Evaluation

Carla Reinken[(✉)] [iD], Nicole Draxler-Weber [iD], and Uwe Hoppe [iD]

Osnabrück University, Osnabrück, Germany
`carla.reinken@uni-osnabrueck.de`

Abstract. There is currently a global movement toward open, digital, reusable educational resources. However, despite the often existing infrastructure and resource capacities of many higher education institutions (HEIs), the introduction of Open Educational Resources (OER) has not yet become a normative practice in all faculties and disciplines. The reasons for this are not immediately apparent to HEIs, and it is difficult to make an assessment of how well a HEI is positioned with regard to OER. For this purpose, the paper presents an initial draft of a maturity model for OER, consisting of six dimensions and five levels. This maturity model was subsequently evaluated and assessed by various higher education stakeholders through an online survey. The evaluation confirmed the dimensions and levels, but identified the need for adaption within the dimension and in the gradation of the levels. The model represents a first step to provide HEIs with important information about the current state regarding OER and to identify areas in need of improvement. The aim is to increase the acceptance of OER in practice by supporting HEIs.

Keywords: Maturity model · Open educational resources · Higher education institutions · Model evaluation

1 Introduction

Digitalization is increasingly leading to the development of numerous electronic teaching and learning innovations. In addition, educational content is more frequently being provided cooperatively [1]. Open Educational Resources (OER) have gained increasing attention as they transcend demographic, economic, and geographical educational boundaries and promote lifelong, personalized learning [2]. The OER movement has successfully promoted the idea that knowledge is a public good and has expanded the aspirations of organizations and individuals to promote OER [3]. Such rapid growth of OER offers new opportunities for teaching and learning. However, the potential of OER to transform teaching in higher education institutions (HEIs) has not yet been realized [2, 3]. An overview of OER research in recent years shows the challenges related to OER no longer lie in the availability or accessibility of those resources, but rather the challenges lie in the area of use. The necessary framework conditions for the use of

M. A. Bach Tobji et al. (Eds.): ICDEc 2022, LNBIP 461, pp. 94–111, 2022.
https://doi.org/10.1007/978-3-031-17037-9_7

OER at HEIs often remain unresolved. The current situation can thus be characterized as follows: Although OER are high on the agenda of social and inclusion policies and are supported by many actors in education, their use in higher education (HE) has not yet reached a critical threshold [3].

The conceptualization of a maturity model for HEIs in the context of OER addresses this problem and can serve as a tool for HEIs. By determining a maturity level that indicates how far an HEI's current circumstances have matured for the inclusion and steady use of OER, universities could position themselves to identify problem areas and develop concrete solutions. Maturity in this context refers to "an evolutionary improvement towards a target state or to a natural end state" [4]. Maturity can also refer more specifically to competencies, skills, business processes, or products [5]. The maturity development to a higher, more advanced stage takes place in steps and is described by maturity levels [6].

To develop such a maturity model, it is necessary to know process models for conceptualization. De Bruin et al. created a generic framework describing the different developmental phases of a maturity model, which serves as a basis here [5]. In this context, maturity models were identified and developed specifically for the field of HEI. Many existing maturity models in the education domain can be found. There are two different approaches to these maturity models. On the one hand, specialized models focus on a subsystem of education, while, on the other hand, more comprehensive models represent the educational institution as a whole [7]. In this context, no maturity model for OER in HEI could be found. Based on the problem description, an OER maturity model should be developed. Due to the lack of empirical research in this area and no comparable established maturity model for OER in HE, a subsequent evaluation of the developed maturity model with different higher education stakeholders from diverse higher education institutions seems reasonable and necessary. The target group includes HEI management, support institutions such as platform operators, media competence centers, and didactics, as well as lecturers, i.e. professors, research assistants, and tutors. By developing a model in the first step, it is now possible for the respondents to express specific suggestions for improvement and criticism and not to come up with their own model in a purely hypothetical and very abstract way. For this reason, an online survey was conducted to evaluate the developed model. The results provide information on how the model can be adapted and optimized in a target-oriented manner. Accordingly, the research subject is guided by the following two research questions (RQs):

RQ 1: What might a first draft of an OER maturity model for HEI look like?

RQ 2: How do higher education stakeholders evaluate the developed OER maturity model draft and which necessary adaptations emerge from it?

To answer the research questions in a targeted manner, this paper is structured as follows. First, the theoretical basis for OER and maturity models is presented in the following section *Theoretical Background*. The third section deals with the development of a maturity model and the framework used for this purpose. The developed model is then shown and explained in more detail. This is followed by the evaluation, which is divided into methodology and results. In the end, the results are summarized, interpreted and specific adaption measures are derived.

2 Theoretical Background

2.1 Open Educational Resources

Open Educational Resources (OER) have been part of the educational landscape since 2001, through the announcement of MIT's OpenCourseWare project, and even longer if the Learning Objects movement is considered as a precursor to OER [8]. The term OER was first introduced at a conference organized by UNESCO in 2000 and was promoted in the context of free access to educational resources on a global scale. There are now several definitions of OER, but they largely overlap. The William and Flora Hewlett Foundation, which funded the MIT project, defines OER as resources that include full courses, course materials, modules, textbooks, streaming videos, tests, software, and any other tools, materials, or techniques that support access to knowledge [9]. However, the most recent definition of OER from UNESCO is "Open Educational Resources (OER) are learning, teaching and research materials in any format and medium that reside in the public domain or are under copyright that have been released under an open license, that permit no-cost access, re-use, re-purpose, adaptation and redistribution by others" [10].

OER help to reduce access barriers to educational materials and support the opening of HEIs, as well as open education in all educational sectors with the active participation of all interested parties [11]. Therefore, OER have gained increasing attention in recent years because of their potential and promise to reduce such barriers as demographic, economic, and geographic boundaries in education and to promote lifelong and personalized learning [2]. The potential benefits of OER are widely advocated [12] and include improving access to higher education, lowering its cost, promote the culture of sharing and improving the quality of materials that result from collaboration and peer review [13, 14]. In general, OER have come to be seen as an invaluable educational resource for institutions and faculty in every region [15]. According to the OER Atlas 2017, the number of OER-based events has increased fivefold compared to 2015, while the number of OER projects has almost tripled, and the supply has increased by 70% [16].

However, previous studies of OER use have suggested that while educators are beginning to embrace open educational practices, understanding of the breadth of teaching and learning practices that OER enables is still limited. This problem may be exacerbated by the tendency of education-related change efforts to focus on educational content or resources, such as OER [3, 17]. Studies have found that limited teacher adoption of OER is influenced by factors at both the individual level [18–20] and the organizational/institutional level [21–23]. OER have not yet been able to sustainably establish themselves in the mainstream discourse of digitalization [24]. The reasons for the still rather low use of OER by teachers and learners are complex and multi-layered (pedagogical, technical, and organizational) [25]. It could therefore be important for an HEI to question its own framework conditions for the use and creation of OER and to be able to classify them in a maturity model.

2.2 Maturity Models

"A maturity model consists of a sequence of maturity levels for a class of objects" [6]. These models show which characteristics need to be assessed to determine the maturity of an object. Those characteristics are then collected and evaluated to determine the corresponding maturity level specific to the organization. Therefore, predetermined procedures, like questionnaires, can be used for application. The highest maturity level represents the total maturity of an object that can be achieved by an organization [6]. With the maturity principle, a distinction can be made between a stage model and a continuous maturity model. The former is characterized by the fact that the next higher level is only reached when all elements of the previous level have been fulfilled [26]. In the latter, however, the dimensions can be at different levels [27].

Many various maturity models can be found in the literature. The most popular maturity model is the Capability Maturity Model (CMM) from 1986, which has achieved global acceptance [5]. The development of CMM occurred at the Software Engineering Institute (SEI) of Carnegie Mellon University in Pittsburgh, USA and was commissioned by the US Defense Department. CMM was intended to be used to assess the US Defense Department's software suppliers. It distinguishes a total of five maturity levels: Initial, Repeatable, Defined, Managed, and Optimizing. Each level contains process goals that must be achieved to increasingly stabilize the software development process. Processes in the Initial level are ad hoc and only defined to a small extent. In this step, project planning is lacking, so success depends on individuals and is not systematically repeatable. The second level, Repeatable, represents a process discipline, which is characterized by project planning, so that previous successes of similar projects can be repeated. A documented and standardized development process is found in the third level, Defined. Within the fourth level, Managed, quantitative quality targets for products and processes as well as measurement parameters are defined. The Optimizing level focuses on continuous improvement of the development process [28]. Over time, CMM has been applied in other fields, such as system and product development, so that the model was further advanced to Capability Maturity Model Integration (CMMI) in the 1990s. The levels of CMMI correspond to CMM, except for a change in the designation: Initial, Managed, Defined, Quantitatively Managed, and Optimizing. In contrast to CMM, maturity levels in CMMI refer to the entire process areas [29]. Both the CMM and later CMMI provided the basis for many other maturity models [6].

Published literature reviews have identified and analysed existing maturity models in the higher education field [7, 30], which provides a basis for this study. The analyses have shown that most educational maturity models have CMM or CMMI as their basis, despite different emphases like e-learning, online courses, or information and communication technologies. Maturity models explicitly related to OER have not been identified in previous papers [7, 30]. Different institutions have been involved in the development of the maturity model in the education sector. These have included educational companies, research organizations, as well as academic experts [7]. In the development process, a distinction is made between specialized models for a particular education sub-system, such as senior management training or project management, and broader models, which represent the education institution as a whole. Maturity models for education are at an early stage of development and need further improvement [7].

3 Development of a Maturity Model for OER in HEI

3.1 Development Framework

In the past, many maturity models have been developed. In most cases, it is not possible to retrace how the development and evaluation of the maturity model took place [6]. To address this, de Bruin et al. created a generic framework that divides the development of maturity models into generic phases [5]. The present study is based on this framework. The phases are divided into *Scope, Design, Populate, Test, Deploy* and *Maintain* and must be followed in this sequence [5]. In response to the research questions, the approach is followed within the first three phases *Scope, Design* and *Populate*.

In the first phase, the *Scope* of application is defined, which significantly influences the subsequent phases. A key decision that needs to be made in this phase relates to the focus of the model and development stakeholders. Regarding the focus of the model, it must be decided whether it should be a domain-specific or general model [5]. The aim of the contribution is to develop a maturity model specifically for OER at HEIs. Thus, the focus of the model is domain-specific, as the framework conditions for OER at HEIs are to be classified. The question about stakeholders is about who is involved in the development of the maturity model. The authors of this paper undertake the development of the maturity model as academics with practical experience in the use and creation of OER.

Design is the content of the second phase, in which the structure of the model is determined. The goal of this phase is to capture the complexity of reality in a simplified maturity model. Therefore, it must be decided which target group the maturity model is intended for, whether it is to be used internally or externally, and who are the respondents in the maturity survey [5]. The target group of this maturity model being developed is the management of several HEIs to get an assessment of the maturity of OER. The application is internal, and all stakeholders of the institution can be involved. In addition, existing maturity models for HEIs were considered from published literature reviews and examined for the most thematic overlap with OER. The Online Course Quality Maturity Model (OCQMM) was used as a basis due to the interfaces between OER and online courses. As already mentioned, within most existing models, the levels of CMM or CMMI are the basis, and so it is also in OCQMM. For this reason, the present maturity model, like OCQMM, is based on the five levels of the CMM: Initial, Repeatable, Defined, Managed, and Optimizing, and is designed as a continuous model.

In the next phase, *Populate*, the structure of the maturity model is filled. Characteristics are identified that indicate the level of maturity. Methods such as literature research or exploratory survey methods are suitable for this purpose [5]. Since published literature reviews have revealed that there are no existing maturity models on the topic, a pure literature-based creation of the maturity model is not sufficient, and therefore a survey was chosen as the method. However, an exploratory survey with higher education stakeholders would have been very abstract and not very promising in terms of results. With the help of a model as a basis, the respondents were presented with something tangible to consider and form their opinions on. To form this base for the survey, the contents of the model were independently formulated in the initial step. The fundamental structure of the model was provided by the dimensions from the selected OCQMM, which were adopted to the content of OER. For each dimension and each level, the characteristics were defined, which the authors derived from experience values and literature and discussed in depth. The developed maturity model for OER in HEIs is presented in Subsect. 3.2 and provides a basis for the survey by evaluating the content and gradations of the model by a range of stakeholders from several HEIs. The evaluation of the developed model is shown in section four.

During the Test, the developed model is examined for its relevance, validity, reliability, and generalizability. In the *Deploy* phase, the model must be provided for the application. The last phase, *Maintain*, includes the further development and update of the model. In order to maintain the relevance of the model, framework conditions must be continuously monitored, and adjustments must be made [5]. The last two phases go beyond the research questions and are for this reason not considered further in the approach of this paper.

3.2 Developed Maturity Model

The represented model in Table 1 includes six different dimensions derived from a literature review of existing maturity models in the field of higher education. The dimensions *Learning Resources, Teaching Process, Teaching Platform, Faculty Conditions, Monitoring & Evaluation, and Management* were taken from the OCQMM and were applied to the OER context. Each dimension contains different characteristics and criteria, which have been assigned in the table. These criteria are classified according to an ascending numbering of levels to distinguish between the five different levels of maturity. Accordingly, the maturity level of the respective dimension is lowest in level 1 and highest in level 5.

The five maturity levels, Initial, Repeatable, Defined, Managed, and Optimizing, were taken from CMM. Each level contains process goals that must be achieved to increasingly stabilize the development process. In the first level, *Initial*, the processes are defined ad hoc and only to a limited extent. The next level, *Repeatable*, represents a process discipline characterized by project planning so that previous successes of similar projects can be repeated. In the third stage, *Defined*, a documented and standardized development process takes place. Quantitative quality targets for products and processes as well as metrics are defined in the fourth level, *Managed*. The final stage, *Optimized*, focuses on continuous improvement of the development process [28].

In the following, the content of the dimensions in the respective levels will be discussed in more detail. The first dimension, *Learning Resources*, reflects OER as learning content. Here, the criteria for creating OER as a learning resource, the quality assurance, the specification of metadata, and licensing surrounding OER are all considered. For example, in level one, no OER are used as learning resources in teaching, while in level five, OER are permanently created and checked by a standardized quality assurance process, and well-maintained metadata (e.g. author information, learning objectives, description text, etc.), and free licensing are specified. The *Teaching Process* represents the second dimension and describes the degree to which OER is integrated into the teaching process. The extent to which OER is used in teaching can vary greatly, so the degree of integration is an important criterion for determining an HEI's OER maturity. In level three, the lecturers in this context already have experience with the creation and

Table 1. Initial draft of a maturity model for OER in HEI

	Level 1 Initial	Level 2 Repeatable	Level 3 Defined	Level 4 Managed	Level 5 Optimizing
Learning Resources	OER are not used as learning resources	Single OER are created; Quality of OER is characterized by rudimentary scientific standards; Meta data are missing; License details are missing	More OER are created; Quality of OER are optimized by adjustments; Further quality criteria are considered; Important meta data are given; License details are missing	Regular creation of OER; Individual quality assurance; Meta data are given; License details with limited openness are given	Permanent creation of OER; Standardized quality assurance process; Meta data are given; License details with the highest degree of openness are given
Teaching Process	OER are not integrated into teaching process	Single OER are made available; OER are not integrated into teaching process	Created OER are offered as an addition to the teaching process; OER are not integrated into teaching process	Created OER are complementary integrated into teaching process and represent a mandatory learning outcome	complete course and are fully integrated into the teaching process
Teaching Platform	No OER platform	Creation of a platform pilot for internal OER	Establishment of an internal OER platform	Internal OER platform with links to external repositories	Internal OER platform with links to external repositories; External repositories include internal OER
Faculty Conditions	No knowledge of OER; No willingness to create and use OER	Knowledge of OER; Willingness to use external OER; No willingness to create OER	Knowledge of OER; Willingness to use external OER; Willingness to create OER	Knowledge of OER; Use of external OER; Creation of OER; OER are shared within HEI	Knowledge of OER; Use of external OER; Creation of OER; OER are shared within HEI and others outside the education sector
Monitoring & Evaluation	No internal (students) and external (OER community) feedback; No usage data is collected	One-time internal feedback from students on single OER; No external feedback from OER community; No usage data is collected	Regular internal feedback from students; No external feedback from OER community; Usage data is collected	Regular internal feedback from students; One-time external feedback from OER community; Usage data is collected	Regular internal feedback from students; Regular external feedback from OER community; Usage data is collected

(*continued*)

Table 1. (*continued*)

Management No OER awareness; No provision of resources for OER; No recognition of students' achievement provided with OER; No OER strategy	OER awareness at single department chairs; External resources are requested; No recognition of students' achievement of OER; only certificate of achievement possible; No OER strategy	OER awareness at departmental level; Departmental provision of available resources; Recognition of students' achievements of OER must be requested by students; No OER strategy	OER awareness at departmental and faculty level; Faculty provision of available resources; Recognition of students' achievements of OER is reviewed by course coordinator; No OER strategy	OER awareness at departmental, faculty and HEI management level; HEI management provides resources for OER; recognition of students' achievements of OER regulated HEI-wide; HEI management anchors OER in strategy

use of OER and integrate these as additional offerings in their own teaching. In this level, however, OER use by students is voluntary, so the OER is not an integral part of the teaching process. In stage five, on the other hand, complete courses are based on OER content, so the OER is fully integrated into teaching. The third dimension, *Teaching Platform*, refers to the technical requirements necessary to enable the use and dissemination of OER. Central characteristics are whether an HEI has its own OER platform, the provision of external OER offerings (e.g. via links), and the availability of internal OER on external platforms so that the content can be used outside the HEI. In stage three, for example, this means that an OER platform is available at one's own HEI where lecturers can upload their OER and students at this HEI can access it. In terms of *Faculty Conditions*, the focus is on faculty and their use and creation of OER. The lecturers' criteria knowledge about OER, the readiness to create or use OER and the readiness to share the created OER across the HEI are addressed. For example, universities are in level four if the use of external OER is established among the lecturers but the teaching staff also create and use OER themselves. The *Monitoring & Evaluation* dimension includes the collection of usage data (e.g. downloads, retrieval numbers, dwell time) and the collection of feedback from users and learners. Accordingly, the criteria of internal feedback by students, external feedback by the OER community, and the collection of usage data are considered. Consequently, in level one, neither feedback nor usage data are collected. In level five, feedback is regularly collected from students, and the usage data is collected and evaluated. Regular exchanges within the OER community and peer support are also promoted in this context. The last dimension, *Management*, focuses on the leadership and strategy of the HEI. Special attention is paid to the criteria of OER awareness at different levels (department, faculty, HEI management), the provision of resources for OER, performance recognition of OER offerings, and the HEI's OER strategy. In level three, for example, OER are already established at the department level and are used regularly. For this purpose, internal departmental resources are made available, and the students themselves must check and inquire whether performance recognition is provided by the respective department.

4 Evaluation

4.1 Method

As already mentioned in Subsect. 3.1, an acknowledged maturity model development process is followed according to de Bruin et al. [5]. Regarding the third phase, *Populate*, a survey was chosen as the method for filling in the designed framework of the maturity model for OER in HEIs. However, to provide a basis for the survey, a first potential draft of such a maturity model was developed (see Subsect. 3.2). Using the model, respondents were given something specific to think about and be questioned on. To analyse the developed maturity model for OER and to answer the RQ2, an online survey was chosen. The survey was addressed to staff of HEIs throughout Germany where OER are used and/or created, which were identified by research. In the first step, a search on seven major German OER repositories (e.g. HOOU, OpenRUB, Twillo) helped to identify HEIs and the persons who provide OER. Based on this, online research was conducted to determine additional contacts at the identified HEIs. Independently, an additional general online search was undertaken to identify additional HEIs and the associated contacts related to OER. Since our study was aimed at participants from German HEIs, the survey was also conducted in German. Before the online survey was launched, a pretest was done with eight researchers to check the survey for comprehensibility and feasibility.

An embedded mixed-method approach was used to create the survey using the online survey tool LimeSurvey (www.limesurvey.org). With this approach, quantitative and qualitative data can be collected simultaneously or sequentially [31, 32]. The survey consists of qualitative and quantitative elements, so these data were collected simultaneously. A welcome text appeared at the beginning of the online survey explaining the purpose of the study and defining OER and maturity model to help develop a common understanding among participants. This was followed by the survey questions[1], which were divided into three question groups. The quantitative research design dominated, which was supplemented by qualitative data. The first set of questions addressed each dimension of the maturity model by presenting each dimension individually with its content and levels. Questions were asked about each dimension separately and were answered by indicating "Yes" or "No" (quantitative data). Only when assigning a level to a dimension there were the answer options "Yes", "No" and "Partly". To get additional information from the respondents on their assessments of the dimensions, they had to justify their responses in the comment field (qualitative data). After the questions on each of the six dimensions were answered, questions concerning the maturity model in its entirety followed. In this question group, too, the answers were given via a "Yes"/"No" selection (quantitative data) with a justification in the comment field (qualitative data). Questions with a drop-down menu and one five-point scale (quantitative data) about the respondents' demographic data and knowledge about OER follow at the end. The survey results were exported and evaluated to analyse the quantitative survey data. The response options were counted, which can be seen in Subsect. 4.2. In addition, the qualitative data were evaluated by using the qualitative content analysis (QCA) according to Mayring

---

[1] The questionnaire is available at: https://drive.google.com/file/d/19BCTFpeNB9KMZQDLo qRJkB1bIdWBJ7yc/view?usp=sharing.

[33]. First, the text from the comment fields were sorted and then paraphrased. This was followed by a generalization of the paraphrases, and, in a third step, the first reduction was carried out by shortening semantically identical paraphrases. In a second reduction, identical paraphrases were grouped, which were then formed into categories. This is in accordance with the inductive approach, since the categories were not determined in advance but derived directly from the analyzed material [33].

In total, the survey was online over a period of four weeks between October and November 2021. The link to the survey was sent to the respondents by e-mail. A sample of 51 fully completed questionnaires were included in the evaluation. The average time to complete the survey was 30 min. The sample is composed of 22 females, 27 males, and two diverse participants. The 40–49 age group represents the largest respondent group with 19 participants, followed by the 30–39 age group with 16 participants. Eight of the respondents were between 50–59 years old and five of the respondents were between 20–29 years old. The smallest group surveyed was the 60–69-year-olds with only three participants. All respondents were from German HEIs from eight states in total. With the largest share of 49%, the respondents were lecturers (25 persons). This includes professors, research associates, and visiting lecturers. Employees at other higher education establishments like libraries or examination offices made up 27,5% of the respondents (14 persons). Eight out of 51 respondents (15,7%) were academic project staff. One respondent was from IT support of an HEI, and three surveyed persons (5,9%) stated other. All respondents were asked to rate their own knowledge of handling OER on a scale of 1 to 5, with 1 representing no knowledge and 5 representing the regular use and creation of OER. The arithmetic mean of value was 3.55. Most respondents (21) rated themselves a 4 on the scale.

4.2 Results

This subsection presents the results of the online survey on the maturity model for higher education institutions in the context of OER. In the survey, initially the same questions were asked for each dimension (1st question group), so that the results are described below for each dimension as well. The questions on the respective dimensions are divided into "Yes"/"No" selection options and free text fields. The "Yes"/"No" selection options provide a direct overview of clear agreement or disagreement on the part of the respondents, so that a first impression becomes apparent. The results of the quantitative questions can be seen in Table 2. After the presentation of the findings for the individual dimensions, a summary of the results is provided for the second question group, which asked questions about the maturity model in general. The third group of questions includes the demographic data, which was already examined in more detail in the previous section.

A total of 51 questionnaires were collected from various higher education stakeholders across Germany (N = 51). Table 2 shows the count of "Yes"/"No" responses based on the sample size 51. The table highlights the five questions, with the corresponding question number, that were asked in the context of each dimension. The count is given in percentages, and the particularly high values (> 70%) are shown in bold in the table. To be able to better classify these values, the answers from the comment fields are of particular interest. The most important findings from the free-text fields are discussed below.

Table 2. Quantitative results (based on N = 51)

Dimension	Comprehensibility of Level (in %)		Supplementary Criteria (in %)		Exclusion of Criteria (in %)		Importance of Dimension (in %)		Assignment to Level (in %)		
	Yes	No	Yes	No	Yes	No	Yes	No	Yes	Partly	No
Learning Resources	41,2	58,8	49,0	50,9	19,6	**80,4**	**80,4**	19,6	13,7	47,1	39,2
Teaching Process	64,7	35,3	27,5	**72,5**	17,6	**82,4**	70,6	29,4	21,6	25,5	52,9
Teaching Platform	68,6	31,4	41,2	60,8	23,5	**76,5**	62,7	37,3	54,9	19,6	25,5
Faculty Conditions	56,9	43,1	39,2	60,8	21,6	**78,4**	**88,2**	11,8	21,6	37,3	41,2
Monitoring & Evaluation	64,7	35,3	23,5	**76,5**	9,8	**90,2**	86,3	13,7	29,4	19,6	51,0
Management	58,8	41,2	29,4	**70,6**	23,5	**76,5**	84,3	15,7	33,3	21,6	45,1

With regard to *Learning Resources*, there is strong support for this dimension, with 41 respondents rating the dimension as relevant for determining OER maturity at HEIs. It is also positive to note that over 80% of respondents would exclude none of the criteria presented, which emphasizes the high relevance of the criteria. One of the few statements on the exclusion of certain criteria simply states that *"The degree of openness of the licenses does not say much about the degree of maturity. The choice of license is quite context dependent after all, e.g., the question whether commercial use is excluded, CC BY NC."* In addition, some suggestions for improvement were made in order to make the dimension and the associated criteria even more understandable and comprehensible. With regard to the comprehensibility of the levels, 58,8% of the respondents stated that there was a need for optimization. For example, the gradations of the quality criterion were criticized, so that the terms should be better distinguished from each other and explained in a more comprehensible way. The license criterion was also misunderstood by many respondents, as most argued that an OER without a license is not an OER and therefore there can only be a yes or no gradation. For metadata, examples should be given to clarify what the important metadata are, and level 1 should not mention usage but rather creation like the other levels. In this context, it was also stated that usage is a crucial criterion in dealing with OER and should be included as an additional criterion. Almost half of the respondents (49%) agreed to add criteria. File formats and aspects such as OER policy and the didactic preparation of resources were mentioned as further additions.

The levels of the *Teaching Process* dimension were rated as comprehensible by around 64,7% of respondents. Those for whom the levels were not intelligible gave wording and lack of information as their reasons. The survey participants would like to see a more precise definition of the term "teaching process", i.e. what is meant by it. In addition, it was questioned how OER can represent a learning outcome or a complete course. The term "mandatory" used in level four of the dimension caused particular irritation among the respondents. One respondent commented that an obligation to use OER would be contrary to the basic idea of OER. One related comment was: *"Here I see a restriction on the freedom of research and teaching"*. Among 72,5% of the respondents, the criteria of the dimension were perceived as complete. Only 12 of all respondents would exclude criteria from the dimension. Here, primarily the obligation to use OER was mentioned, which was already questioned by the respondents in the previous questions. In addition, it was doubted whether an entire OER course could be regarded as the highest maturity or whether this criterion should also be excluded or adapted: *"I don't really know whether I would regard it as a sign of high maturity whether OER represents an entire course"*. With a majority of 70,6%, the dimension was considered important by the respondents. However, there were a few hesitations about the extent to which this dimension could be adequately determined. The teaching process is seen as very heterogeneous, in that it can neither be centrally categorized nor uniformly determined for the whole HEI. This is also reflected in the analysis, where a slight majority of respondents (49%) considered it difficult to assign their own HEI to a level, while 29,4% would only be able to do it partially. In general, it is assumed that there is heterogeneity in each HEI regarding the dimension. It is pointed out here that a survey would have to be carried out within the respective HEI to be able to create a holistic picture.

The relevance of the *Teaching Platform* dimension for the determination of OER maturity was again confirmed by the survey participants. Respondents also overwhelmingly (70%) acknowledged the logical comprehensibility of the levels. However, it became quite evident, through many mentions, that the criterion of internal platform did not seem to make sense, although 76,5% of respondents indicated that the exclusion of criteria is not necessary. Many of the respondents expressed their opposition to the inclusion of this criterion because it was not a suitable indicator of OER maturity. Furthermore, the cooperative idea of OER was affirmed, so it seems to make more sense to rely on already existing infrastructures of, for example, portals at the state level, such as Twillo for Lower Saxony. In addition to the exclusion of the criterion of internal platform, recommendations were given for content-related extensions. Overall, 41,2% of respondents voted in favor of adding criteria, including interoperability (import and export of certain media and formats), accessibility (for which can OER be used), and the addition of certified OER platforms. In general, reference was often made to external platforms, which should play an overriding role in the context of the *Teaching Platform* dimension. Interactive potentials should also be included and further promoted in this dimension by including integrated modules in learning platforms for the development and provision of OER rather than focusing on pure file provision.

The *Faculty Conditions* dimension was rated by the respondents as very relevant for the determination of the OER maturity at higher education institutions and achieved the highest agreement, with almost 90% compared to the other dimensions. Furthermore, all selected criteria seemed to be important, as 78,4% of the respondents stated that no criterion should be excluded. In addition, only a few recommendations for supplements to criteria were made, as the majority, with 60,8%, of the respondents considered a supplement of further criteria unnecessary. In this context, criteria such as digital competencies or knowledge of OER platforms were mentioned as potential additions. The greatest challenge for the *Faculty Conditions* dimension was the gradation of the criteria for the participants. Level 1 should be adjusted accordingly, as it was argued that if there is no knowledge, the question about willingness to use or create OER is invalid. In addition, the order of use and creation seems to be very individual, as it was stated that some teachers either first used external OER and then created some themselves or not, or that teachers directly created OER themselves because they did not find suitable OER or did not trust the quality of external resources. The difficulty of grading these criteria also made a clear classification harder.

Regarding *Monitoring & Evaluation*, the majority (64,7%) confirmed that the levels were logically comprehensible. However, the wording in this dimension also led to difficulties in understanding. Potential for adaptation was seen in the areas of *"OER community"*, *"feedback"*, and *"usage data"*. Here, the respondents expressed a need for more information. This also applies to the other questions on the dimension as well. When asked about supplementary criteria, which the respondents saw as necessary, the specification of the OER community was mentioned to ensure that all important actors were considered. The expert community was mentioned, which was considered important for internal feedback. In addition, in terms of quality assurance, it was suggested: *"If feedback is available, there should also be an adjustment loop for quality improvement"*. Further, 90,2% saw no need to exclude criteria in this dimension. Only one respondent questioned the extent to which usage data was relevant for determining the maturity level. It is interesting to note that two respondents suggested a division of the dimension into monitoring and evaluation in order to make the levels even more comprehensible. A clear majority (86,3%) considered the dimension important, but an alignment change *"much more from quality assurance point of view"* is recommended. The respondents considered a classification into a level only division-specific (19,6%) or not at all (51%) realistic.

Within the dimension *Management*, the participants saw heterogeneous organizational differences as a special challenge in the dimension. Of all respondents, 58,8% considered the levels as comprehensible. In this context, the respondents criticized that no gradation was made within the OER strategy and suggested a differentiation. Better wording was called for regarding recognition of students' achievements of OER and resources for OER. In the latter case, there was a particular lack of information on what was specifically meant by resources. One respondent asked: *"What kind of resources should we be talking about? Time? Money? Technology? Personnel?"* In addition, an overlap regarding the OER awareness criterion was seen, because *"awareness has already been addressed with teachers"*. Therefore, it is considered a duplication of the criterion knowledge of OER within the *Faculty Conditions* dimension. Additionally, 70,6% of the respondents saw no need to add more criteria to the dimension. However, additions arose from among the remaining respondents. Incentives for teachers, OER policy, and legal frameworks were mentioned several times as additions. The majority of participants (76,5%) also saw no need to exclude criteria. Among the minority, on the other hand, the exclusion of OER awareness was recommended, due to the overlap already described above. In addition, the recognition of students' achievements of OER was also mentioned. One of the reasons given was: *"Recognition of students' achievements of OER is not so much linked to the use of OER as to appropriate exams. I am not sure if this is a reflection criterion for the university to OER"*. Overall, the dimension was given high importance as confirmed by 84,3% of the respondents.

Regarding assigning their own HEI to a level (QN 5), there was a tendency across all dimensions with the exception of *Teaching Platform*. With respect to *Teaching Platform*, the assignment was often perceived as easier by the respondents, since it is relatively simple to find out whether the HEI uses its own or external platforms and which ones. With regard to the other dimensions, the majority of respondents were able to assign their own HEI either partially or not at all to a level. There are always two justifications for this. Either there is a lack of knowledge among respondents to make a holistic assessment due to the heterogeneity within each institution, or there are different classifications within the criteria of a dimension, which makes it difficult for participants to make an overall classification. Regarding the first reason, it is noted here that a survey would need to be conducted across the HEI to make a classification.

After the first group of questions on the six dimensions, five further questions were asked about the maturity model in general (question group 2). As a result, the most important stakeholder groups (QN 6, Yes 50,9%, No 49,1%) and dimensions (QN 9, Yes 72,5%, No 27,5%) were covered in the model. Only support units such as the libraries and administration, as well as ministries and the student group, were named as additions for other relevant stakeholder groups. Among the few suggestions for additions to the dimensions (QN 10, Yes 29,4%, No 70,6%), support activities, legal frameworks, and continuing education offerings were listed most prominently. The general comprehensibility was rated as very high with 43 agreements (QN 7, Yes 84,3%, No 15,7%). Participants who found the model incomprehensible stated that the gradations of the individual criteria needed to be improved as a reason. Furthermore, it was emphasized that the level division was good, *"especially for an orientation about where one stands. However, in some cases a clear assignment to the levels is not possible or difficult"*. Here, there is a need to improve the operationalizability and thus the applicability of the model. Still, it should be emphasized that the number of levels was mainly considered appropriate and sufficient (QN 8, Yes 76,5%, No 23,5%).

All of these findings culminate in an adapted OER maturity model[2] that provides the basis for further research.

5   Conclusion

Maturity models optimize processes and provide an aid to better assess the current state of an organization [34]. In the education sector, in particular, such a maturity model for OER in HEI was lacking. In this context, two research questions were posed related to the draft and evaluation of a maturity model. The first research question asks what a first draft of an OER maturity model might look like. For this purpose, a model based on the development framework of de Bruin et al. was developed [5]. In addition, both the levels and the dimensions are based on different models that have been transferred and adapted

---

[2] The adapted OER maturity model is available at: https://drive.google.com/file/d/1-U9QMym lojNoM259OQlwYFkoCMnRHqdL/view.

to the OER context. To assess the developed model, an evaluation was conducted with 51 higher education stakeholders intended to answer the second research question. The most important findings are summarized below.

The survey confirms the high relevance of such a maturity model for HEI. The general comprehensibility of the overall model was also considered being given by almost 85% of the respondents in the survey. The respondents rated the selected number of levels, criteria, and dimensions as applicable and comprehensible. Among the exceptions that did not agree with the number of dimensions, only a split of the Monitoring & Evaluation dimension into two separate dimensions and support services (technical, legal, didactical) as additional dimensions were suggested. In this context, however, it was also stated that these structural support services represent an important framework condition for OER to find its way into HEI in the first place. Another criticism from the respondents relates to the selection of stakeholder groups. It was emphasized that students and support units, such as administration and IT support, should be included. Despite the confirmation of a high relevance of the maturity model for HEIs, some criticisms were made by the respondents in the evaluation with regard to the criteria and their gradations. In this context, several recommendations and suggestions for improvement were made, which are reflected in all dimensions and criteria. Among them were often difficulties in understanding, showing the need for more information and examples, e.g. the meaning of metadata or specific formulations should be adapted. Furthermore, the gradation of some criteria was criticized, and the differentiation of individual criteria should be made more precise in some cases. For some criteria, the assignment was also described as very individual, so that some kind of prioritization is required to be able to cover all circumstances. Only a few criteria were listed that should be excluded from the maturity model. Instead, there were some ideas regarding additions to various criteria that could be subsequently included. The assignment to a specific level was found to be particularly difficult. The reason frequently given was that there may be different variations in the criteria, making it impossible to assign them unambiguously. Furthermore, a lack of information and department-specific knowledge were cited as constraints to assigning the entire HEI to a particular level.

The results have been incorporated into numerous adjustments, so that the adapted OER maturity model is no longer a first draft model, but an empirically based model. However, the applicability and operationalizability of the model must be facilitated by a survey instrument for the necessary data. This tool needs to be developed in follow-up research. According to de Bruin et al., this still takes place in the *Populate* phase, which is then followed by the *Test*, *Deploy*, and *Maintain* phases [5]. In general, however, it should be noted that the numerous suggestions for adjustments that have emerged in the evaluation have led to a highly modified model. For this reason, the evaluation of the conceptual design during the *Populate* phase is considered only partially successfully completed. Rather, a further evaluation of the adapted model is desired to re-examine all adaptations. The goal is to use a subsequent Delphi study to successfully conclude the conception phase with expert knowledge and, at the same time, to provide an instrument that is ready for use. Figure 1 illustrates the steps that have already been carried out and those that are still necessary in the *Populate* phase. Thus, the first three steps towards an adapted OER maturity model for HEIs have already been completed (highlighted in gray) and the remaining steps (highlighted in white) will be considered in a further contribution of the follow-up research.

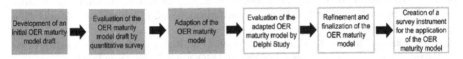

Fig. 1. Procedure of the populate phase

Nevertheless, the existing evaluation confirms the first draft of an OER maturity model for HEI in its basic structure with six dimensions and five levels. The evaluation was important and useful, as many good optimization approaches were identified. In this way, a big step was made towards a final maturity model, which lays the foundation for further research.

References

1. Bergamin, P., Filk, C.: Open educational resources – ein didaktischer kulturwechsel? In: Bergamin, P., Pfander, G.: Offene Bildungsinhalte (OER): Teilen von Wissen oder Gratisbildungskultur?, pp. 25–38 Hep, der Bildungsverlag, Bern (2009)
2. Yuan, L., MacNeill, S., Kraan, W.: Open Educational Resources – Opportunities and Challenges for Higher Education, JISC CETIS (2008)
3. Ehlers, U.-D.: Extending the territory: from open educational resources to open educational practices. Journal of Open, Flexible and Distance Learning **15**(2) (2011)
4. Marx, F., Wortmann, F., Mayer, J.H.: Ein reifegradmodell für unternehmenssteuerungssysteme. Wirtschaftsinformatik **54**(4), 189–204 (2012)
5. de Bruin, T., Freeze, R., Kaulkarni, U., Rosemann, M.: Understanding the main phases of developing a maturity assessment model. In: Proceedings of the 16th Australasian conference on information systems (ACIS) (2005)
6. Becker, J., Knackstedt, R., Pöppelbuß, J.: Developing maturity models for IT management. Bus. Inf. Syst. Eng. **1**, 213–222 (2009)
7. Carvalho, J.V., Pereira, R.H., Rocha, À.: Maturity models of education information systems and technologies: a systematic literature review. In: 13th Iberian Conference on Information Systems and Technologies (CISTI), pp. 1–7 (2018)
8. Weller, M.: Battle for Open: How Openness Won and Why it Doesn't Feel Like Victory. Ubiquity Press, London (2014). https://doi.org/10.5334/bam
9. Hewlett Foundation: White Paper: Open Educational Resources - Breaking the Lockbox on Education. Retrieved from http://www.hewlett.org/library/hewlett-foundation-publication/whitepaper-open-educational-resources (2013)
10. UNESCO: UNSECO-Empfehlung zu Open Educational Resources (OER). In: Records of the General Conference, 40th session, Resolutions, Paris, November 2019 (2019)
11. Arnold, P., Kilian, L., Thillosen, A., Zimmer, G.M.: Handbuch E-Learning: Lehren und Lernen mit Digitalen Medien. utb GmbH, Stuttgart, Deutschland (2018). https://doi.org/10.36198/9783838549651
12. West, P.G., Victor, L.: Background and action paper on OER: a background and action paper for staff of bilateral and multilateral organizations at the strategic institutional education sector level. Report Prepared for The Williams and Flora Hewlett Foundation (2011)

13. Daniel, J., Kanwar, A., Uvalić-Trumbić, S.: A tectonic shift in global higher education. Change: The Magazine of Higher Learning **38**(4), 16–23 (2006). https://doi.org/10.3200/CHNG.38.4.16-23

14. Robra-Bissantz, S., Bott, O.J., Kleinefeld, N., Neu, K., Zickwolf, K.: Teaching Trends 2018. Die Präsenzhochschule und die Digitale Transformation, vol. 158. Waxmann, Münster, New York (2019)

15. Katsusuke, S., Mitsuyo, K., Hiroyuki, S., Yasuhiro, T., Rieko, I., Naoshi, H.: A survey of the awareness, offering, and adoption of OERs and MOOCs in Japan. Open Praxis, Universidad Nacional de Educacion a Distancia **9**(2), 195 (2017)

16. Neumann, J., Muuß-Merholz, J.: OER ATLAS 2017: Open Educational Resources – Deutschsprachige Angebote und Projekte im Überblick, Köln; Hamburg: Hochschulbibliothekszentrum des Landes Nordrhein-Westfalen (hbz); Zentralstelle für Lernen und Lehren im 21. Verlag, Jahrhundert e.V (2017)

17. OPAL: Beyond OER: Shifting focus to open educational practices. OPAL Report 2011. Open Education Quality Initiative, Essen, Germany (2011)

18. Littlejohn, A., Hood, N.: How educators build knowledge and expand their practice: The case of open education resources. Br. J. Educ. Technol. (2016)

19. Littlejohn, A., Pegler, C.: Reusing resources: open for learning. J. Interact. Media Educ. **2014**(1), 2 (2014). https://doi.org/10.5334/2014-02

20. McAndrew, P.: Inspiring creativity in organisations, teachers and learners through open educational resources. European Journal of Open, Distance and E-learning **14**(2), 1–9 (2011)

21. Banzato, M.: Barriers to teacher educators seeking, creating and sharing open educational resources: an empirical study of the use of OER in education in Italy. In: 2012 15th International Conference on Interactive Collaborative Learning (ICL), pp. 1–6 (2012)

22. Beetham, H., Falconer, I., McGill, L., Littlejohn, A.: Open practices: briefing paper. JISC (2012)

23. Carey, T., Davis, A., Ferreras, S., Porter, D.: Using open educational practices to support institutional strategic excellence in teaching, learning and scholarship. Open Praxis **7**(2), 161–171 (2015)

24. Deimann, M.: Hochschulbildung und digitalisierung – entwicklungslinien und trends für die 2020er-Jahre. In: Digitalisierung in Studium und Lehre gemeinsam gestalten, pp. 25–41. Springer, Wiesbaden (2021). https://doi.org/10.1007/978-3-658-32849-8_3

25. Glennie, J., Harley, K., Butcher, N., van Wyk, T.: Open educational resources and change in higher education: reflections from practice, Commonwealth of Learning, Perspectives on Open and Distance Learning, 136–149 (2012)

26. Egeli, M.: Erfolgsfaktoren von mobile business. Ein Reifegradmodell zur digitalen Transformation von Unternehmen durch Mobile IT. Springer, Wiesbaden (2016)

27. Christiansen, S.-K., Gausemeier, J.: Klassifikation von Reifegradmodellen. ZWF Zeitschrift für wirtschaftlichen Fabrikbetrieb **105**(4), 344–349 (2010)

28. Paulk, M.C., Curtis, B., Chrissis, M.B., Weber, C.V.: Capability maturity model, version 1.1. IEEE Softw. **10**, 18–27 (1993)

29. Team, C.P.: Capability maturity model® integration (CMMI SM), version 1.1. CMMI for systems engineering, software engineering, integrated product and process development, and supplier sourcing (CMMI-SE/SW/IPPD/SS, V1. 1) (2002)

30. Duarte, D.V., Martins, P.: A maturity model for higher education institutions. J. Spat. Organ. Dyn. **1**, 25–45 (2013)

31. Yu, X., Khazanchi, D.: Using embedded mixed methods in studying IS phenomena: risks and practical remedies with an illustration. Commun. Assoc. Inf. Syst. **34**, 555–595 (2017)

32. Dhanapati, S.: Explanatory sequential mixed method design as the third research community of knowledge claim. Am. J. Educ. Res. **4**(7), 570 (2016)

33. Mayring, P.: Qualitative Content Analysis: Theoretical Foundation, Basic Procedures and Software Solution. Beltz Verlag, Klagenfurt (2014)
34. Khoshgoftar, M., Osman, O.: Comparison of maturity models. In: IEEE International Conference on Computer Science and Information Technology, pp. 297–301 (2009)

IT User Behavior and Satisfaction

Relationship Between Culture and User Behavior in the Context of Information Security Systems: A Qualitative Study in SMEs

Olfa Ismail[(⊠)] [iD]

Nantes University, Nantes, France
Olfa.Ismail@univ-nantes.fr

Abstract. This paper examines the relationship between information system (IS) security culture and IS user security behaviors, which is little examined in the literature [1]. This article first goes through a review of literature in the field of information security systems, then the proposal of a framework based on [2] three-level culture model and finally the presentation of a qualitative study conducted with twenty-two users from eight French small and medium enterprises (SMEs). The results of this study show that there is a strong relationship between IS security culture and user behaviors related to IS security, in the sense that a positive security culture is conducive to creating security behaviors.

Keywords: IS security culture · Security-related behaviors · Organizational culture · IS users

1 Introduction

Information systems (IS) are both essential to the daily management of companies and to the achievement of strategic business objectives [3]. Therefore, the protection of these information systems is a major issue for organizations in order to keep their information safe and to guarantee their sustainability. At the literature level, a study by [4] shows that the level of IS security effectiveness had a positive influence on organizational performance, including performance focused on financial and operational processes.

Organizations are investing in the security of their IS infrastructures and implementing technical measures. A number of studies have applied various techniques to motivate employees to adopt secure intentions and behaviors, but despite these efforts, employees remain the "weak link" in organizational IS security [5]. We thus find that there are first and foremost human behavior issues, where people lack the understanding of the threat and risks. For [6] organizations face security risks related to their information assets, which can also come from their own employees. Organizations need to focus on employee behavior to limit security failures, if they want to establish an effective security culture. IS security culture should be considered as part of the IS security program to guide employee behavior. Such a culture can help protect the IS and minimize the risk posed by employee behavior [7]. Security researchers have consistently argued

M. A. Bach Tobji et al. (Eds.): ICDEc 2022, LNBIP 461, pp. 115–128, 2022.
https://doi.org/10.1007/978-3-031-17037-9_8

that creating an IS security culture is essential to changing attitudes, perceptions, and instilling good security behaviors [8, 9].

[10] show that there is a significant and positive relationship between decisions that concern information security and information security culture. Such that improving an organization's information security culture will have a positive influence on employee behaviors, which can mitigate information system risks. But according to [1] few empirical studies have examined the relationship between security culture and behaviors, and there is not enough empirical evidence on the actual effect of security culture on security behavior.

[2] postulated that organizational culture is a powerful and often unconscious force that establishes employee behaviors. Thus, the relationship between organizational culture and employee behaviors must be taken into account when implementing security practices, as it has an impact on the behavior of employees in organizations [11]. According to [2], a culture can be analyzed at several different levels, the term level meaning the degree to which the cultural phenomenon is visible to the observer. And he proposes a model called the three levels of culture that we will mobilize in order to understand by analogy the levels of security culture.

In this paper, we study the relationship between culture and behavior, how a strong security culture can lead the IS user to adopt security behaviors such as using strong passwords that are difficult to retrieve and hard to guess, making regular backups, controlling the dissemination of personal information and company data, etc. This leads us to ask the following questions: What is the relationship between IS culture and IS user security-related behavior? Does culture influence behavior, or vice versa? To answer these questions, we will review the literature in the field of IS, propose a conceptual framework, and present the results of our qualitative study conducted in the field.

2   Theoretical Foundations

According to [12], IS security culture is often explained using a variety of established theories and principles from other research fields. Indeed, security culture is a new and emerging research area. Therefore, it makes sense to use other theories as a basis for research. Among these theories, we note the strong presence of theories related to organizational culture. We cite as an example the research of [13], which includes [2] cultural model and [14] national cultural framework; both of which come from organizational science.

2.1   Organizational Culture

Organizational culture is defined by [15] as "a pattern of shared basic assumptions that the group has learned in solving its external and internal adaptation problems." [2] made distinctions between three cultural layers, namely, artifacts, shared beliefs and values, and basic assumptions which are presented in the following figure (Fig. 1):

These layers range from the very tangible manifestations that we can see and feel to the deeply embedded base, the unconscious assumptions that Schein defines as the

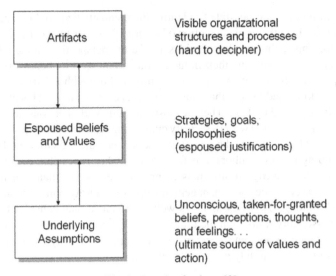

Fig. 1. Levels of culture [2]

essence of culture. In between these layers are various beliefs, values, norms, and rules that members use as a way to represent culture to themselves and to others.

Organizational culture may have different subcultures based on sub-organizations or functions. For [16], IS security culture is a subculture with respect to the general functions of the company. It should support all activities in such a way that IS security becomes a natural aspect in the daily activities of every employee.

Through two case studies, [17] found that organizations with a consistent culture, characterized by employees who follow a code of practice or ethics, will be able to implement and adopt IS security policies more easily. Another study by [18] shows that security culture is influenced by organizational culture, through an in-depth case study within a large organization. And then another, more recent study by [19] shows that organizational culture has a strong causal influence on IS security culture.

2.2 IS Security Culture

Based on the elements that define what an information system is, what culture is and the definitions proposed in the literature on information security culture, we propose a definition of IS security culture which is as follows:

"Information systems security culture is the set of visible and invisible manifestations shared by the members of an organization. These manifestations include assumptions, beliefs, values, artifacts, and formal and informal practices that influence the actions and behaviors of users regarding the protection of the organization's information system" (Author).

This definition makes it possible to identify the elements that could be particularly important in describing the implementation of security practices by the users of an information system. This definition also provides a different perspective on the relationship between elements of culture and their influence on certain security behaviors.

[20] propose a holistic framework of IS security culture with a distinction between factors that constitute and factors that influence this security culture. This classification was previously proposed by [21]. They proposed a framework that considers the major key human factors associated with IS security culture suggested by previous frameworks, and that adds new factors to see the potential link between these factors and IS security culture. According to these authors, this framework makes it possible both to improve and to evaluate the security culture. It is composed, on the one hand, of the factors that influence IS security culture: management support, security policy, ethics, security education and training, risk assessment, as well as organizational behavior factors (job satisfaction, personality traits). On the other hand, we find the factors that make up IS security culture: security awareness, security ownership, and security compliance, which we will explain more accurately in the following lines:

Security Ownership: Security ownership refers to how employees perceive their responsibilities, roles, and willingness to act constructively to improve their security performance and that of the organization [21]. Security ownership means when the users show interest in IS security first, then whether they admit having a share of responsibility in their company's IS security, starting with their workstation and the data concerning their scope of responsibility, and then moving on to a sense of responsibility for their company's IS security as a whole.

Security Awareness: Security awareness is when users understand the potential problems related to IS and become aware of the importance of their role in security. This is what leads to their commitments on this topic [22]. In this research, we refer to security awareness as everything that is the knowledge of the security measures taken in the SME, that is, does the user know the security measures implemented in the company? Then, the knowledge of the threats, which means whether the user is aware of the possible threats that can put the company's information system in danger, and also, whether the user is aware of how to protect himself or how to handle these security threats.

Security Compliance: According to [22] in an organization where there is a strong or healthy security culture, compliance would be expected to be a visible feature of the culture. Compliance is reflected in the staff's knowledge of security policies and procedures. The role of security awareness as an antecedent of compliance was identified by [23], who found that security awareness influences users' intentions to comply with security policies. For [24] security awareness is associated with user perception of sanctions (through perceived certainty and perceived severity of sanctions), which in turn determines user compliance. For example, an employee who takes part in security training or who has read a security charter or a security policy, has complied with security. This compliance may be converted to a security behavior such as the application of security measures recommended during the training or written in the charter, for example the regular change of passwords, backups, protection of confidential data, etc. But if an employee has complied with security, attended training or read a security policy, and then failed to demonstrate any security behavior, then we are talking about compliance and not actual security behavior.

If we take Schein's theory of the three levels of culture (1985), we see that each factor making up security culture corresponds to a level of culture proposed by Schein. Thus, security ownership corresponds to the basic assumptions, security awareness corresponds to the shared values and finally, security compliance corresponds to the artifacts, as shown below (Fig. 2):

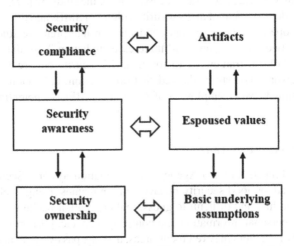

Fig. 2. Positioning of the factors that constitute IS security culture on three levels of culture (Schein, 1985)

Relationship Between Basic Assumptions and Security Ownership

For [2], culture as a set of basic assumptions defines for us what to pay attention to, what things mean, how to react emotionally to what is happening, and what actions to take in various types of situations. We believe that the security ownership can be placed on the first culture level 'Basic Assumptions', this security ownership refers to how employees perceive their responsibilities, roles, and willingness to act in a constructive way to improve their own safety performance and that of the organization [21].

Relationship Between Shared Values and Security Awareness

Security awareness defines when users understand the potential problems related to the IS and become aware of the importance of their role in terms of security. This is what leads to their commitments on this topic [22]. We have placed this awareness at the second level of Shared Values Culture, which is all group learning that reflects one's beliefs and values, one's sense of what should be [2].

Relationship Between Artifacts and Security Compliance

On the surface is the artifact level, which includes all the phenomena one sees, hears, and feels when encountering a new group with an unfamiliar culture. Artifacts also include the organizational processes by which behavior becomes routine, and structural elements such as charters, formal descriptions of organizational functioning, and organizational charts. If the observer spends enough time in the group, the meaning of the artifacts becomes increasingly clear [2]. Within this level of culture, we placed security compliance. According to [22] in an organization where there is a strong or healthy security culture, compliance would be expected to be a visible trait of culture. Compliance results in staff knowledge of security policy and procedures.

Research on IS security culture in SMEs: Some research has focused on the study of security culture in SMEs [25, 26]. Take the example of the study by [27], which explores the subject of the development of an IS security culture in SMEs and the national context in which SMEs operate. These authors conducted an interpretative study based on a literature review, two focus groups, and three case studies in Australian SMEs. Then, they proposed a holistic framework to foster an IS security culture in SMEs within a national framework. The study showed that cooperation, collaboration, knowledge sharing and learning between employees of Australian SMEs is a potentially interesting activity.

2.3 Security-Related Behaviors

According to the French National Agency for Information Systems Security (ANSSI), it is important to adopt good security behavior in companies: using quality passwords that are difficult to find and difficult to guess, making regular backups, controlling the dissemination of personal information and company data, etc. [10] proposes a tool that measures security behaviors in seven focus areas, namely, password management, email use, internet use, social media use, mobile devices, information processing, and incident reporting. We are concerned here with actual behavior, not to be confused with behavioral intention, which is a measure of the strength of intention to perform a specific behavior depending on attitudes and subjective norms, as distinguished in [28] TRA (Theory of Reasoned Action) and [29] (1991) TBP (Theory of Planned Behavior). In the IS field, effective security-related behaviors can be, for example, choosing a strong password, regularly backing up information, regularly running updates and anti-virus software, or locking one's office.

2.4 Relationship Between IS Security Culture and Security-Related Behavior

First, according to [30] security behavior refers to a set of basic security activities that end users must follow in order to maintain the security of the information system, as defined by the security policy. And according to Schein (2010) culture is "a set of structures, routines, rules, and norms that guide and constrain behavior". Several authors in the security field have suggested that creating a security culture will influence employee security behavior (Alhogail et Mizra, 2014, Da Veiga et Eloff, 2010).

A study by [31] showed that security culture, job satisfaction, and perceived organizational support positively affect employees' security compliance intentions. Another study by [10] presents three aspects of IS security decision making, namely, knowledge of policies and procedures, attitude toward policies and procedures, and self-reported behavior that were examined in conjunction with organizational factors that may increase human cyber vulnerabilities. Their results from a survey of 500 Australian employees revealed a significant positive relationship between IS security decision making and IS security culture. This suggests that improving an organization's security culture will positively influence employee behavior, which in turn should also improve compliance with security policies. This means that the risk to an organization's IS and data will be mitigated. And according to a more recent study conducted by [32] the concept of security culture has also been found to be significant in influencing security policy compliance behavior.

3   Conceptual Framework and Methodology

3.1   Framework of the Relationship Between IS Security Culture and Security-Related Behavior

From our literature review and the factors we have presented above: security ownership, security awareness, security compliance that we have linked by analogy to the three levels of organizational culture proposed by Schein. And also from the analysis of the relationship between IS security culture and security-related behavior, we are going to propose a framework that presents the factors making up IS security culture and the relationship between this culture and the security behaviors. Our framework is shown in Fig. 3:

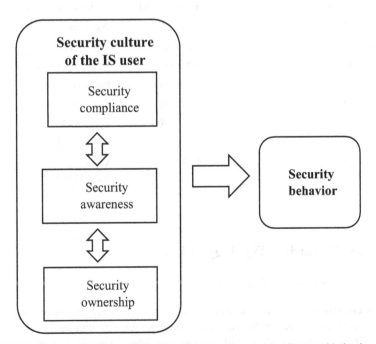

Fig. 3. Framework of the relationship between IS security culture and behaviors

We will try to verify our framework and enrich it from our field study where we present our research methodology in the following title.

3.2 Research Methodology

In order to confront our theoretical and conceptual framework with the field, we adopted a qualitative research through this method. The researcher more specifically observes "behaviors, life histories, social interactions, organizational functioning or social movements" [33]. We carried out this qualitative study based on semi-directive interviews with 22 IS users in 8 French SMEs details in Table 1. The interviews lasted on average 25 min per person. Each interview was recorded after obtaining permission from the interviewee. Then, each interview was transcribed in order to be able to draw a larger part of the "discussion." The multiple case study is a methodology frequently used by researchers who carry out comparative studies, multiplying the points of view and the cases in order to tend towards a global understanding of the phenomenon. According to [34], the use of several cases increases the strength of the evidence, and the multiplication of examples and points of view is a vector of variance and guarantees greater robustness of the results compared to the single case study. We used the Nvivo software to code and analyze our results, which will be presented in the following section.

Table 1. Characteristics of the SMEs studied

SME	Size (number of employees)	Turnover (€)	Activity area
A	80	35.074.500	Wholesale
B	35	12.795.200	Wholesale
C	40	500.283	Landscaping service
D	70	20.000.000	Processing and preservation
E	30	2.138.400	Sealing works
F	19	2 .029.300	Retail trade
G	250	13.389.000	Sorting and recycling
H	20	1.011.500	Vegetable processing and preservation

4   Results: Towards a Typology of Users

4.1   The Security Culture of IS Users

In order to classify users and estimate their security culture levels, we have gone through the three topics that represent the factors making up security culture: security ownership, security awareness, and security compliance. Each theme is divided into several subtopics that will be presented below:

Security Ownership: for this theme, we used the following subtopics: interest in security, responsibility for security and who is responsible for security? Each sub-theme is composed of several questions from the interview guide. We present in Table 2 an example of a sub-theme which is the interest in security expressed by the respondents with the categories of answers, the number of respondents in each category, and examples of verbatims expressed by the respondents.

Table 2. Interest expressed by users in IS security

Subtopic	Category	Number out of 22 users	Example of verbatims
Interest in security	Interested	13	*"Yes, it's important to know how to pay attention to what we say, to know how to use our computer in a very controlled way"*
	Not interested	9	*"it's not a field that interests me"*

Security Awareness: security awareness is composed of the following subtopics: knowledge of measures taken, knowledge of other types of threats, and how to protect oneself against IS security risks and threats. Table 3 represents the subtopic "knowledge of other types of threats."

Table 3. Knowledge of the types of threats and potential risks related to IS security

Subtopic	Category	Number out of 22 users	Example of verbatims
Knowledge of other types of threats	Knowledge	9	*"But it can come from within the company and not necessarily from an external threat! Afterwards, there are viruses, emails where you have to click on the file and then you will be infected by a virus"*
	No knowledge	13	*"No! I don't know!"*

Security Compliance: for the compliance sub-theme, we considered the aspect of training, whether the users had had IS security-related training, or not. Among all the users, 3 of them from company A have received security training. Only one user from company B has received RGPD training that we consider related to information security.

Estimation of the Security Culture of Each User:
We will estimate the level of security culture of the users through the matrices by referring to our interview guide and more precisely, the questions regarding security culture, consisting of: security ownership, awareness and compliance. We took the estimation method proposed in the COBIT (Control Objectives for Information and Related Technology) repository to measure each area to be audited (IT risk management, data management, etc.) through a rating of: 0 Non-existent, 1 Initialized, 2 Repeatable yet intuitive, 3 Defined, 4 Managed and measurable, 5 Optimized. So we were inspired by this method to estimate the level of security culture and we adapted its measures according to our interview themes:

Knowledge of measures taken/other types of threats
0: No knowledge
1: Knowledge

Interest in security
0: Not interested
1: Interested

How to protect yourself	Participation in training	Who is responsible
0: Non-existent	0: No participation	0: Don't know
1: Low knowledge	1: Low participation	1: Management responsibility
2: Good knowledge	2: Participation	2: Everyone is responsible

Then, from the participants' answers, we assigned an estimate defined below to have a total score for each participant, and we classified these users into three levels:

Level 1: Low level of security culture (5 users)
Level 2: Medium level of security culture (10 users)
Level 3: High level of security culture (7 users)

4.2 Security-Related Behaviors Performed by Users

In this element, we will estimate the level of security-related behaviors such as the frequency of password changes, the strength of the chosen passwords as well as the backup of data by users. We have adapted the same method used to estimate security culture. The rating scale is as follows:

Change password	Reference to personal items	Backup of data
0: Never	0: Referred	0: Non-existent
1: Not often	1: Referenced and I know it is wrong	1 : Initialized
2: When asked	2: Referenced but difficult to determine	2 : Repeatable yet intuitive
3: Often	3: Do not refer	3 : Defined
		4 : Managed and measurable
		5 : Optimized

After evaluating the security behaviors of each user, we will classify them into three levels:

Level 1: Low security behaviors (8 users)
Level 2: Medium security behaviors (8 users)
Level 3: Strong security behaviors (6 users)

From these results and estimates, we conclude that 17 users out of 22 (77%) keep the same level in security culture as in security behaviors, those who have a strong level in security culture (ownership, awareness and compliance) remain on level 3 (strong) in the classification of security behaviors (password policy, backups), those who have an average level in culture keep an average level in behaviors, and finally, those who are classified at a low level of security culture also have a low level of security behaviors. With the exception of two users whose levels of security-related behaviors go down a level compared to their security culture. These level changes may be due to other factors, such as the age or position of the user. We will present some opinions of the participants:

One of the participants expresses: *"Training is clear! But then is it useful, I don't know! Because, if someone works here, will they be interested in this?! You see! It depends on the positions, maybe a little more in the office."*. Another example: *"Nope! Because I am from a generation where we were not concerned about computer security, I think that my children or my grandchildren will be more aware of that for sure!"*.

In view of these significant results, 77% of respondents have the same level of security culture as for their security-related behaviors, we conclude that the higher the level of security culture, the more security-related behaviors improve.

5 Discussion

Our results are consistent with the study by [10], which shows that IS security culture has a significant influence on employees' attitudes toward security policy and procedures. Let's consider the study by [35], which examines the relationship between IS security culture and security behavior. Although they did not focus solely on the effect of the IS security culture construct on security behavior, their findings provided more comprehensive results on the relationship between security culture and employee security behavior compared to other studies. Specifically, they found that security culture had a significant effect on attitude and normative belief in social engineering resistance. Another study by [36] shows the influence of organizational culture, countermeasures, and security procedures on employees' security behaviors. Their study shows that the deterrent effect of procedural security countermeasures increases IS security awareness. This awareness, in turn, tends to prevent malicious actions by employees and encourages secure behaviors. A more recent study by [19] shows the significant influence of IS security culture on user security compliance behaviors. Our results add to these studies to show the importance of a security culture that results from several factors, including executive security awareness, training and awareness, etc., in influencing security behaviors.

Our study also showed that other factors can influence the relationship between culture and behavior such as the age of the user, where we found that the youngest users feel more comfortable with the IT tools and therefore with the security of its tools. According to research by [37] regarding the cultural and generational influence on privacy concerns, when it comes to age, they found that young people feel more positive, more responsible, and more confident in their ability to prevent possible misuse of data, and they also have more confidence than adults in the effectiveness of legal protection. Conversely to these findings, other studies show that people aged 18–25 were more vulnerable to phishing than older age groups [38]. And [10] found a significant positive relationship between age and behavior in the domain of IS security, indicating that older people may have better behavior. Our results are more in line with those of Miltgen and Guillard (2014), in the sense that the younger the person, the stronger their security culture is likely to be, which means their security-related behavior may be better, as well. This can be explained by the familiarity of young people (between 18 and 40 years old) with computer tools, social networks, and new technologies, which can promote greater ease in processing information through these tools and technologies, which may explain the less rigidity in terms of understanding and applying security measures.

We also found that the position held by the user plays a role in the relationship between security culture and actual security behavior, where the type of position held can reinforce security behaviors if it is linked to sensitive or confidential data. Going back to the literature, it has been found that the positions (ranks) of employees have a positive impact on compliance with IS security policy [39]. To our knowledge, we have not identified other studies that have tested the effect of the position occupied by the user on his IS security culture. This could be explored and tested through future quantitative studies.

6 Conclusion

This paper presents a qualitative study in the field of IS security carried out in eight French SMEs by integrating 22 IS end-users, with the objective of studying in depth the relationship between IS security culture and IS user security-related behaviors. Our conceptual framework is based on [2] model of the three levels of culture in order to present the three levels of IS security culture. The results of our study show that most of the users interviewed have the same level in security culture as in security behaviors. Those who have a strong level in security culture remain on level 3 (Strong) in the classification of security behaviors, and vice versa. This allows us to assert that a positive IS user security culture is favorable to create security related behavior such as regular password change, backup and regular updates. Our results are consistent with several findings [10, 19, 35] that show the significant influence of IS security culture on security-related behavior. The great contribution of this research is that it proposes a model that simplifies the components of an IS security culture and its relationship with security behaviors. On a practical level, our research shows that SMEs, despite their modest means compared to large companies, can set up training and awareness-raising actions on IS security within the SME, intended for users of the company's IS. These actions must be adapted to the context of the SME, with a simple and inexpensive approach. Nevertheless, our research has its limits regarding the generalization of the data and the model that we have designed. This is why our next step is to test our model on a larger sample of SMEs, with more participants. Another very interesting point to integrate into such a study is to test the theory of reasoned behavior to verify the relationship between security culture and security behavior.

References

1. Akhyari, N., Ruzaini, A., Mohd, R.A.: A dimension-based information security culture model and its relationship with employees' security behavior: a case study in Malaysian higher educational institutions. Information Security Journal: A Global Perspective (2019)
2. Schein, E.H.: Organizational Culture and Leadership, pp. 358. Jossey-Bass, Publishers, San Francisco (1985)
3. Laudon, K., Laudon, J., Fimbel, E., Costa, S. : Management des systèmes d'information. Pearson, 551 (2010)
4. Moon, Y.J., Choi, M., Armstrong, D.J.: The impact of relational leadership and social alignment on information security system effectiveness in Korean governmental organizations. Int. J. Inf. Manage. **40**(2018), 54–66 (2018)
5. Silic, M., Lowry, P.B.: Using design-science based gamification to improve organizational security training and compliance. J. Manag. Inf. Syst. **37**(1), 129–161 (2020)
6. Tolah, A., Steven, M. Furnell, S., Papadaki, M.: An empirical analysis of the information security culture key factors framework. Comput. Secur. **108**, 102354 (2021). ISSN 0167-4048
7. Martins, N., Da Veiga, A.: An Information security culture model validated with structural equation modelling. In: Proceedings of the 9th International Symposium on Human Aspects of Information Security and Assurance, HAISA 2015, Haisa, 11–21 (2015)
8. Da Veiga, A., Astakhova, L.V., Botha, A., Herselman, M.: Defining organizational information security culture-perspectives from academia and industry. Comput. Secur. **92**, 101713 (2020)
9. Wiley, A., McCormac, A., Calic, D.: More than the individual: examining the relationship between culture and information security awareness. Comput. Secur. **88** (2020)
10. Parsons, K.M., Young, E., Butavicius, M.A., McCormac, A., Pattinson, M.R., Jerram, C.: The influence of organizational information security culture on information security decision making. J. Cogn. Eng. Decis. Mak. **9**(2), 117–129 (2015). https://doi.org/10.1177/155534341 5575152
11. Thomson, K.L., Von Solms, R., Louw, L.: Cultivating an organizational information security culture. Comput. Fraud Secur. 7–11 (2006). October 2006
12. Ngo, L., Zhou W., Warren, M.: Understanding transition towards information security culture change. In : Proceeding of the 3rd Australian Computer, Network and Information Forensics Conference, Edith Cowan University, School of Computer and Information Science, pp. 67–73 (2005)
13. Karlson, F., Astrom, J., Karlson, M.: Information security culture – state-of-the-art review between 2000 and 2013. Inf. Comput. Secur. **23**(3) (2015)
14. Hofstede, G.H.: Cultures and Organizations : Software of the Mind. McGraw-Hill, New York (1997)
15. Schein, E.H. : Organizational Culture and Leadership, vol. 2. John Wiley & Sons (2010)
16. Schlienger, T., Teufel, S.: Information security culture: the socio-cultural dimension in information security management, security in the information society: visions and perspectives. In: IFIP TC11 International Conference on Information Security (Sec2002). Kluwer Academic Publishers, Cairo, Egypt (2002)
17. Kokolakis, S., Karyda, M., Kiountouzis, E.: The insider threat to information systems and the effectiveness of ISO17799. Computer Security **24**(6), 472–484 (2005)
18. Tang, M., Li, M., Zhang, T.: The impacts of organizational culture on information security culture: a case study. Inf. Technol. Manage. **17**(2), 179–186 (2015). https://doi.org/10.1007/s10799-015-0252-2
19. Solomon, G., Brown, I.: The influence of organizational culture and information security culture on employee compliance behaviour. J. Enterp. Inf. Manag. **34**(4), 1203–1228 (2020)

20. Tolah, A., Furnell, S.M., Papadaki, M.: A comprehensive framework for cultivating and assessing information security culture. In: The Eleventh International Symposium on Human Aspects of Information Security & Assurance (HAISA), HAISA 2017, pp. 52–64 (2017)
21. Alnatheer, M., Chan, T., Nelson, K.: Understanding and measuring information security culture. In: Pacific Asia Conference on Information Systems, pp. 144 (2012)
22. Da Veiga, A., Martins, N.: Defining and identifying dominant information security cultures and subcultures. Comput. Secur. **70**, 72–94 (2017)
23. Haeussinger, F., Kranz, J.: Information security awareness: its antecedents and mediating effects on security compliant behavior. In: Proceedings of the International Conference on Information Systems, ICIS 2013, Milan, Italy (2013)
24. D'Arcy, J., Greene, G.: The multifaceted nature of security culture and its influence on end user behavior. In: IFIP TC 8 International Workshop on Information Systems Security Research, pp. 145–157 (2009)
25. Kuusisto, T., Ilvonen, I.: Information security culture in small and medium size entreprises. Frontiers of E-business research, Tampere University of Technology: University of Tampere, Finland (2003)
26. Santos-Olmo, A., Sánchez, L.E., Caballero, I., Camacho, S., Fernandez-Medina, E.: the importance of the security culture in SMEs as regards the correct management of the security of their assets. Future Internet **8**, 30 (2016)
27. Dojkovski, S., Lichtenstein, S., Warren, M.: Fostering information security culture in small and medium size enterprises: an interpretive study in Australia. In: European Conference on Information Systems (ECIS) (2007)
28. Davis, F.D., Bagozzi, R.P., Warshaw, P.R.: User acceptance of computer technology: a comparison of two theoretical models. Manag. Sci. 982–1002 (1989)
29. Ajzen, I.: The theory of planned behavior. Organ. Behav. Hum. Decis. Process. **50**(2), 179–211 (1991)
30. Padayachee, K.: Taxonomy of compliant information security behavior. Comput. Secur. **31**(5), 673–680 (2012)
31. D'Arcy, J., Greene, G.: Security culture and the employment relationship as drivers of employees' security compliance. Inf. Manag. Comput. Secur. **22**, 474–489 (2014)
32. Nasir, A., Arshah, R.A., Hamid A.M.R.: A dimension-based information security culture model and its relationship with employees' security behavior: a case study in Malaysian higher educational institutions. Information Security Journal: A Global Perspective **28**(3) (2019)
33. Wacheux, F.: Méthodes Qualitatives et Recherche en Gestion. Economica, Paris (1996)
34. Yin, R.K.: Applications of Case Study Research (Applied Social Research Methods). Sage Publications, Inc. (2003)
35. Flores, W.R., Ekstedt, M.: Shaping intention to resist social engineering through transformational leadership information security culture and awareness. Comput. Secur. **59**, 26–44 (2016). ISSN 0167-4048
36. Connolly, L.Y., Lang, M., Gathegi J., Tygar, D.J.: Organizational culture, procedural countermeasures, and employee security behaviour: a qualitative stud. Inf. Comput. Secur. **25** (2017)
37. Miltgen, C.L., Peyrat-Guillard, D.: Cultural and generational influences on privacy concerns: a qualitative study in seven European countries. Eur. J. Inf. Syst. **23**(2), 103–125 (2014)
38. Sheng, S., Holbrook, M., Kumaraguru, P., Cranor, L.F., Downs, J.: Who falls for phishing?: a demographic analysis of phishing susceptibility and effectiveness of interventions In: Proceedings of the Sigchi Conference on Human Factors in Computing Systems. ACM, pp. 372–382 (2010)
39. Guo, K.H., Yufei, Y.: The effects of multilevel sanctions on information security violations: A mediating model. Inf. Manag. **49**(6 (2012)

Possibilities and Limitations of the Croatian Police in Communication via Social Networks

Ivana Radić[1]([✉]), Robert Idlbek[2], and Irena Cajner Mraović[3]

[1] Ministry of the Interior, Pozesko-Slavonska County Police Administration, Zagreb, Croatia
iradic0@gmail.com
[2] Polytechnic in Pozega, Pozega, Croatia
ridlbek@vup.hr
[3] Faculty of Croatian Studies, University of Zagreb, Zagreb, Croatia
icajner@gmail.com

Abstract. There is a large amount of research on the application of social networks in companies' business activities. Still, their application and usefulness in the business activities of the public sector are much less researched. Their application for police purposes poses significant challenges because there are substantial risks that can cause great damage to the reputation and work of the police and police officers. There are currently no systematic guidelines and forms of social media use regarding the police in the Republic of Croatia, and this research is one of the first to provide a basis for further work in this area.

The research aims to identify and describe the possibilities and limitations of the Croatian police in communication via social networks. Also, the study aims to determine the current forms of communications of the Croatian police with the public through social networks and the level of preparedness for managing digital communication channels regarding human, organizational and technological resources.

The research was approached by a qualitative focus group research procedure, given that no research on police communication through social networks has been conducted in Croatia yet.

Keywords: Croatian police · Social networks · Focus group

1 Introduction

The speed of development of social network technology, its reach and impact on humanity is the subject of many scientific articles. We are seeing a large number of users and that number is growing significantly. As technology is becoming cheaper, the Internet is more accessible, and apps are easier to use, social networks are becoming available to a large number of people no matter the age group they belong to. This "Era of the Internet", recently hit by a global pandemic as a catalyst, has significantly influenced the transition of much of communication into virtual space. It should be noted that in addition to providing opportunities to improve communication, social networks can also cause problems if used without a prepared communication strategy. Despite possible

M. A. Bach Tobji et al. (Eds.): ICDEc 2022, LNBIP 461, pp. 129–144, 2022.
https://doi.org/10.1007/978-3-031-17037-9_9

problems, police forces around the globe provide security to their residents by using social networks as one of the channels of communication. Social networks have become a strong communication channel between the police and the community, as well as a daily means of collecting data from the field.

This paper presents a study of the Croatian police communication with the public via social networks. The research was conducted using a qualitative focus group research process, given that no research on police communication via social networks has been conducted in Croatia thus far, and in order to start the research, it was necessary to encourage in-depth discussion of police public relations officers on this topic.

2 Social Networks and Their Significance for Society

Research has shown that 53.6% of the world's population use social media for an average of 2 h and 25 min a day (DataReportal 2021). According to the latest Eurostat research, the largest portion of citizens using social networks is in Denmark, approximately 87% (Eurostat 2021). The European average presence on social networks is 57% (research on a sample of people aged 16 to 74), and this also includes citizens of the Republic of Croatia.

The Internet in Croatia, in addition to collecting information on products and services (93%), reading daily news (91%), collecting health information (79%), using e-mail (74%), sending messages via phone apps (87%), is largely used for access to social networks, in 73% of cases (Croatian Bureau of Statistics 2019). According to data provided by DataReportal (2021b), 68.4% of the total population of Croatia use social networks, and most of them use Facebook 50.2% (population 13+), YouTube 70.5% (18+), Instagram 36.3% (13+), Facebook Messenger 39.1% (13+), LinkedIn 20.1% (18+), Snapchat 14.6% (13+) and Twitter 3.6% (13+).

Over time, Croatian social networks were created and shut down: for example Iskrica, Tulumarka, Trosjed, Teen and Zrikku. However, the number of their users has always been negligible compared to the number of users of global social networks in Croatia (Grbavac and Grbavac 2014).

Speaking of apps used for accessing certain social networks, the latest research for the first quarter of 2021 shows that 36.6 billion downloads of apps in the "social network" category were recorded worldwide. This is an increase of 8.7% over the same period last year. Figure 1 shows how TikTok was again the most successful mobile app in terms of downloads worldwide. Telegram is in second place in Europe, with a 40% increase compared to the same period last year, achieving approximately 27.3 million downloads in the first quarter. Due to the pandemic, Zoom and Microsoft Teams reached highest download numbers (SensorTower 2021). The primary reason for this are online activities related to teaching, business meetings and work from home.

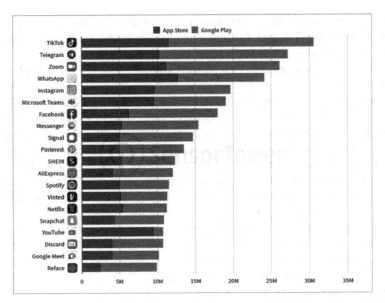

Fig. 1. App downloads in Europe during the 1st quarter of 2021 (SensorTower 2021)

3 Application of Social Networks as a Communication Channel for Policing

Certain authors cite social networks as one of the modern technologies that will have a strong impact and application in policing (O'Connor and Zaidi 2020), and the importance of social networks in policing is best shown by a fact from September 2021. At the American Conference of the most influential International Association of Police Chiefs (IACP), which has more than 30,000 members from 165 countries, several presentations spoke about the possibilities of using social networks during mass protests. The presentations emphasized the need for establishing a system of best practices in the use of social networks, the need to clarify legal norms related to social networks, instructions on what to do when well-intentioned posts are wrongly accepted by the public and the like (IACP 2021).

Police communication with the wider community via social media must have a defined mission, as is the case with the New York Police Department (NYPD), which categorize all of their social media posts (Facebook, Twitter, Instagram and Snapchat) into groups, with two distinct larger categories of posts, the first with the goal of protection (keeping people safe) and the second with the goal of connecting (strengthening relationships with the community). In their posts, they use dedicated hashtags to promote these goals (#NYPDProtecting and #NYPDConnecting), and the hashtag #NYPDTips is also important, which is used for seeking information about perpetrators and offering rewards. It is already a well-established practice of the police to use social media to post pictures and videos in order to seek public help that would lead to the identification and arrest of suspects in criminal or misdemeanour cases (Ruddell and Jones 2013; Colbran 2020). In the UK, direct police communication via social media is made possible by direct inquiries to police officers, for example on Twitter or Facebook, using a specific hashtag, such as #AskTheChief. Citizens who click on this hashtag can see what other users are saying or asking (Scholes-Fogg 2015).

Social media campaigns are often planned with targeting the demographic group that is likely to receive the desired message (Ruddell and Jones 2013), which can mostly include younger and more educated residents as they are most present on social media.

There are other interesting approaches in the application of social networks related to the publication of police content. An example is the Australian approach, which was based on increasing the presence on social networks by publishing contents from the so-called meme domain. A new police communication strategy was implemented in 2017 with the aim of increasing the number of post followers on Facebook. In order to boost Facebook's algorithm for displaying posts, the posts featured humour and amicable additions such as pictures of police dogs. The goal of the strategy was to demystify and humanize the police force and enable important announcements to a large number of people (Wood 2019), i.e. to reach millions of users, which would be more than 850 thousand people who follow the NYPD's Facebook profile, the most famous example of the application of social networks within the police.

The cooperation of emergency services in the field is also moving into the digital space. Institutions close to the police (fire-fighters, Mountain Rescue Service, etc.) often post police announcements, and the police also post announcements by the emergency services (Fernandez et al. 2017). By researching police communication via social media, in a small town in the southern region of the United States, Boateng and Chenane (2020) discovered that there are no defined rules and regulations that would specify what and how to post and there is a lack of defined responsibility for reading and removing inappropriate comments. Research dealing with defining the strategy and rules of conduct (Meijer and Thaens 2013; Meijer and Torenvlied 2016; Coomber 2018; Jungblut and Jungblut 2021) is increasing in proportion to the increase in the use of social networks.

Recent research shows that social networks have enabled the police to bypass the media and thus take their "gatekeeping" function away, i.e. it enabled the police to bypass the media's thorough checks of police communications prior to presenting them to the public (Grygiel and Lysak 2020). Recent research also address the strengths and weaknesses of proactive police communication via the Internet (Williams et al. 2019), the need to form inter-agency collaborations to make better use of information and resources (Fallik et al. 2020) and treating users as co-development operators from which the organization learns (Dekker et al. 2020).

Certain scientists such as Davis, Alves and Sklansky (2014) suggest using an informal tone when communicating on social networks, but with maximum professionalism and supervision by experts in the field of communication via digital channels. They note that in defining the strategy of such specific communication, one should not only count followers and "social engagement" such as retweets, likes, shares, etc., but also observe the outcome, i.e. improving community safety and other contributions. The effectiveness of informal expressions in posts on social media networks in the United States has been confirmed through research (Hu and Lovrich 2019a, 2019b).

Furthermore, it should also be emphasized that the quality of the police response to digitally obtained information is important, which has not been achieved according to research conducted in the 10 most populous US cities (Brainard and Edlins 2015). Without this reaction, the basic purpose of communication via social media is lost, and it is necessary to clearly define the steps to be taken when useful information from the citizens is obtained.

The negative effect of social networks was also felt by the police in Kensington (Ross 2016) when on their official Facebook page they tried to associate the drivers who violate traffic regulations to listening to the music of a certain band using a funny post and using a hashtag. This resulted in a public apology from the police officer, the author of the controversial post. Since the post was quickly picked up by news organizations around the world, it spread widely and many citizens did not find it witty. In other words, the attempt to get closer to the community ended in a negative reaction due to misinterpretation. Although the use of social networks has great potential due to its two-way communication in public relations, it also brings potential problems. Therefore, before any activity, it is necessary to think critically and plan wisely, and to establish a communication plan in order to be able to strategically respond to a problem without delay.

Gilkerson and Tusinski Berg (2017) explain the term "Hashtag Hijacking" by warning that using a hashtag (#) as a tool used to tag and organize conversations on social media pages can easily become a means of ridicule and negative criticism. Hastag Hijacking has become a strategic tool for individuals and activist groups that use hashtags to publicly name and try to influence a certain organization.

Research conducted approximately ten years ago (Denef et al. 2012) shows that the application of new information and communication technologies in the police is an inevitable step in adapting to new trends.

4 Research Objective and Research Questions

The aim of the research is to determine the current forms and characteristics of the Croatian police communication with the public via social networks and the level of preparedness for managing digital communication channels with regard to human, organizational and technological resources.

Accordingly, the following research questions have been defined:

Q1. To what extent is the Croatian police organizationally prepared to manage digital communication channels on social networks?
Q2. To what extent is the Croatian police prepared to manage digital communication channels on social networks with regard to human resources?
Q3. To what extent is the Croatian police technologically ready to manage digital communication channels via social networks?
Q4. How to overcome problems when adopting the document Police Communication Strategy on Social Networks?

5 Methods

5.1 Sample

The sample of participants in this research is based on the principle of homogeneity, i.e. belonging to a group with common interests, and in this case that is professional public relations in the police and the Ministry of the Interior of the Republic of Croatia.

The Ministry of the Interior of the Republic of Croatia is structurally divided into several organizational units. Thus, the Police Directorate was established for performing police work, as an administrative organization within the Ministry, while police administrations operate at the local level. One of the organizational units of the Ministry of the Interior is the Civil Protection Directorate, whose activities are also directly related to the protection and rescue of life and property. The Central Public Relations Service is structurally defined in the Cabinet of the Minister, along with several individuals in other organizational units. Since it is difficult to separate the communication of the police from the communication of other components of the Ministry of the Interior, this paper uses and analyses the experiences of communication with the public of all organizational units and uniformly applies the terms "police public relations" and "public relations of the Ministry of the Interior". Accordingly, the target population for this survey is 57 public relations officers of the police and the Ministry of the Interior.

The research was conducted on one focus group consisting of six participants, which is 10% of the overall target population. This number is optimal because it allows each member to express their own views and opinions, and is also sufficiently big to allow the development of group dynamics (Onwuegbuzie and Collins 2007), especially considering that communication takes place at a distance.

One individual in the focus group is male, which is proportional to the share of male individuals in the target population. The Civil Protection Directorate, the Police Directorate, the Public Relations Service of the Cabinet of the Minister and the Police Administration of various categories are represented. All participants are long-term employees of the Ministry of the Interior and individuals who contact the public on a daily basis via various communication channels. It should be noted that some of the participants know each other superficially, which did not affect the relations between the participants, i.e. the introduction of external dynamics (Skoko and Benković 2009).

5.2 Instrument

For the needs of the research, a Protocol for a semi-structured interview was prepared, developed from the aspect of Communication Theory and Shannon–Weaver's communication model. The interview is thematically divided into five parts:

1. Problems of communication in general (four questions)
    The topic of this group of questions aims to create preconditions for quality and open communication of participants. Four issues sparked a discussion on the changes that digital technology brings to everyday life. At the same time, a particular focus is placed on digital communication, for both private and professional purposes.

2. Problems of police communication via social networks (five questions)

The topics of the second group of questions were prepared in a way that would enable the collection of information on the current attitude of each individual participant regarding the digital communication of the police with citizens. In doing so, the emphasis was on researching their attitude towards social networks and the usefulness of social networks in the work of the police in general.

3. Problems of organizational, technological and human readiness of the Ministry of the Interior to communicate via social networks (eleven questions)

Most of the questions are dedicated to the analysis of the current state of the Croatian police and the state of their readiness to introduce additional communication channels with citizens. In doing so, the focus was placed on social media presence. An important aspect of the observation is focused on the issues of how educated and ready police officers are for new forms of communication. Several questions examined the attitudes of focus group participants on the possibility of adapting the police considering the current work positions and the regulations within which the police operate. The idea of this thematic unit is to collect and then analyse the experiences of individuals already involved in public relations and determine what would need to be adopted or changed in order to increase the required level of readiness for new forms of digital communication.

4. The problem of the impact of the police presence on social networks on the community in terms of police legitimacy, citizens' trust in the police and procedural justice (seven questions).

Having in mind the possibility of solving specific business problems, the topic of this group of questions is related to understanding the area of possible applications of digital communication between the Croatian police and citizens. Participants should share their ideas regarding in which cases the use of social networks is justified, when such communication is applicable and how often (and in what way) can social networks be used to create a positive climate and socially responsible business from a community perspective.

5. Concrete suggestions for improving communication and other issues that need to be mentioned (two questions).

Two open-ended questions allow the participants to clarify concepts, ideas, or critiques that they did not have the opportunity to express during the interview. Through this topic, they are able to further argue their views, point out problems and make suggestions based on their many years of experience in policing or participation in public services.

5.3 Data Collection and Processing Methods

At the very beginning of the focus group discussion, a verbal consent of the participants for the recording was requested, emphasizing that the complete protection of the participants' identities will be respected in result processing and presentation. Two moderators, based on a pre-prepared protocol for a semi-structured interview, conducted a group discussion for 90 min in accordance with the recommendations for conducting interviews (Skoko and Benković 2009). In addition to the moderators, the participants encouraged each other to get involved in the conversation and thus enabled the collection of additional information during the interview.

In accordance with the mechanisms proposed in Grounded Theory (Corbin and Strauss 1990/2015; Strauss 1987/2003; Willig 2008), notes were kept during the empirical research of the focus group. They were used to record areas that need to be further analysed in order to identify ideas that could be a potential source of information in the preparation of proposals for the Croatian police communication models on social networks.

The recorded material was transcribed and the transcript was used for further analysis of the results. A constant comparative analysis was applied, according to the Grounded Theory (Glaser and Strauss 1967), as a result of which the results were coded and compared. The data were analysed by systematizing the answers according to the questions, by monitoring non-verbal communication and by using notes taken during the focus group.

Based on the processed and analysed data, a transcript and a narrative report of the focus group were drafted (Krueger and Casey 2000).

5.4 Ethical Aspect of the Research

Participation in the focus group was voluntary and anonymous.

First, the consent for the implementation of this research was requested and obtained in writing from the competent persons of the Ministry of the Interior, the Public Relations Service and the Police Directorate. Consent for research participation was then requested and obtained from selected members of the target population.

At the very beginning of the focus group discussion, a verbal consent of the participants for the recording was requested, emphasizing that the complete protection of the participants' identities will be respected in result processing and presentation. The participants were then presented with the goal and method of work as well as the rules of conduct during this form of research. Each participant was made aware of the possibility to withdraw from the research at any time.

Focus group participants are marked with abbreviations P1, P2, P3, P4, P5 and P6 and there is no possibility of their identification.

5.5 Research Limitations

Based on the interview, it can be concluded that focus group members are well selected since they represent people who actively use modern information and communication tools and are well aware of the current situation, needs and problems in public reporting on police work. However, the results obtained should be viewed in the context of research limitations that are primarily related to the fact that only one focus group with six participants was held. The limitation of the research is to some extent the disproportion between the topicality and scope of the research topic on the one hand and the time frame of the focus group interview on the other.

6 Results

The results were determined by analysing the transcript of the focus group, which clearly show how the participants perceive police communication via social networks as an important segment of communication. There is a growing tendency for this form of communication to be present in everyday business processes.

6.1 Communication Problems in General

The focus group started with general questions on communication in order to introduce the participants to the conversation, but also to acquaint them with the issues covered by the research.

Participants believe that the change in the way of communication in the past ten years represents mostly positive developments. They immediately state that these changes are especially visible in police work and the presence of the police in the media as well as on social networks.

P4: "We have brought the speech closer to the citizens, we no longer speak in a way that no one understands us. We have simplified our official speech."

P2: "At the beginning of the Corona crisis, everything was urgently opened (social network profiles), so that we could be as accessible to the public as possible, which in many segments proved to be very good, like the great earthquake in Zagreb. Everyone is mobile, they are not sitting at home in front of the TV, because they are running away from a real life danger."

Regarding everyday private and business communication, participants state that they use a number of applications for social networks, which shows that it is necessary to accept changes and adopt new knowledge in the field of communication, especially in the segment of digital communication. They also point out that an essential feature of today's communication is the feedback "speed" and the transition to new forms, noting that new generations do not distinguish messages sent via SMS compared to other communication tools such as Messenger, Viber etc.

P1: "WhatsApp, Viber and Telegram are used internally, because it is the fastest method to share something important. Instagram, Twitter, Facebook, LinkedIn are used in official communication with citizens."

P1: "When people ask questions through these channels and media, they want an answer immediately, not in two days, but in twenty minutes. They have a concrete problem and expect an answer immediately."

Discussing whether the mass media tends to sensationalism, the discussion moved in the direction of practical examples, noting the importance of the type of content that is posted. Namely, the participants commented on the quality of media reporting based on the information provided by the police, and it is possible to conclude that certain media strive for sensationalism. That reduces the quality of information passed on to citizens and can sometimes lead to unnecessary problems in the work of the police.

Respondents believe that with more frequent and better information through digital channels, the police can provide accurate information to citizens. In doing so, it can avoid potential noise in communication. That can reduce the quality of information placed on citizens and can sometimes lead to unnecessary problems in the work of the police.

P1: "If we talk about placing some kind of press release in terms of preventive matters, such as fraud on the Internet and such, in almost 99% of cases the message is transmitted the same way as it was sent."

P5: "Official information must go out as soon as possible, since in fact they create their stories (journalists), especially if we are speaking about some smaller rural areas… in the latest case of an attempted robbery, two or three slightly larger media that are followed by the national media managed to obtain video surveillance and recordings within half an hour or an hour after the said incident. They were already announcing the identities of possible suspects."

6.2 Problems of Police Communication via Social Networks

This was followed by the topic of police communication via social networks, i.e. issues related to the communication of the Ministry of the Interior employees with the public, which encompasses the tasks of the participants.

The discussion defined how all organizational units of the Ministry of the Interior use e-mail to communicate with citizens and social networks to a lesser extent. However, that information about the work of the police ends up on social networks, as various media report them. It was noted that different social networks target different groups of people who are divided mainly by age. For example, Facebook is more aimed at the middle-aged and older generations of people, while young people and children use other social networks such as TikTok and Instagram. Accordingly, it is necessary to prepare materials for social network posts depending on the target group, but also to include as many social networks as possible. The participants understand the issue of preparing texts and visuals for posting on various social networks, but are not familiar with the possibilities offered by tools for central and uniform publishing such as HootSuite and Contentino.

P2: "As far as Facebook is concerned, I think it is used by older populations. I see it in my kids who say 'mom you have Facebook, you are old'. Twitter is something newer. Teenagers at the age of 14 used Instagram, Snap… you need several different networks at various points of time in order to cover everything."

Talking about whether posts on social networks can negatively affect the perception of the police, the problem of comments on social networks arose. Nevertheless, the common position of the focus group is that with the help of a quality presence on social networks, one can increase the reputation and favourable public opinion about the police. The participants state that "uniformed" and "cold" announcements often provoke negative comments from citizens, while, for example, announcements about the search dog were positively accepted. In addition to negative comments, there are also positive comments on social networks that can influence public opinion about the police, and some of them result in operationally interesting information. As an important segment, it was emphasized that the police communicate with the public on topics such as: completed criminal investigations related to crimes and misdemeanours, missing and wanted persons and other illegal forms of behaviour, which can also ensure helpful feedback.

P6: "There will always be someone who will write something in a negative context."

P2: "Civil Protection Directorate, our Gizmo, our search dog, the most famous paw of Croatia. Earthquake in Albania, what were we recognized by? By his fantastic photo of rescuing people from the ruins taken from a plane."

P5: "Sometimes maybe certain comments within these Facebook posts bring us some new knowledge and we can react based on these comments and messages."

6.3 Problems of Organizational, Technological and Personnel Readiness of the Ministry of the Interior to Communicate via Social Networks

The next block of questions discussed the findings, but also the thoughts, of the participants related to the level of preparedness for digital channel management with regard to personnel, organizational and technological resources in the Ministry of the Interior.

Since it was previously determined that posts can negatively affect public opinion, which certainly needs to be reduced to the lowest level, the participants see additional training of public relations personnel to work with social networks as one possible solutions. They also believe that it is necessary to develop and actively use agreed standards (e.g. book of standards for graphic design) and have clear instructions on how to post and draft social network contents. The current situation, according to the participants, requires the definition of a comprehensive strategy for police communication via social networks.

P1: "The Ministry does not have any handbook, as far as the book of standards is concerned, for the visual presentation of anything..."

Discussing which social networks the police should post on, the participants concluded that it was important to initially define the content and determine on which social network posting would be "most profitable" given the age of its users. The role of influencers as relevant representatives of a certain demography and through which the information sent can reach a larger audience was also mentioned.

P1: "If there is a preventive operation in traffic, we should definitely use Instagram to reach young high-flying drivers who like to take pictures while driving 230 km/h on a highway."

All participants believe that among their own employees they have the personnel with the necessary knowledge to create content and post on social networks, noting that any additional form of education would be desirable. Some of the focus group participants believe that more intensive use of social networks is needed at the level of Police Directorates, and that they might already be falling behind in this segment.

P3: "We even had a proposal ten years ago for launching a pilot project of the Police Directorate Facebook..."

When discussing whether it is necessary to keep statistics on posts, post reach, and social engagement of posts made on social networks, the participants have a divided opinion. They agreed that analyses and statistics should be done, but that the basic measures of the effectiveness of such posts should not be valorised and measured in the same way in the public sector (police) as in the real sector in which advertising is mainly done. Metrics exist, but their application is questionable.

All participants agreed that it would be helpful to establish a central team for managing the presence on social networks and a list of all public profiles of organizational units of the Ministry of the Interior on social networks. That statement opened the question of lack of personnel. Namely, as a definite problem, the participants state the lack of human resources for deeper acceptance of social networks in terms of communication channels. Introduction of so-called two-way communication, in which the police would answer questions and comments asked via social networks, is seen as a process that cannot be achieved with the current distribution of tasks and number of people and without significant changes in the functioning of public relations services.

There was also talk of inappropriate communication via social networks, about which the participants have a divided opinion. Namely, some of them think that it is common knowledge what the appropriate way of communication is, while others think that it is necessary to define the rules in this area as well.

P5: "I think that the Code of Ethics says it all... whether it is a cadet at the Police Academy or an officer who has been in the police for 10 years..."

6.4 The Problem of the Impact of the Police Presence on Social Networks on the Community in Terms of Police Legitimacy, Citizens' Trust in the Police and Procedural Justice

This was followed by questions on how police communication on social networks could/should reflect on the legitimacy of the police, citizens' trust in the police and procedural justice with regard to improving communication via social networks.

The discussion on improving police communication via social networks through an increased number of contacts reopens the issue of lack of personnel and other components of successful communication.

I2: "We lack resources, we lack technology, we lack humanity, we lack knowledge... we always have some limitations, inability to access something, finances and lack of personnel. I think that there would be more will if there were some incentives and opportunities for people to be educated a little more."

The participants agreed that police use social media to respond quickly to emergencies such as earthquakes, apprehending criminals and searching for missing persons with the announcement of new technologies in the area such as the introduction of Facebook's AMBER warning for missing children. They also agreed that the contact of citizens with the police via social networks enables equal treatment of different social groups. Discussing whether improving police communication via social media can heighten people's sense of obligation to act in accordance with police instructions has imposed the importance of two-way communication. The possibility of using social networks to explain certain decisions and reasons for some actions was also accepted as desirable. What certain participants find unacceptable is the reporting of criminal offenses and misdemeanours via social networks, emphasizing that direct contact is more useful in such situations.

P6: "It is better to personally go to a Police Station and file a criminal complaint and say everything you have and provide more information than you would by sending an e-mail, etc."

Through various preventive activities and cooperation with institutions, associations and other organizations, the police is involved in solving social problems, news of which is also published via social networks. Often, social networks and communication via them are a source of information about social problems, but also about the possibilities of solving them.

P3: "Organizing humanitarian actions… collecting books for the Association that cares for children with developmental disabilities…. in this way we get involved in community work."

6.5 Suggestions for Improving Communication

At the end of the discussion, the participants were invited to make concrete suggestions for improving communication, but also other facts that could be relevant to the focus group topic.

A discussion followed on whether individual organizational units should have their own social network profiles, on which opinions were divided. The participants are aware that communication via social networks would bring the police closer to the community, but they also point out a number of limitations that currently arise when thinking about intensifying this form of communication. They agree that in this situation it would be desirable to have a centre (e.g. in Zagreb) that would be the starting point for new forms of communication with citizens. This centre should run complete administration of police public profiles on social networks in one place, have an advisory role and provide the technology and knowledge (education) needed for quality public relations.

P2: "Social networks are an engagement practically 24 h a day. There is no delay."

P3: "We should somehow define the whole procedure in order to ensure that this communication via social networks is of good quality. However, even though it may be a slightly more informal way of communication, we would still communicate as an institution, so it should be within a certain policy framework."

7 Discussion and Conclusion

The implementation of this empirical focus group research gathered information, ideas and attitudes of selected participants dealing with public relations of the police and other organizational units of the Ministry of the Interior.

Since the aim of the research was to determine the current forms and characteristics of the Croatian police communication with the public, with particular emphasis on modern digital communication channels and social networks, the information collected is the basis and a motive for further research on this topic. The conclusions drawn through the analysis of available literature, interviews with the participants and analysis of their formed attitudes on this topic indicate that the selected research area is engaging, relevant and insufficiently researched in the Republic of Croatia. The results of the focus group's conclusions show that, at the moment, the presence of the police and other components of the Ministry of the Interior on social networks is not given sufficient attention. It is interesting to find out how the participants identify opportunities and problems that may arise from a stronger application of new digital channels in communication with the community.

Bearing in mind that police administrations in other countries have been actively trying to master the methodology and technology of using social networks for many years, it is unquestionable that this topic deserves appropriate attention in the Republic of Croatia. However, unlike the approaches that are already well known in the business environment, the police approach towards the community via social networks should differ significantly both in the metrics for measuring performance and in the way of addressing, i.e. posting information.

Given the broad scope of issues and the susceptible area in which public sector institutions, especially the police, operate, additional efforts are required for developing procedural guidelines and methodologies that are simple and applicable. It is also necessary to focus on additional training of public information personnel, describe procedures and instructions for the preparation and publication of information, and adopt a joint position of all police services regarding the configuration and subject matter of posted information. In addition, there is a need to adjust the current regulations in order to carry out these activities without hindrance. This includes the development of the necessary methodological framework that would define competencies, processes and procedures, organization and technological infrastructure through which the Croatian police could manage their presence on social networks and new digital channels.

References

Boateng, F.D., Chenane, J.: Policing and social media: a mixed-method investigation of social media use by a small-town police department. Int. J. Police Sci. Manag. **22**(3), 263–273 (2020). https://doi.org/10.1177/1461355720927429

Brainard, L., Edlins, M.: Top 10 U.S. Municipal Police Departments and their social media usage. Amer. Rev. Public Admin. **45**(6), 728–745 (2015). https://citeseerx.ist.psu.edu/viewdoc/download?doi=10.1.1.836.3792&rep=rep1&type=pdf

Colbran, M.: Policing, social media and the new media landscape: can the police and the traditional media ever successfully bypass each other? Policing Soc. **30**(3), 295–309 (2020). https://doi.org/10.1080/10439463.2018.1532426

Coomber, N.: Police Use of Twitter: 21st Century Community Policing. Theses and Dissertations (Comprehensive) 2095 (2018). (https://scholars.wlu.ca/cgi/viewcontent.cgi?article=3211&con text=etd

Corbin, J., Straus, A.: Basics of Qualitative Research: Techniques and Procedures for Developing Grounded Theory, 4th edn. Sage, Thousand Oaks, CA (1990/2015)

DataReportal: Digital 2021: Global Overview Report (2021). https://datareportal.com/reports/dig ital-2021-global-overview-report. Accessed on 22 Aug 2021

DataReportal: Digital 2021b Croatia (2021b). https://www.slideshare.net/DataReportal/digital-2021b-croatia-january-2021b-v01

Davis, E.F., Alves, A.A., Sklansky, D.: Social Media and Police Leadership: Lessons From Boston. New Persp. Policing. https://www.ojp.gov/pdffiles1/nij/244760.pdf. Accessed on 10 Aug 2021

Dekker, R., Brink, P.V., Meijer, A.: Social media adoption in the police: barriers and strategies. Gov. Inf. Quart. 37(2) (2020). https://doi.org/10.1016/j.giq.2019.101441

Denef, S., Kaptein, N., Bayerl, P.S., Ramirez, L.: Best Practice in Police Social Media Adaptation. COMPOSITE – Comparative Police Studies in the EU (2012). https://repub.eur.nl/pub/40562. Accessed on 28 Aug 2021

Državni zavod za statistiku Republike Hrvatske: Primjena informacijskih i komunikacijskih tehnologija (IKT) u kućanstvima i kod pojedinaca u 2019., prvi rezultati. (2019). https://www. dzs.hr/Hrv_Eng/publication/2019/02-03-02_01_2019.htm. Accessed on 17 Aug 2021

Eurostat: Do you participate in social networks? (2021). https://ec.europa.eu/eurostat/web/pro ducts-eurostat-news/-/edn-20210630-1. Accessed on 21 Aug 2021

Fallik, S.W., et al.: Policing through social media: a qualitative exploration. Int. J. Police Sci. Manag. 22(2), 208–218 (2020). https://doi.org/10.1177/1461355720911948.-28.08.2021

Fernandez, M., Dickinson, T., Alani, H.: An analysis of UK policing Engagement via Social Media. In: Ciampaglia, G., Mashhadi, A., Yasseri, T. (eds.) SocInfo 2017: The 9th International Conference on Social Informatics, Oxford, UK, 13–15 Sep 2017, pp. 289–304. Springer, Cham (2017). https://doi.org/10.1007/978-3-319-67217-5_18

Gilkerson, N., Tusinski Berg, K.: Social media, hashtag hijacking, and the evolution of an activist group strategy. In Austin, L., Jin, Y. (ed.) Social Media and Crisis Communication, pp. 141–157. Routledge, New York (2017). https://toc.library.ethz.ch/objects/pdf03/z01_978-1-138-81199-7_01.pdf

Glaser, B., Strauss, A.L.: The Discovery of Grounded Theory. Adline, Chicago (1967/2006)

Grbavac, J., Grbavac, V.: Pojava društvenih mreža kao globalnog komunikacijskog fenomenaPO-JAVA DRUŠTVENIH MREŽA KAO GLOBALNOG KOMUNIKACIJSKOG FENOMENA. Media Cult. Pub. Relat. 5(2), 206–219 (2014). https://hrcak.srce.hr/127963

Grygiel, J., Lysak, S.: Police social media and broadcast news: an investigation into the impact of police use of Facebook on journalists' gatekeeping role. Journalism Pract. (2020). https://doi. org/10.1080/17512786.2020.1759123

Hu, X., Lovrich, N.P.: Small police agency use of social media: positive and negative outcomes noted in a case study. Policing J. Policy Pract. (2019). https://doi.org/10.1093/police/paz077

Hu, X., Lovrich, N.P.: Small police agency use of social media: positive and negative outcomes noted in a case study. Policing J. Policy Pract. https://www.researchgate.net/publication/338158780_Small_police_agency_use_of_social_media_Positive_and_negative_outcomes_noted_in_a_case_study

International Association of Chiefs of Police IACP: IACP Conference 2021, September 11–14, New Orleans, Louisiana https://www.theiacpconference.org/. Accessed on 22 Aug 2021

Jungblut, M., Jungblut, J.: Do organizational differences matter for the use of social media by public organizations? A computational analysis of the way the German police use Twitter for external communication. Pub. Admin. 1–20 (2021). https://doi.org/10.1111/padm.12747

Krueger, R.A., Casey, M.A.: Focus Groups: A Practical Guide for Applied Research, 5th edn. Sage, Thousand Oaks, CA (2000)

Meijer, A.J., Thaens, M.: Social media strategies: understanding the differences between North American police departments. Gov. Inf. Quart. Int. J. Inf. Technol. Manag. Policy Pract. **30**(4), 343–350 (2013). https://doi.org/10.1016/j.giq.2013.05.023-22.08.2021

Meijer, A.J., Torenvlied, R.: Social Media and the New Organization of Government Communications: An Empirical Analysis of Twitter Usage by the Dutch Police. Amer. Rev. Public Admin. **46**(2), 143–161 (2016). https://www.utwente.nl/en/bms/csd/research/Meijer%20en%20Torenvlied%202014.pdf

O'Connor, C.D., Zaidi, H.: Communicating with purpose: image work, social media, and policing. Police J. Theory Pract. Princip. (2020). https://doi.org/10.1177/0032258X20932957

Onwuegbuzie, A.J., Collins, K.: A typology of mixed methods sampling designs in social science research. Qual. Rep. **12**(2), 281–316 (2007). https://doi.org/10.46743/2160-3715/2007.1638

Ross, S.: Kensington police officer apologizes to Nickelback for Facebook post (2016). http://www.cbc.ca/news/canada/prince-edward-island/pei-kensington-nickelback-apology-1.3879808. Accessed on 23 Aug 2021

Ruddell, R., Jones, N.: Social media and policing: matching the message to the audience. Saf. Commun. **12**(2), 64–70 (2013). https://doi.org/10.1108/17578041311315030

Scholes-Fogg, T.: Independent Police Commission: Police and Social Media (2015). https://www.researchgate.net/publication/278677308_Independent_Police_Commission_Police_and_Social_Media. Accessed on 22 July 2021

SensorTower (2021) Q1: Store Intelligence Dana Digest. https://go.sensortower.com/rs/351-RWH-315/images/Sensor-Tower-Q1-2021-Data-Digest.pdf. Accessed on 21 Aug 2021

Skoko, B., Benković, V.: Znanstvena metoda fokus grupa – mogućnosti i načini primjene. Politička misao. **46**(3), 217–236 (2009). https://hrcak.srce.hr/509

Strauss, A.L.: Qualitative Analysis for Social scientists. Cambridge: Cambridge University Press (1987)

Williams, M., et al.: Offensive communications: exploring the challenges involved in policing social media. Contemp. Soc. Sci. **16**(2), 227–240 (2019). https://doi.org/10.1080/21582041.2018.1563305

Willig, C.: Introducing Qualitative Research in Psychology, 2nd edn. McGraw Hill & Open University Press, Berkshire (2008)

Wood, M.A.: Policing's 'meme strategy': understanding the rise of police social media engagement work. Curr. Issues Crim. Jus. **32**(1), 40–58. https://doi.org/10.1080/10345329.2019.1658695

Digital Marketing

Cause-Related Marketing: Towards an Exploration of the Factors Favoring the Purchase Intention of the Tunisian Consumer

Molka Triki Ellouze[1]([⊠]) [iD] and Amel Chaabouni[2] [iD]

[1] Marketing Research Laboratory (FSEG Sfax), Higher Institute of Management of Tunis, Sfax, Tunisia
molkatriki00@gmail.com
[2] Higher Institute of Management of Tunis, ARBRE Laboratory (ISG Tunis), Tunis, Tunisia

Abstract. Cause-related marketing (CRM) is an important type of corporate social responsibility that offers engagement initiatives to consumers, brands and non-profit organizations. This study aims to explore the factors affecting Tunisian consumers' intention to participate in cause-related marketing campaigns. Building on the previous literature on CRM, the authors focused on the factors that predict consumer's intention to purchase products supporting social causes. Taking into consideration these determinants, a qualitative study was conducted with ten consumer-members of a Tunisian virtual community via individual semi-structured interviews conducted online. The results show that the three types of fit (cause-brand fit; cause-consumer fit; brand-consumer fit), consumer-cause identification, the involvement in the product category, the attribution of altruistic motivations and the attitudes towards CRM are the factors favoring the purchase intention of the Tunisian consumer. These results corroborate prior research and provide more particular information on Tunisian customers. The present findings can help companies in Tunisia design stronger cause-related marketing initiatives.

Keywords: Cause-related marketing (CRM) · Consumer behavior · Cause-brand fit · Consumer-cause identification · Altruistic motivations · Purchase intention

1 Introduction

Nowadays, companies are increasingly obliged to respond to various consumer concerns and behave ethically in order to be more competitive and to penetrate markets in emerging economies. In this context, Cause-Related Marketing (CRM) has found its place in recent years as corporate social responsibility becomes a key strategic priority. Indeed, according to Cone communication's CSR report, 87% of US consumers buy products from companies engaged in social problem-solving initiatives, [1]. In fact, cause-related marketing is an important type of corporate social responsibility initiative, [2]. It is a promising marketing strategy to improve the company's competitiveness and its economic and social conditions [3]. These cause campaigns allow the company to increase sales while strengthening its sense of social responsibility.

Indeed, *"Cause-related marketing (CRM) is almost ubiquitous as brands of all price points participate in this marketing strategy in the United States and internationally, as well. The value that CRM brings to the firm, the consumer, and the nonprofit organization has made it a popular and valuable tool for marketers."* [4]. Moreover, CRM is *"a fundraising activity or marketing strategy consists of a contribution to a cause through a purchase of a product/service by consumers"* [5]. This definition emphasizes the mutual benefit of this strategy for all three stakeholders.

It should be noted that academic research on cause-related marketing (CRM) has grown in recent years in emerging countries by addressing the effect of a cause-brand congruence on consumer behavior [6, 7].

Despite the effectiveness and success of CRM are amplified in the case of congruence (fit) between the cause and the brand, there is in the literature a controversy among researchers as to the results of the impact of congruence cause brand (cause-brand fit) on the intention to purchase.

In addition, little research has been suggested that when a consumer identifies with the cause, he or she will go to CRM programs and purchase products associated with them [7]. Despite all the studies developed, there is a gap in studies focused on identifying the consumer at the cause and its consequences.

Another factor that has been mentioned in the literature and which has a real impact on the intention to buy products supporting a social cause is «the attribution of altruistic motivations» while emphasizing the key role of the consumer attribution system in the processing of societal data [8].

However, it is time to fill the literature gap and shed light on the controversies mentioned about the factors favoring the intention to purchase products supporting social causes.

Therefore, a qualitative exploratory study among 10 consumers and members of a Tunisian association «DARNA» allows providing elements of response to the objectives of this research work. The choice of this community is justified by the knowledge of the concept "cause-related marketing" by the members of the latter, since this concept has not yet been sufficiently known in Tunisia.

In the following, we present in a first part the literature review, then a second part deals with the research methodology and the third part will be devoted to the presentation of the results.

2 Theoretical Framework

2.1 Cause-Related Marketing

The first and most cited definition of CRM in the literature is that of Varadarajan & Menon, [9], which corresponds to *"process of formulating and implementing marketing activities that are characterized by an offer from the firm to contribute a specified amount to a designated cause when customers engage in revenue providing exchanges that satisfy organizational and individual objectives"*. CRM is the association of a brand with a cause by involving consumers: the brand's support for the cause is contingent on consumers purchasing the brand's products. It is a type of corporate social responsibility initiative, fundraising innovation, and interactive business mechanism. It is a form of association where a product or brand supports a cause over some time. Furthermore, CRM requires consumer participation via purchasing behaviors [5]. Companies regularly use CRM campaigns to change consumers' overall attitude towards the company and its brands [10]. Several studies have shown that approximately 85% of US consumers have preferred organizations or brands or products associated with a social cause or issue [4]. Thus, the majority of previous research on CRM has found that consumers generally have positive attitudes towards CRM, companies supporting social causes and charities sponsored by it [11–15]. These favorable attitudes can have an impact on consumer purchases and create awareness for a social cause [16, 17]. Other works such as Bergkvist [6], Durate [7], Shree [18], Christofi [19], Bigné [16] have worked on the effectiveness of cause marketing and the success of CRM campaigns and that this effect is amplified in the case of congruence between the cause and the brand.

2.2 Cause-Brand Congruence

Congruence or fit are related concepts expressing similarity or complementarity, it is the overall perceived fit between cause and brand, [20]. It is "the fact that two (or more) entities fit together well." [21]. A better congruence between the brand or company and the social cause will lead to a positive consumer attitude towards the brand or company hence a favorable consumer response.

The literature in consumer behavior or psychology shows that congruence positively affects judgment, while incongruence has a negative effect [22, 23].

Furthermore, according to Nan [14], Bigné [16], Chéron [12] and Pracejus [24], cause-brand congruence is a particularly critical factor for the success of CRM campaigns and they have shown that the impact of cause-brand fit on consumer responses has a significant effect.

2.3 Consumer-Cause Identification

Consumer-cause identification is the degree of overlap between consumers' self-concept and their perceptions of the cause [25].

Consumer-cause identification is the convergence of a consumer's self-concept and their perception of the cause [25, 26]. Therefore, when designing CRM campaigns, companies should choose a cause that could be recognized by customers [27]. Furthermore, being able to get customers to identify with the cause is an important indicator of an effective CRM campaign [28] and leads to its success [29]. Furthermore, this idea has been discussed by Zdravkovic [30], who state that when a consumer associates with a cause, there is a predisposition to patronize CRM programs and purchase the associated products.

2.4 Purchase Intention

Purchase intention is one of the most important concepts in the study of consumer behavior. Purchase intention refers to the "disposition of a consumer who declares himself favorable to the purchase of a good or service" [31].

In the literature, purchase intention can be defined either according to the probabilistic dimension as "the subjective probability of buying a given product or brand" [32] or according to the planning dimension while integrating the planning character of the intention and is defined as "the result of a desire, or a need, processed cognitively which leads to purchase planning" [33, 34].

3 Methodology

The understanding and exploration of the factors impacting the purchase intention of the Tunisian consumer towards CRM, allowed us to fill the gap in the literature and shed light on concepts little studied in Tunisia.

A qualitative exploratory approach is adopted in this research. A semi-directive interview guide was developed, which is a written document that structures the interview, specifies the terms to be explored and the specific prompts for each theme in order to gather individual, differentiated and subjective points of view. We used individual interviews as a data collection method to validate the themes identified in the literature. Participants were interviewed around five main themes. The semi-structured interviews were transcribed in full and a thematic analysis of the discourse was carried out (Table 1).

Table 1. Topics of the interview guide

Topic 1	Respondents' views on cause-related marketing strategy
Topic 2	The relationship between cause-brand congruence, consumer-cause congruence, consumer-brand congruence and purchase intention
Topic 3	The relationship between consumer cause identification et purchase intention
Topic 4	Motivation of the purchase of products using cause related marketing by the respondents
Topic 5	Attitude and Intention to buy products using cause related marketing

Ten semi-directive interviews were conducted with members of a Tunisian virtual community, the "Darna[1] Association", and we chose consumers who are part of a virtual community based on social networks, particularly Facebook, and who share the same interests. Thus, through Facebook, the present study had the opportunity to explore the perceptions of these consumers towards the cause-related marketing strategy. The choice of this community was based on CRM actions that it has published and also on the knowledge of consumers of these kinds of shares. This allowed us to collect a set of

---

[1] Tunisian non-profit association that helps children without family support, it was created in March 2014.

data, to have a sufficiently complete corpus. This allowed us to collect a set of data, to have a sufficiently complete corpus.

In order to determine the minimum sample size for satisfactory validity of the results, we used the theoretical saturation principle [35]. In this sense, the study stops when there is no additional information [36]. We reached thematic saturation at the end of the 10th interview; no new ideas emerged thereafter. We were, therefore, able to determine a sample of 10 people a posteriori. Our sample is fairly balanced according to several criteria (see Annex 1). We thus tried to respect the theoretical representativeness of the qualitative sample recommended by Miles and Huberman [37].

4 Research Results

The interviews thus conducted, recorded, and transcribed are processed using content analysis. The various results of our empirical investigations are identified from the analysis of the ten interviewees' speeches to interpret them. These results are to be deduced through thematic analysis, using the "QDA Miner" software, which enables us to draw up a vertical and horizontal analysis table (see Annex 2) and a horizontal analysis table. (See Annex 2) and on the other hand, the co-occurrence and similarity which are calculated from the Jaccard coefficient (see Annex 3: The dendrogram). The use of the QDA miner software facilitated the division of the corpus and allowed us to select the corresponding verbatim at the level of each paragraph and to assign them a code which is called a category.

At the end of our thematic analysis, we were able to identify 5 themes that could favor the Tunisian consumer's intention to purchase the CRM and which are presented in the table below (Table 2).

Table 2. Factors favoring purchase intention identified in the literature and in qualitative studies

Catégories	Sources
Brand cause congruence	Qualitative study [12, 14, 16, 24]
Consumer cause congruence	Qualitative study [38]
Consumer brand congruence	Qualitative study [28, 39]
Consumer cause identification	Qualitative study [7]
Involvement in the product category	Qualitative study
The Attribution of Altruistic Motivations	Qualitative study [40]
Attitude towards CRM	Qualitative study [41]

- **Congruence (or Fit):**
  The importance of the theme of congruence is felt in the interviews with the participants where they mentioned that to participate more in the action there must be a congruence and this is in line with the literature which shows that perceived

congruence amounts to evaluating the extent to which a brand and another entity (another brand, event or cause) go well together [34] and this perceived congruence acts positively on the attitude of consumers towards CRM [30, 42].

Some respondents emphasized the importance of cause-brand congruence [43, 44], *"the brand has to align with the cause, they have to have the same purpose, the same category e.g. Pampers, a brand aimed at children so it has to support a cause related to babies"* (individual 1). And others mentioned the effectiveness of consumer-cause congruence [38] to participate in CRM action *"I think it would be good to have a relationship and a fit between the consumer and the cause supported to participate"* (individual 2). And even respondents spoke of brand-consumer congruence [39], *"a beneficial relationship between the brand or company and the consumer does favor the intention to participate in these CRM actions, for example when there is a high-level connection with the company, commonalities this will indicate my intention to participate"* (individual 4). These results are supported in the literature by Mandler's [45] congruence theory.

- **Consumer- cause identification**

    All the interviewees clearly expressed the idea that there must be a degree of shared value and familiarity with the cause and that the consumer must feel a psychological link with the cause to be motivated to defend it. *"When I identify with the cause i.e. I will live the cause, I share values, principles with it" "I feel that my values and objectives are met, I feel that it is an opportunity to participate in this action"* (individual 4).

    Returning to the related marketing cause literature, Durate [7] work confirmed the positive relationship between consumer identification with the cause and purchase intention while building on social identity theory.

- **Involvement in the product category**

    Product category involvement according to Rothschild (1984, p. 217) in the work of Perrin-Martinenq, [46] corresponds to an *"unobservable state of motivation, excitement, and interest in a product category"*.

    Thirty percent of the interviews seek to be involved in the product category as a motivation for purchase intention from companies engaged in social initiatives [47, 48]. *"When the company produces goods for a well-defined target so it has to support a cause that affects this target to influence them to participate because when I got involved in the product that will satisfy my need I will participate"* (individual 10). *"I participate in the action if the product concerns me, the product must be important for me I need it I consume it, it interests me this pushes me to buy it"* (individual 6).

- **Attribution of Altruistic Motivations**

    Three dimensions of motivations perceived by consumers on the company cited by Öberseder [49] and were evoked by the interviewees, the motives considered as a marketing tool where the company takes advantage of CRM practices to obtain more profit *"It's a marketing used to maximize customers and inflate sales"* (individual 6) or as an interconnected relationship estimating the beneficial effect on the whole society *"I hope that these companies continue to make profit to carry out these actions and to develop their social commitment"* (individual 8) and finally as a give-and-take relationship *"I encourage these actions, I find that they have a mutual impact, it's a win-win relationship"* (individual 9).

- **The attitude towards CRM**

The success or failure of CRM engagement is determined by how customers perceive corporate motives [50].

Consumer perceptions of cause-related marketing have been studied in the literature [43, 51]. The data demonstrate that cause-related marketing methods can improve people's perceptions of a sponsored company's products or services [51]. This was mentioned by the interviewees *"it makes a lot of sense to me to find a congruent action because the company is working in its field so it's going to be interested in its target and the causes of its target. I find it legitimate; I believe in this company more, it will raise the level of belief in this brand behavior. And this will generate a positive attitude towards the action and I value it more"* (individual 3).

5   Discussion

This paper is a modest contribution to the ongoing discussions about the factors promoting purchase intention towards related marketing in developing countries such as Tunisia. Although our study is still in an exploratory phase, the findings can be used to suggest some theoretical and practical implications which will be presented below:

Theoretical implications: This study adds to the research agenda on consumer behavior towards cause-related marketing by addressing a theoretically important area of research that has been neglected by Tunisian marketing researchers: the factors favoring consumer purchase intention towards cause-related marketing actions.
Managerial implications: CrM is beneficial to the business, the cause, and even the customer in Tunisia. With a focus on the business side of CrM, this study can assist businesses better understand what makes customers more likely to participate in CrM campaigns, improving buy intent and increasing revenue.

Since the study was conducted with members of a non-profit association who already like to get involved in causes and like to be socially responsible, CRM might even be better applied to them. This research demonstrates the importance of designing CRM marketing efforts before launching them, as to how they are carried out has a significant impact on their success or failure.

This study adds to the list of suggestions for companies who want to support a good cause. Tunisian Companies should cherry-pick the cause that the brand wants to support, because this not only affects the consumer's perception of the firm's motivations, but it can also make the consumer more willing to buy the brand and indirectly have a better perception of the firm if the consumer identifies with the cause.

This study will help marketers to conduct cause-related marketing strategies. Thus, marketers should develop strategies where the cause is aligned with the brand and with the consumer. Also, managers should take into consideration the involvement of the consumer in the product category. We recommend supporting for example causes that touch their targets. And finally, managers should take seriously the importance of attributing altruistic motivation as a predictor of purchase intention, i.e. the more consumers believe that a company is acting for purely altruistic reasons, the more they will participate in the action through their purchase behavior, which is in line with the CSR literature [52, 53]. Indeed, to improve consumer attitudes towards cause-related marketing, companies need to highlight their altruistic commitment to social causes and their commitment to the welfare of society.

6 Conclusion

There is a growing interest in finding how to use CRM more effectively, taking into consideration the perspective of customers, and how to use it to improve the success of these initiatives. This study aids in determining which factors have an impact on CRM and which are the most important. The study's key finding is that there are determinants that have an impact on the consumer's intention to acquire a CRM campaign product.

Like any other qualitative research, this study is limited by the sample size used for data collection and the results are not intended to be generalizable to the entire population. Despite all efforts to complete this study, a number of limitations need to be highlighted. Firstly, we have limited ourselves to a qualitative exploratory study using interviews, and a quantitative phase will be necessary. Secondly, the main limitation of the present study is the small sample size, thus, it seems necessary to duplicate this study with a larger sample in order to confirm the results.

Annex 1

Table 1. Profile of participants interviewed during the semi-structured interviews

Nature	Gender	Age	Professional category	Family situation	Duration of interview
Interview 1	Woman	28 years	Engineer	Unmarried	30 min
Interview 2	Woman	40 years	Teacher	Married	45 min
Interview 3	Man	36 years	Engineer	Married	43 min
Interview 4	Man	28 years	Businessman	Unmarried	35 min
Interview 5	Woman	35 years	Human resources manager	Married	1 h 15 min
Interview 6	Woman	32 years	Teacher	Married	55 min
Interview 7	Woman	25 years	PhD student	Unmarried	40 min
Interview 8	Woman	45 years	Housewife	Married	47 min
Interview 9	Man	34 years	Project Manager	Married	58 min
Interview 10	Woman	40 years	Administrative officer	Married	1 h 05 min

Annex 2

Table 2. Horizontal and vertical analysis table

Category	Code	Absolute frequency	Relative frequency
Congruence	Cause brand congruence	28	13,70%
Congruence	Consumer cause congruence	22	10,80%
Congruence	Consumer company congruence	4	2,00%
Identification	Consumer cause identification	25	12,30%
Implication	Involvement in product category	9	4,40%
Attitude	Attitude toward CRM	6	2,90%
Purchase	Purchase intention	16	7,80%
Motivations	Attribution of Altruistic Motivations	9	4,40%

Annex 3

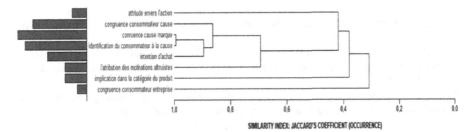

Fig. 1. Dendrogramme: Indice de similarité et de proximité entre codes

References

1. Lee, J.Y., Johnson, K.K.P.: Cause-related marketing strategy types: assessing their relative effectiveness. J. Fashion Market. Manage. Int. J. (2019)
2. He, H., Chao, M.M., Zhu, W.: Cause-related marketing and employee engagement: the roles of admiration, implicit morality beliefs, and moral identity. J. Bus. Res. **195**, 83–92 (2019)
3. Porter, M.E.: Creating shared value: redefining capitalism and the role of the corporation in society. Harvard Bus. Rev. 62–77 (2011)
4. Lafferty, B.A., Lueth, A.K., Mccafferty, R.: An evolutionary process model of cause-related marketing and systematic review of the empirical literature. Psychol. Market. **33**(11), 951–970 (2016)

5. Nelson, M.R., Vilela, A.M.: Exploring the interactive effects of brand use and gender on cause-related marketing over time. Int. J. Nonprofit Voluntary Sector Market. **122**(3), 580 (2017)

6. Bergkvist, L., Zhou, K.Q.: Cause-related marketing persuasion research: an integrated framework and directions for further research. Int. J. Advert. **138**(1), 5–25 (2019)

7. de Oliveira Duarte, P.A., Silva, S.C.: The role of consumer-cause identification and attitude in the intention to purchase cause-related product. International Marketing Review (2018)

8. Benoît-Moreau, F., Larceneux, F., Parguel, B.: La communication sociétale: entre opportunités et risques d'opportunisme. Décis. Market. **159**, 75–78 (2010)

9. Varadarajan, P.R., Menon, A.: Cause-related marketing: a coalignment of marketing strategy and corporate philanthropy. J. Market. **52**, 58–74 (1988)

10. Till, B.D., Nowak, L.I.: Toward effective use of cause-related marketing alliances. J. Prod. Brand Manage. (2000)

11. Boenigk, S., Schuchardt, V.: Cause-related marketing campaigns with luxury firms: an experimental study of campaign characteristics, attitudes, and donations. Int. J. Nonprofit Volunt. Sect. Market. **18**, 101–121 (2013)

12. Chéron, E., Kohlbacher, F., Kusuma, K.: The effects of brand-cause fit and campaign duration on consumer perception of cause-related marketing in Japan. J. Consum. Market. (2012)

13. Ladero, M.M.G., Casquet, C.G., Singh, J.: Understanding factors influencing consumer attitudes toward cause-related marketing. Int. J. Nonprofit Volunt. Sect. Market. **20**, 52–70 (2015)

14. Nan, X., Heo, K.: Consumer responses to corporate social responsibility (CSR) initiatives: examining the role of brand-cause fit in cause-related marketing. J. Advert. **36**(2), 63–74 (2007)

15. Youn, S., Kim, H.: Antecedents of consumer attitudes toward cause-related marketing. J. Advert. Res. **48**(1), 123–137 (2008)

16. Bigné, E., Curras-Perez, R., Aldas Manzano, J.: Dual nature of cause-brand fit. Eur. J. Market. (2012)

17. Human, D., Terblanche, N.S.: Who receives what? The influence of the donation magnitude and donation recipient in cause-related marketing. J. Nonprofit Public Sect. Market. **24**(2), 141–160 (2012)

18. Shree, D., Gupta, A., Sagar, M.: Effectiveness of cause-related marketing for differential positioning of market entrant in developing market: an exploratory study in Indian context. Int. J. Nonprofit Volunt. Sect. Market. **22**(2), 573 (2017)

19. Christofi, M., Leonidou, E., Vrontis, D., Kitchen, P., Papasolomou, I.: Innovation and cause-related marketing success: a conceptual framework and propositions. J. Serv. Market. **29**(5), 354–366 (2015)

20. Goldsmith, R.E., Yimin, Z.: The influences of brand-consumer and cause-congruence on consumer responses to cause related marketing. J. Appl. Market. Theory **5**(2), 74–95 (2014)

21. Maille, V., Fleck, N.: Congruence perçue par le consommateur: vers une clarification du concept, de sa formation et de sa mesure. Rech. Appl. Mark. **26**(2), 77–111 (2011)

22. Cohen, J.B., Basu, K.: Alternative models of categorization: Toward a contingent processing framework. J. Consum. Res. **13**(4), 455–472 (1987)

23. Fiske, S.T., Pavekchak, M.A.: Category-based versus piecemeal-based affective responses: Developments in schema-triggered affect (1986)

24. Pracejus, J.W., Qian, D., Douglas Olsen, G., Messinger, P.R.: Fit in cause-related marketing: an integrative retrospective. J. Glob. Scholars Market. Sci. **30**(2), 105–114 (2020)

25. Vanhamme, J., Lindgreen, A., Reast, J., van Popering, N.: To do well by doing good: improving corporate image through cause-related marketing. J. Bus. Ethics **109**(3), 259–274 (2012)

26. Lichtenstein, D.R., Drumwright, M.E., Braig, B.M.: The effect of corporate social responsibility on customer donations to corporate-supported nonprofits. J. Market. **68**(4), 16–32 (2004)
27. Hoeffler, S., Lnae Keller, K.: Building brand equity through corporate societal marketing. J. Public Policy Market. **21**(1), 78–89 (2002)
28. Gupta, S., Pirsch, J.: The company-cause-customer fit decision in cause-related marketing. J. Consum. Market. (2006)
29. Berger, I.E., Cunningham, P.H., Drumwright, M.E.: Identity, identification, and relationship through social alliances. J. Acad. Market. Sci. **34**(12), 128–137 (2006)
30. Zdravkovic, S., Magnusson, P., Stanley, S.M.: Dimensions of fit between a brand and a social cause and their influence on attitudes. Int. J. Res. Market. **27**(12), 151–160 (2010)
31. Lehu, J.M.: Back to life! Why brands grow old and sometimes die and what managers then do: an exploratory qualitative research put into the French context. J. Market. Commun. **10**(12), 133–152 (2004)
32. Dussart, C.: Comportement et Stratégie de Marketing. McGraw Hill, Quebec (1984)
33. Darpy, D.: Une variable médiatrice du report d'achat: la procrastination. chez XIIIème Congrès de l'Association Française de Marketing (1997)
34. Fleck-Dousteyssier, N., Roux, E., Darpy, D.: La congruence dans le parrainage: définition, rôle et mesure. chez 6ème congrès international des tendances du marketing Nancy, Paris (2005)
35. Allard-Poesi, F.: Méthodes de recherche en management. Dunod, Paris (2004)
36. Conchon, A.E.: Les méthodes d'évaluation de la validité des enquêtes qualitatives en marketing. chez Congrès des Tendances du Marketing (2003)
37. Miles, M.B., Michael Huberman, A.: Analyse des données qualitatives. De Boeck Supérieur (2003)
38. Sung, H., Kim, J., Choi, H.: Effects of consumer–cause fit and consumer–product fit of cause-related marketing on product purchase intention. J. Consum. Behav. **20**(3), 791–802 (2021)
39. Menichini, M., Rosati, F.: A fuzzy approach to improve CSR reporting: an application to the Global Reporting Initiative indicators. Proc. Soc. Behav. Sci. 355–359 (2014)
40. Alcañiz, E.B., Caceres, R.C., Curras Perez, R.: Alliances between brands and social causes: the influence of company credibility on social responsibility image. J. Bus. Ethics **96**(2), 169–186 (2010)
41. Myers, B., Kwon, W.S., Forsythe, S.: Creating effective cause-related marketing campaigns: the role of cause-brand fit, campaign news source, and perceived motivations. Cloth. Text. Res. J. **30**(3), 167–182 (2012)
42. Lafferty, B.A., Goldsmith, R.E., Hult, G.T.M.: The impact of the alliance on the partners: a look at cause–brand alliances. Psychol. Market. **21**(7), 509–531 (2004)
43. Barone, M.J., Miyazaki, A.D., Taylor, K.A.: The influence of cause-related marketing on consumer choice: does one good turn deserve another? J. Acad. Market. Sci. **28**(2), 248–262 (2000)
44. Lafferty, B.A., Goldsmith, R.E.: Cause–brand alliances: does the cause help the brand or does the brand help the cause? J. Bus. Res. 423–429 (2005)
45. Mandler, G.: The structure of value: accounting for taste. In: Clark, M.S., Fiske, S.T. (eds.) Affect and Cognition: Annual Carnegie Symposium, pp. 3–36. Lawrence Erlbaum Associates, Hillsdale, NJ (1982)
46. Perrin-Martinenq, D.: The role of brand detachment on the dissolution of the relationship between the consumer and the bran. J. Market. Manage. **220**(9–10), 1001–1023 (2004)
47. Lucke, S., Heinze, J.: The role of choice in cause-related marketing–investigating the underlying mechanisms of cause and product involvement. Procedia Soc. Behav. Sci. **213**, 647–653 (2015)

48. Kureshi, S., Thomas, S.: Testing the influence of message framing, donation magnitude, and product category in a cause-related marketing context. J. Market. Commun. **26**(3), 268–289 (2020)
49. Öberseder, M., Schlegelmilch, B.B., Murphy, P.E.: CSR practices and consumer perceptions. J. Bus. Res. **66**(10), 1839–1851 (2013)
50. Tsai, S.-P.: Modeling strategic management for cause-related marketing. Market. Intell. Plan. **27**(5), 649–665 (2009)
51. Ross, J.K., Patterson, L.T., Stutts, M.A.: Consumer perceptions of organizations that use cause-related marketing. J. Acad. Market. Sci. **20**(1), 93–97 (1992)
52. Sen, S., Bhattacharya, C.B.: Does doing good always lead to doing better? Consumer reactions to corporate social responsibility. J. Market. Res. **38**(12), 225–243 (2001)
53. Simmons, C.J., Becker-Olsen, K.L. (2006)

What Leads Customer to Create and Participate in Anti-brand Community: A Netnographic Approach

Latifa Mednini[(✉)] [iD] and Mouna Damak Turki [iD]

Economics and Managment Sciences Faculty of Sfax, Sfax, Tunisia
Latifamednini@yahoo.com

Abstract. This study aims to explore the antecedents that lead a consumer to create and participate in an anti-brand community. A qualitative exploratory study based on the netnography method with three anti-brand communities was conducted. As a first result, the antecedents that motivate consumers to create an anti-brand community are brand hate, social approval, and not real hater. As a second result, consumers participate in an anti-brand community due to three antecedents, namely: negative brand relationship, community identification, and patriotism. Thus, this paper provides insight for brand managers to understand the antecedents that drive consumers to engage in anti-brand communities.

Keyword: Anti-brand community · Brand relationships · Virtual brand community · Negative emotion

1 Introduction

Some consumers might have experienced dissatisfaction with a product or service [24], which brings them to stop consuming it and participate in anti-brand activities. Actually, consumers engaged in anti-branding have a long term commitment to brand rejection [3, 31]. Their objective is to refuse brands, imposed meanings, ideologies, and practices [14]. Specifically, such customers engage in an anti-brand community to participate in anti-consumption. Participation in this community is a development phenomenon in online and offline contexts, as proposed by some researchers such as Hollenbeck and Zinkhan (2006, 2010); Krishnamurthy and Kucuk (2009) [15, 16, 19]. In an online context, the anti-brand site exchanges negative experiences with others, organizes boycott events and influences negative WOM [8].

Recently, joining an anti-brand community has known a great interest, however, reasons for its creation have not been explained yet. Some researchers have investigated the learning processes by negotiating brand meaning in the context of anti-brand communities [16]. Other studies have demonstrated the drivers of participating in these communities [7, 8]. Dessart and al. [7] introduced the antecedents that push the consumer to engage in an anti-brand community. Additionally, Dessart and al. [8] focused on understanding how an intense negative resentment reinforces consumers as individuals acting independently to participate with others and establish collective behavior [1].

© The Author(s), under exclusive license to Springer Nature Switzerland AG 2022
M. A. Bach Tobji et al. (Eds.): ICDEc 2022, LNBIP 461, pp. 159–169, 2022.
https://doi.org/10.1007/978-3-031-17037-9_11

To the best of our knowledge, there are no studies that focus on the antecedents of creating online anti-brand. Moreover, there are limited concerns about the drivers that drive consumers to participate in these communities. In addition, most of previous studies has investigated the dark side of virtual anti-brand. From a positive perspective, scholars did not take into consideration consumers who engage in a community to defend the brand. Therefore, this paper attempts to discuss this subject.

The rest of this paper is structured as follows: Sect. 2 presents the theoretical backgrounds of the anti-brand community. In Sect. 3, we illustrate our methodology. Results are presented in Sect. 4 which is followed by discussion, theoretical and managerial implications in Sect. 5. Finally, Sect. 6 includes the conclusion of this research.

2 Theoretical Framework

Because of growing Tunisian consumer empowerment and the proliferation of social media such as Facebook, anti-brand communities are being emerged. In Tunisia, "Facebook" is gaining an increasing interest. In 2022, the statistics of "Digital Discovery Tunisia" announced the presence of 7,737,800[1] "Facebook" accounts. Online community based on Facebook allows consumers express their positive and especially their negative emotions towards a brand.

2.1 Anti-brand Community

Anti-brand hate sites play a crucial role in damaging or developing companies. Kucuk [21] was the first researcher to introduce this concept. His research indicated that consumer's voice is increasing with the development of the Internet and the anti-brand websites, more precisely, with a new form of boycott and protest of consumer activism. Kucuk [21] noted that when customers seek information about the brand, the anti-brand sites show up in the top ten search results because this brand was searched on major search engines. In this line, Kucuk [21] presented a new theory, which is Negative Double Jeopardy (NDJ). This theory demonstrate that "the most valuable brands attract more anti-brand sites while less valuable brands do not have such hate attraction on the Internet". Dessart and al. [8] defined an anti-brand community as "groups of people who have negative feelings towards a brand and self-select to join this kind of community to express their feelings to the brand". As a matter of fact, the online community creates relationship between individual from different places in the world, and defines a common need, goal, and identity [15]. The objectives of these communities are: reducing the brand value and expressing the feeling of revenge (Grégoire and al., 2009; Cooper and al., 2019) [6–13]. Drawing on Hollenbeck and Zinkhan [16], community is considered as a powerful agency and information resource for consumers. The members share their negative experiences with others and affect negative WOM [19]. On the other hand, can be as a source of valuable information for a company to understand and manage brand haters [19].

---

[1] https://www.digital-discovery.tn/.

2.2 Creating an Anti-brand Community

The creators of anti-brand sites have a good knowledge of markets and business practices surrounding brand that they hate. They are capable of following market changes in the real world (for example killercoke.org announces the news about Coca-Cola on a daily basis from many reliable sources such as Associated Press, etc.) [21]. Most of the prior studies overlook the motivation of creating an anti- brand community. According to motivation theory, the work of Oh and Syn (2015) [27] provides an understanding of individuals motivations. Motivation can be categorised into intrinsic and extrinsic [27]. Intrinsic motivation is presented by self-encouragement or self-interest in doing such activities. Extrinsic motivation is demonstrated by relying on external factors and reasons. Romani and al. [29] announced that consumers engage in anti-brand communities because they perceive injustice from brands. As a consequence, they respond by expressing feelings of hate which include disgust, anger/fear, and contempt. Indeed, several studies in the literature have been proposed to explain the negative consequence of hate like consumer boycott [23], brand revenge [11, 14], and negative WOM [14, 38].

In another perspective, Kucuk [22] demonstrated that the firm need to engage in listening efforts. In other words, it can assist the company decide whether the hate feeling is expressed by a real person, a troll, a review-farm, or a competitor-associated source such as a paid-blogger. For example, an anti-brand community creator may be not a real hater who has a negative experience toward a brand.

2.3 Participating in an Anti-brand Community

Dessart and al. [7] explained three antecedents that affect a participation group, namely: individual-related, brand-related, and social factors. According to uses and gratifications theory, media use is a method to satisfy needs or interests such as searching for information to reduce uncertainty and solve personnel problems [30]. Stafford and Gonier [34] defined several gratifications that motivate the individual to use the Internet such as web searching, acquisition of information, and the ability to engage in interpersonal communication and socialization.

Social Factors. Dessart and al. [7] suggested three social factors, which are community identification, community engagement, and social approval. First, community identification refers to feeling identified as a member, and belonging to a community (Bagozzi and Dholakia 2006; Dholakia and al. 2004) [4–9]. This identification includes conscious, cognitive, and affective process, which influence members' community memberships [1]. Second, certain customers engage in the community to share their experiences with others. Community engagement is the intrinsic motivation of members to interact, communicate, and find benefits they extract from this engagement [1]. In fact, Hollenbeck and Zinkhan [15] showed that communities are considered as essential source and powerful agency for the consumer. Third, social approval from other participants in the community is an important element influencing membership [7]. Dessart and al. [8] illustrated that the person who has high level of social approval is more likely to be an active participant in the community. Previous works on brand community indicated that gaining social acceptance and approval are the drivers of member engagement [9]. Hollenbeck and Zinkhan [15] found that the participant's objective is the social movement. This term refers to "the coming together of relatively large numbers of people around a commonly held set of values or notion of rights (human and/or social) in order to bring about social change" (Dykstra and Law 1994, p. 122 cited by Hollenbeck & Zinkhan, 2006). According to the social exchange theory, it is one of the most influential theories that have been used to demonstrate the participation of consumers in online communities. In fact, partaking in communities has been recognized as social exchange [12].

Individual-Related. Individual factors consists of two elements, which are oppositional attitudinal loyalty and brand material value. Oppositional attitudinal loyalty refers to consumer loyalty to another brand [7]. Several researchers found that this factor leads the consumer to actively engage and identify with the community of opposers. Therefore, driving to the growth of the anti-brand community [8–15, 20]. In addition, Dessart and al. [7] discussed another individual factor, which is the brand material value. This concept illustrates the importance of brands in consumer life.

Brand-Related. Brand factors comprise the negative relationship and collective memory. Recently, researchers have a great attention on the positive relationships [7]. In fact, Park and al. [28] noticed that the traditional notion of positive brand relationships (attachment) include a negative side (aversion). Prior studies have suggested that a negative relationship can lead to rejection, dislike, or hate [14], depending on the emotional degree and associated behavioral intensions [2]. Veloutsou [35] demonstrated that consumer-brand relationship has two aspects, which are emotions and communication. Moreover, Dessart and al. [7] proposed the second element of brand factors which is collective memory. This term is defined as the degree to which the members of a social network share information and feelings toward a specific brand (Veloutsou and Moutinho 2009, Dessart and al., 2016) [7–36].

3   Methodology

In the proposed qualitative approach, we follow the netnographic study on Tunisian consumers in the context of the anti-brand community. The netnographic method adapts to the collection of information from sensitive subjects, such as topic suggested in our research. More specifically, customers can freely express their feelings within the virtual community which is difficult to obtain by assisting a traditional quantitative method. We have chosen the social network "Facebook" in order to collect rich data. Facebook allow this research "to offer a high level of interactivity, a large number of communicators and heterogeneous participants" [18, 32].

According to Kozinet [17], the netnographic study is composed of five steps. The first step is entry. Our interest is to obtain an understanding of the antecedents that drive the consumers to create and participate in the anti-brand communities. We choose to work on three anti-Tunisair communities as shown in appendix 1. The choice of the latter can be explained by the classification of Air Help,[2] in 2018, "Tunisair" ranks 85 among

---

[2] https://www.espacemanager.com/classement-mondial-des-compagnies-tunisair-loin-derriere-au-85-eme-rang-sur-87.html.

87 airlines in the world. Additionally, referring to the article published in the Money-inc.com[3] 2019, "Tunisair" was the worst airline in the world. This company has caused a strong intensity of negative emotion among customers and as a result, consumers have created and joined anti-brand communities. Similarly, we choose these brand communities based on Bernard's [5] selection criteria. Indeed, these are the ones that most match our research goals. Likewise, the traffic intensity, the number of participants, and the descriptive richness of data (the existence of positive and negative comments in the community) satisfy our research goals. Then, we logged in "Facebook", and joined the anti-brand communities to be an active member in order to understand the culture of the three virtual communities, the behavior and the rituals of participants. the second step consists of collecting data from the selected communities. According to Bernard [5], the netnography steps includes the non-participating and participating observation. In a non-participating observation, we collected 150 comments from the three communities. More precisely, we read the comments and choose the information adapted to our research objective. As a part of participatory observation, referring to Bernard [5], we launched an online discussion group on the social networking site "Facebook," and asked actives members to participate in the conversation. We contacted 30 participants from the three anti-Tunisair communities using the focus group technique. Only 14 participants joined the focus group. Regarding the fewest received responses, we decided to invite 16 other customers to participate in the individual interviews. The appendix 2 demonstrates our sample characteristics. In this perspective, we prepared our guide interview (see appendix 3). After that, the third step is based on information analysis and interpretation. We coded the interview guide using the open coding (inductive coding applied on first reading). Then, we used the software "Lexico 3" that categorise the themes in a theme grid and extract the necessary ones from the verbatim of each participant. The fourth step refers to have permission from members before posting their comments and messages. In the last step, Bernard (2004) [5] noted that this step allows, "To obtain additional and more specific elements on the meanings of consumers". We had several messages about our study, for example, " You are doing a good research but you are wasting your time by choosing Tunisair, it is a crappy company!".

4   Findings

In this section, we present our results based on data collection on three online anti-brand communities hosted on Facebook. The findings are focused on two specific themes: 1) what are the antecedents that leads consumers to create an anti-brand community?, and 2) what are the antecedents that drive them to participate in this community?

4.1   The Antecedents of Creating and Participating in Anti-brand Community

The Antecedents of Creating an Anti-brand Community. According to our netnography study, our individual interview with the creator of the anti-brand community

---

[3] https://www.tunisienumerique.com/tunisair-classee-pire-compagnie-aerienne-au-monde-en-2019/#:~:text=Selon%20l'article%20pbli%C3%A9%20dans,a%C3%A9rienne%20de%20l'ann%C3%A9e%202,019.

"Boycottons Tunisair et ses tarifs indécents" noted that he created this community for two reasons. First, he has negative feelings towards Tunisair, in other words, he has many failed experiences with this brand. Therefore, he decided to alert the other passengers to boycott it. We quote his verbatim illustrating this point of view: "I cannot tell you just one reason, every time I choose Tunisair, there is a problem, I hate this brand, I created this community to inform the other passengers about its poor service quality". Second, the creator of this community wants it to be the virtual space of many haters, which support to resolve Tunisair problem. In this context, we quote: "This community will help Tunisair to solve its problems and satisfy their passengers in the future, Tunisair directors should accept the consumers' haters to construct a good service quality".

From a participant's point of view, some passengers mentioned that the creator of the brand is probably an employee who works with another concurrent or can be a real hater. We quote the next verbatim "Maybe he is not a real hater, he's just a person who works with Tunisair concurrent".

The Antecedents of Participating in an Anti-brand Community. Our   finding revealed that the majority of consumers are active participants in the community anti-brand. Actually, some members are active, others are passive. Active persons have been informed by notification to see all the posts shared by the creator of the community. However, passive consumers just view the post without any reaction. Our qualitative study indicates that the majority of members stated their negative impressions toward Tunisair. Thus, they participate in the anti-brand community to show up their emotions and their negative experience like stolen baggage, price unfairness, retard without any explanation, excuse, or compensation. For example, "Don't waste your time, they don't respect their customers! A delay of 5 h in Tunis without announcement of what is happening! It is a shame!!!!!".

In addition, drawing on our netnography study, the passengers found this community as a free virtual space to present their resentments without any control. In addition, they informed us that this kind of virtual community is more comfortable than the brand virtual community because the majority of members have negative experiences. The anti-Tunisair community is a space to seek a solution to this brand as shown this verbatim "I joined this page just to inform the Tunisair about their poor service and I hope that it will help to correct their mistakes".

In contrast, some passengers have positive emotions toward Tunisair and they engaged in the community just to defend this brand. Actually, they always post positive comments. We quote some verbatim demonstrating this point of view:" Tunisair is our pride, it is the best airline despite all the lies", and," I love Tunisair because it's a part of my country".

5 Discussion

The current paper aims to empirically study the antecedents that push the consumer to create and join an anti-brand community. In this research work, we collect data from members of anti-brand communities on Facebook.

This study underscores both negative and positive aspects of participation in an anti-brand community. From a negative viewpoint, findings show that negative relationship, more specifically, brand hate is one of the reasons to create and participate in an anti-brand community for consumers having negative experience toward a brand. In accordance with Romani and al. [29] and Nguyen and Nguyen [26] demonstrated that the negative feeling of hate influence anti-brand actions. Moreover, the findings of Dessart and al. [8] emphasize the impact of a negative brand relationship on community participation.

From a positive viewpoint, results present the second antecedent for creating an anti-brand community, designed for social approval to solve the brand problems. As reported by Kucuk [20], the anti-brand activities include collected information for the firm. In accordance with Hollenbeck and Zinkhan [15], this community acts as a significant consumer agency and source of data. Kucuk (2019) [20] has proposed that the firm should understand what their consumers say about the brand by developing technologically advanced listening systems. This set community is the best virtual space to detect negative emotions and put solutions to reduce hate customers. Similarly, Hollenbeck & Zinkhan [15] illustrated that the engagement objective in community is the social movement. Moreover, this paper clearly proposed that the person who creates this kind of online community can be an employee who works with concurrent. Kucuk [22] has suggested that the hate can be from a real person or from a competitor-associated source such as a paid blogger.

The results found that the participants are more comfortable in the anti-brand community than the others communities. Consistent with Dessart et al. [8], brand community participation is driven by community identification, consumers desire to find other like-minded individuals in terms of brand interest, to interact, and to be identified as members of the group. In this prospect, the results of Dholakia et al. [9] revealed that individual social identity affects higher levels of intentions to join the online communities.

In addition, we have addressed not only the negative aspect of motivation but also the positive. The main purpose of this paper is to draw attention to the positive comments written by members of a negative brand community. We noticed the patriotism of such members toward the brand. In fact, national product consumption by individuals can be an expression of duty towards the nation through respect and acknowledgment of such product that is representative of the nation. The product or service patriotism defined as" the expression of how an individual lives and expresses his national identity via various the consumption of a nationally-iconic product" [33]. The patriotism is an intense emotion regarding their own country without ignoring the other countries [37]. The findings of Nik Kamariah and al. [25] argued that patriotism is one of the direct motivation that reinforce the consumer purchase.

6   Conclusion

6.1   Theoretical and Managerial Implications

From a theoretical standpoint, the current research explores the antecedents of participating in online anti-brand namely brand negative relationships, community identification, and patriotism. Our results describe at first the patriotism as an antecedent of participating in online anti-brand. Generally, the anti-brand community is considered as the brand's negativity. Most comments written by members were negative. To the best of our knowledge, there are no study that analyze the positive comments in online anti-brand. This paper reveals that such consumers participate in this type of community to defend the brand in reason of patriotism. Moreover, this is the first study that investigates the antecedents that drive the consumer to create an anti-brand community. These antecedents are hate emotion, social approval, and not real hater. In addition, community identification is an important antecedent of participating in the community. Mostly, members were more comfortable in online anti-brand than the other online communities. More precisely, participants feel identified by the other members because they share the same negative experience. Our work enriches the literature of anti-brand, the anti-consumption, the brand- consumer relationship and the brand hate.

Additionally, several scholars have demonstrated the anti-brand community in many sectors like magazine [14]; restoration [14]; technology products [8]. This paper is the first study that focus on the airline sector.

From a practical standpoint, the firm is being well informed by the negative emotion of the customer which assists to put the management strategies to satisfy the hater. In fact, the firm should be conscientious about the profile of the hater. The complaint can be a real hater or just a person who works with concurrent, who wants to destroy the brand image. Consequently, companies need to be aware about this problem. If he is not a hater, brand practitioners should respond to their complaints by defining a strategy that can improve the service quality.

In addition, this paper presents a pilot study to pay attention to listening technologies. Mostly, this method can improve consumer-brand relationships by detecting consumers complaints towards the brand. To conclude, certain brand haters engage in an anti-brand community to suggest some solutions. Therfore, the firm can find proposed action that can allow to satisfy them.

6.2 Limitations and Future Research

The current study has multiple limitations. In terms of the data collection, our research is limited to a qualitative study. In future research, we intend to quantify our findings. Besides, the study on brand negativity in brand community's context is still in its infancy [8]. Our work focuses on the airline sector, whereas many sectors are still on the level of passion [11]. This research do not investigate the level of consumer hate. Further research will study it. In addition, the negative emotion towards a brand has bad consequences like consumer boycott, revenge. Future work would do well to explore the strategies of managing the hate existing in the anti-brand community and investigate the consumer personality.

Appendix 1

Anti-brand communities' characteristics

Anti-brand community	Period	Number of memberships
فضائح الخطوط tunisair «Scandales التونسية»	1 year	6494
« Boycottons Tunisair et ses tarifs indécents »	1 year	2668
« Reclamations Tunisair »	1 year	548

Appendix 2

Sample characteristics

	Member profile	Number in percentage
Gender	Man	33.33%
	Woman	66.67%
Age	Between 15–25	23.33%
	Between 26–30	50%
	Between 31–60	26.67%
Social-professional Category	Student	33.33%
	Employee	36.67%
	Liberal profession	26.67%

Appendix 3

The interview guide

Interview guide
Hello everyone, my name is Latifa MEDNINI, I am Phd Student at FSEG Sfax, I do research about reasons that make customers create and participate in anti-Tunisair community. Your help would be very valuable for my studies. Tell me your response as freely as possible
1. Do you have a negative experience with Tunisair?
2. Are you an active or passive participant in anti-Tunisair community?
3. What do you share in this community?
4. What are the antecedents that make you participate in this anti-brand community?
5. In your opinion, what are the reasons that make a consumer create an anti-brand community?
6. Is there anything else you would like to add about your experience of participation in anti-Tunisair community that we have not mentioned?
Finally, please indicate your age, your gender, and your profession

References

1. Algesheimer, R., Dholakia, U.M., Herrmann, A.: The social influence of brand community: evidence from european car clubs. Journal of Marketing. **69**(3), 19–34 (2005)
2. Alvarez, C., Trudel, R., Fournier, S.: Brand Consensus and Multivocality: Disentangling the Effects of the Brand, the Consumer, and the Consumer-Brand Relationship on Brand Meaning. ACR North American Advances (2013)
3. Awasthi, B., Sharma, R., Gulati, U.: Anti-branding: analyzing its long-term impact. IUP Journal of Brand Management **9**(4) (2012).
4. Bagozzi, R.P., Dholakia, U.M.: Antecedents and purchase consequences of customer participation in small group brand communities. Int. J. Res. Mark. **23**, 45–61 (2006)
5. Bernard, Y.: La netnographie: une nouvelle méthode d'enquête qualitative basée sur les communautés virtuelles de consommation. Décisions marketing. 49–62 (2004)
6. Cooper, T., Stavros, C., Dobele, A.R.: Domains of influence: EXPLORING negative sentiment in social media, Journal of Product & Brand Management (2019)
7. Dessart, L., Morgan-Thomas, A., Veloutsou, C.: What drives anti-brand community behaviours: an examination of online hate of technology brands. In: Let's Get Engaged! Crossing the Threshold of Marketing's Engagement Era. Springer, Cham, pp. 473–477 (2016)
8. Dessart, L., Veloutsou, C., Morgan-Thomas, A.: Brand negativity: a relational perspective on anti- brand community participation. European Journal of Marketing (2020)
9. Dholakia, U.M., Bagozzi, R.P., Pearo, L.R.K.: A social influence model of consumer participation in network- and small-group-based virtual communities. Int. J. Res. Mark. **21**(3), 241–263 (2004)
10. Dykstra, C., Law, M.: Popular social movements as educative forces: Towards a theoretical framework. In: Proceedings of the 35th Annual Adult Education Research Conference, pp. 121–126. University of Tennessee, Knoxville (1994)
11. Fetscherin, M.: The five types of brand hate: How they affect consumer behavior. J. Bus. Res. **101**, 116–127 (2019)
12. Gharib, R.K., Philpott, E., Duan, Y.: Factors affecting active participation in B2B online communities: an empirical investigation. Information and Management. **54**(4), 516–530 (2017)
13. Grégoire, Y., Tripp, T.M., Legoux, R.: When customer love turns into lasting hate: the effects of relationship strength and time on customer revenge and avoidance. Journal of Marketing. **73**(6), 18–32 (2009)
14. Hegner, S.M., Fetscherin, M., Van Delzen, M.: Determinants and outcomes of brand hate. Journal of Product & Brand Management (2017)
15. Hollenbeck, C.R., Zinkhan, G.M.: Consumer activism on the internet: the role of anti-brand communities. Advances in Consumer Research. **33**, 479–485 (2006)
16. Hollenbeck, C.R., Zinkhan, G.M.: Anti-brand communities, negotiation of brand meaning, and the learning process: the case of wal-mart. Consumption. Markets and Culture. **13**(3), 325–345 (2010)
17. Kozinets, R.V.: Netnography : doing ethnographic research online. Sage, London (2009)
18. Kozinets, R.V.: The field behind the screen: Using netnography for marketing research in online communities. Journal of marketing research. **39**(1), 61–72 (2002)
19. Krishnamurthy, S., Kucuk, S.U.: Anti-branding on the internet. Journal of Business Research. **62**(11), 1119–1126 (2009)
20. Kuo, Y.-F., Feng, L.-H.: Relationships among community interaction characteristics, perceived benefits, community commitment, and oppositional brand loyalty in online brand communities. Int. J. Info. Manage. **33**(6), 948–962 (2013)

21. Kucuk, S.U.: Negative double jeopardy: the role of anti-brand sites on the internet. Journal of Brand Management **15**(3), 209–222 (2008)
22. Kucuk, S.U.: Managing brand hate. In: Brand Hate, pp. 163–191. Palgrave Macmillan, Cham (2019)
23. Kucuk, S.U.: Consequences of brand hate. In: Brand Hate, pp. 87–101. Palgrave Macmillan, Cham (2019)
24. Lee, M.S., Motion, J., Conroy, D.: Anti-consumption and brand avoidance. J. Bus. Res. **62**(2), 169–180 (2009)
25. Nik-Mat, N.K., Abd-Ghani, N.H., Esmail Al-Ekam, J.M.: The direct drivers of ethnocentric consumer. In: Int'l Conference on Business, Marketing & Information System Management (BMISM'15) Nov. 25–26, 2015 Paris (France) Intention and Actual Purchasing Behavior in Malaysia. International Journal of Social, Behavioral, Educational, Economic and Management Engineering **9**(4) (2015)
26. Nguyen, H.N., Nguyen, T.B.: Sense of online betrayal, brand hate, and outrage customers' anti-brand activism (2021)
27. Oh, S., Syn, S.Y.: Motivations for sharing information and social support in social media: a comparative analysis of Facebook, Twitter, Delcious, YouTube, and Flickr. J. Asso. Info. Sci. Technol. **66**(10), 2045–2060 (2015)
28. Park, C.W., Eisingerich, A.B., Park, J.W.: Attachment–aversion (AA) model of customer–brand relationships. J. Consu. Psychol. **23**(2), 229–248 (2013)
29. Romani, S., Grappi, S., Zarantonello, L., Bagozzi, R.P.: The revenge of the consumer! How brand moral violations lead to consumer anti-brand activism. Journal of Brand Management. **22**(8), 658–672 (2015)
30. Rubin, A.M.: Audience activity and media use. Communication Monographs **60**, 98–105 (1994)
31. Sandıkcı, Ö., Ekici, A.: Politically motivated brand rejection. Journal of Business Research. **62**(2), 208–217 (2009)
32. Sayarh, N.: La netnographie: mise en application d'une méthode d'investigation des communautés virtuelles représentant un intérêt pour l'étude des sujets sensibles. Recherches qualitatives. **32**(2), 227–251 (2013)
33. Spielmann, N., Maguire, J.S., Charters, S.: Product patriotism: how consumption practices make and maintain national identity. Journal of Business Research **121**, 389–399 (2020)
34. Stafford, T.F., Stafford, M.R., Schkade, L.L.: Determining uses and gratifications for the Internet. Decision sciences. **35**(2), 259–288 (2004)
35. Veloutsou, C.: Identifying the dimensions of the product-brand and consumer relationship. Journal of Marketing Management. **23**(1–2), 7–26 (2007)
36. Veloutsou, C., Moutinho, L.: Brand relationships through brand reputation and brand tribalism. Journal of Business Research. **62**(3), 314–322 (2009)
37. Wel, C.A.C., Alam, S.S., Omar, N.A.: The effect of ethnocentrism and patriotism on consumer buying intention. In: Int'l Conference on Business, Marketing & Information System Management (BMISM'15) **25**(26), 1–5 (2015)
38. Zarantonello, L., Romani, S., Grappi, S., Bagozzi, R.P.: Brand hate. Journal of Product & Brand Management (2016)

Consumer Satisfaction Using Fitness Technology Innovation

Simona Abdo[✉], Tahani H. Nahouli, and Karim Daye

Lebanese International University, Beirut, Lebanon
simona.abdo@gmail.com

Abstract. It is not a surprise that technology is raising increasingly within the people's fitness routine and showing a shift in customer's mindset. Hence, the technological products' companies have to keep on tracking customer's purchase intentions and loyalty for their business growth. Meanwhile, customer satisfaction is essential in determining the purchase intention. Therefore, a research is conducted to find the determinants that lead to customer satisfaction using fitness technology innovation particularly. Various theories, regarding technology, are discussed to reach customer satisfaction determinants; thereby, four of them are under study, as follows, service quality, helpfulness, friendliness, and quickness to investigate their relationship with customer satisfaction. For the benefit and purpose of this study, a quantitative research is applied and data is collected using a self-directed questionnaire. Hence, the obtained results revealed that customer satisfaction is determined by helpfulness, friendliness, and quickness of the devices, in addition to the service quality provided by the companies. However, the research methodology has its limitations and imperfections where the sample's size and selection are limited. Also, the research is not focusing on all the customer satisfaction determinants the theories discussed in the literature review. All in all, this study is vital for fitness technology companies to track the customer's satisfaction for strengthening their Research and Development to meet the customer's expectations that leads to higher satisfaction and business growth. Moreover, further research is necessary to decide whether the obtained results can be generalized across other innovative technological devices.

Keywords: Customer satisfaction · Fitness technology innovation · Friendliness · Helpfulness · Quickness · Service quality

1 Introduction

Lately, the wearable technology retail is expanding rapidly toward the leading technology sector, where smartwatch sales are driving the consumer market growth largely. The modernized wearable devices, which can provide a broad sort of features like wireless connectedness, well-being tracking, smart card payment, etc., are produced heavily by leading companies like Apple and Samsung. On the contrary, the restricted features and capabilities of the fitness trackers are making their popularity drop. Meanwhile, consumers expect wearable devices to eventually be very smart, linking technologies like

AR (Augmented Reality) and AI (Artificial Intelligence), by that rising their applicability to individuals and business users. Ed Thomas (2017), the GlobalData Analyst, declared, "The wearable tech theme incorporates more than just wrist-worn devices. Smart ear-wear, or wearable, has become a more prominent category with the emergence of devices that incorporate voice-activated virtual assistants such as Apple's Siri and Google's Assistant. Audible also has the potential to match, or even exceed, the performance of smart watches when it comes to providing health monitoring services". Generally, the wearable technology market is predicted to expand at a compound annual growth rate (CAGR) of 19% to approach $54 Billion by 2023, while in 2018 it was valued at around $ 23 Billion, as Global Data announced (FinancialBuzz, 2020).

The demand for the fitness tech market is driven by the increase in social media usage and the customers' willingness to stay updated with its related posts. People are using wearable devices since its accessibility is accelerating. The expanding usage of various applications is prompting the Global Wearable Device Market growth. Furthermore, the market growth in the planned period is strengthened by the increase in health awareness globally. As for personal grooming, it is a flourishing industry, for maintaining calorie intake via these devices that affects the market's growth indirectly. On the other side, such device usage is devoted to privacy and security issues. For instance, the populated data of the user in the devices can be to be misused. Also, the constraint that prevents people from purchasing these devices is the short battery life span (Research and Markets, 2020). Therefore, companies need to work harder and enhance Research and Development to stay competitive in the industry. (Research and Markets, 2020).

Referring to Gustafsson et al. (2005), consumers nowadays are more demanding than ever since their expectation level for a product or a service is increasing. Thus, to meet and satisfy their customers, companies have to keep on recognizing and investigate their needs and expectations. Besides, the increase in competition among leading companies is driving them to maintain customer-driven policy (Drosos et al., 2011). Meanwhile, it is regarded that fitness wearable devices are becoming more saleable, lately. Hence, customer satisfaction and how it is measured will be discussed generally. Subsequently, the research will go through customer satisfaction using fitness technology innovation through various theories, diffusion theory, theory of planned behavior, and technology acceptance model, to indicate the satisfaction determinants. The demonstration of customer satisfaction determinants is beneficial for companies for Research and Development and industry competitiveness due the high demand on these innovative products that would lead to companies' market growth. Therefore, that aim of this research is to reveal the determinants that would lead to customer satisfaction using fitness technology innovative devices. Could the service quality, helpfulness, quickness, and friendliness be from the customer satisfaction determinants?

2   Literature Review

This section aims to present a review of the literature concerning customer satisfaction regarding fitness technology innovation, and how it's determined through various theories. It will present the theoretical framework of customer satisfaction and the pivotal theories used in this research in addition to stating the main research question and outlining the underlying hypotheses.

2.1 Customer Satisfaction

Consumer satisfaction is characterized as an "assessment of the apparent disparity among earlier desires and the actual execution and performance of the item or product". Client's satisfaction with the organization's products and services is regarded as a pivotal element that drives competitiveness and achievement.

Rogers (1995) maintains that innovation is endorsed faster than diverse products, since it is perceived as rather simple to understand and use. Customers experience would turn into positive feelings for products capable of communicating in a humanlike way. According to Homburg and Stock (2004), consumer's positive and perceptual evaluation regarding a product or service represent consumer satisfaction. Rogers (1995) asserted that satisfaction is derived from product's competitive advantage. Relatively, smart product manufacturers have to grasp the tie between product smartness and the satisfaction level among consumers, due to the expansion in the smart devices usage. Haba et al. (2017) encountered that customer satisfaction is established by the smart services' quality, since it generates the smart services' usage. Furthermore, the bond between product performance and consumer satisfaction is recognized. Spreng and Olshavsky (2003) revealed that product's perceived performance leads to consumer satisfaction. Consequently, Fornell et al. (1996) noticed that both product quality and value shape consumer satisfaction (Lee and Shin, 2018).

Measuring Customer Satisfaction: Presently, estimating consumer loyalty and satisfaction turned into an essential issue to the vast majority of business association. In such manner, Ruler Kelvin in the nineteenth century declared, "In the event that you can't quantify something, you can't comprehend it". In ongoing decades, significance of consumer satisfaction has expanded in this way numerous association considered estimating consumer satisfaction ought to be set as a parameter. "It additionally considered as dependable input and it gives as compelling, immediate, and significant and target way of the clients' inclinations and desires". Gerson (1993), Wild (1980) and Slope (1996) stated, consumer satisfaction estimation gives a feeling of accomplishment and achievement for all workers associated with any phase of the client benefit process and it spurs individuals to execute just as accomplish larger amounts of profitability. Therefore, what are the determinants that lead to customer satisfaction?

2.2 Diffusion Theory of Fitness Wearable Devices and Customer Satisfaction

In 1962, diffusion of innovation theory, one of the earliest studies, was developed by E.M. Rogers. The theory clarifies how a concept or product acquires energy and diffuses within a particular population or community over time. Thereby, it is people's adoption of a new concept, product, or behavior. Adoption is when a person acts differently than s/he used previously, as acquiring or accepting a new product, have and perform new behavior (LaMorte 2019a).

Theory's Customer Satisfaction Model In the mid-1980s, a chain of effective and multi-stepped research program was initiated by the researcher Parasuraman, concentrating on the service quality concept and measurement. The instrument development technique toward assessing customers' evaluation of service quality achievement, in 1985 afterword the basic service quality "gaps model" conception. According to Parasuraman et al. (1991, 1994), for quantifying the customer's expectations a company meets, SERVQUAL has become logically well-known model. Nonetheless, SERVQUAL requires feedback structure where customer satisfaction count on the gap between customers' expectation and the service quality. Besides, the change in customers' expectations and technology have to be considered, as well as the continuous change of service quality evaluating method and thus customer satisfaction. This suggests that a good decision could not depend on customer satisfaction fixed evaluation. The growth and underinvestment model could be considered the missing significance behind the customer satisfaction archetype (Yeon et al. 2006).

H_1: *A Positive relationship exists between service quality while using of wearable fitness devices and customer satisfaction.*

2.3 Theory of Planned Behavior of Fitness Wearable Devices and Customer Satisfaction

In 1980, the Theory of Reasoned Action was the foundation of the Theory of Planned Behavior (TPB) to anticipate an individual's motive to join an action at a particular place and time. The theory's objective is to clarify all actions taken by people and capable of applying self-control. Behavioral intention is viewed as the model's pivotal element. Attitude influences behavioral intention. The six TPB constructive components that display actual control of the person over the behavior are attitude, behavioral intention, subjective norms, social norms, perceived power, and perceived behavioral control (LaMorte 2019b).

According to Fishbein and Ajzen (2010), the individual's purpose to presume in behavior is the behavior's direct determinant. Ajzen (1991) revealed, that attitude, subjective norms, and perceived behavioral control unitedly predict action intention, as the TPB suggested. Regarding physical exercise, attitude relates to the degree where the individual favors the exercising evaluation. Subjective norm is the referent important idea in person's life for the agree or disagree of exercise, and anticipated social constraint to submit with community (referent). Anticipated behavioral control is the individual's degree of believing in their exercising capability and realizing if they are in control of exercising or not (Zhu et al. 2017).

During the wide presence of fitness trackers and an increasing number of individuals wearing them, it is becoming vital to interpreting the devices' role in altering the exercise intentions. Conner and Sparks (2005) suggested to understand the individuals' intention to exercise, the TPB since it is considered as a practical framework, in addition to other health behaviors, as Freberg 2013 revealed. A conducted study demonstrated social sharing and social competing as two communicative elements of wearable devices. They attempt a broad perspective as information and communication technologies to transform health communication patterns. Lately, wearable devices are influencing individuals' behavior in modern ways, due to the technological growing role that is playing in individuals' lives. Thereby, people's intention to exercise is influenced by the technological devices' social aspects. Fishbein and Ajzen (2010) submitted interventions are altered by the recommended mediation model since its framework is used for expanding and evaluating behavior. For instance, people are realized to be more likely to exercise when their health data are shared; so, potential health campaigns and wearable fitness devices have to involve features that could alter behavior effectively (Zhu et al. 2017). Respectively, social sharing and social challenging are vital in both health communication and wearable fitness devices since they are capable of influencing the individuals' intention toward this technology.

Theory of Planned Behavior and Customer Satisfaction Relationship: Chi (2007) claimed that customers come back to the same company and eager to share their forward-looking experience when they are satisfied. Yoon (2005) stated forward-looking experiences will suggest the word of mouth recommendations in regard to marketing since it is viewed as the most honest and as one of the most seek post information for future customers. According to Opperman (1998), customer satisfaction affects the behavioral intentions;, as the return and recommend intention which will be excessive for various prospects. Besides, Oliver (1997) found that the state of experience of a psychological process refers is referring to satisfaction. Crompton (1995) indicated, the psychological result emerging from the participation in the activities is the experience that prompt satisfaction. Hence, the emotional state of mind, that derive succeeding customer's disclosure to the provider's services attribute, is referred to satisfaction. Further, referring to Blanchard (1994) and Heskett (1990), consumer's perception outcome of the value received in a relationship is consumer satisfaction. Meanwhile, Bitner (1994) argued, consumer's after purchase appraisal and emotional reaction to the experiences maintained by and united with specific products or services purchased is the satisfaction (Mohd Din et al. 2019).

2.4 Technology Acceptance Model of Fitness Wearable Device

Davis (1989) and Davis et al. (1989) stated that the Technology Acceptance Model (TAM) clarifies the client's knowledge or dismisses another innovative technology; thereby this model adjusts the contemplated activity hypothesis. So, the technology acceptance model is a standout among the most usually utilized hypotheses inside the technology perception setting; for instance, the model display is used to comprehend the consumer's acceptance, reception, utilization purpose of managing account advances, PDAs, health services' framework (Holden and Karsh 2010), online purchasing, and innovative advance. Besides, apparent usability and helpfulness are recommended as vital elements that clarify the technology acceptance. TAM indicated that its factors determine the conduct aim and approach for utilizing all technologies, in addition to genuine usage.

Perceived Usefulness: Perceived usefulness is portrayed as "the forthcoming client's abstract likelihood that utilizing an explicit application framework will expand his or her execution" (Bagozzi 1989). The observed effectiveness communicates convictions regarding buyers where the use of technology might enhance execution (Legris et al. 2003). Further, observed effectiveness was admitted to be the greatest variable to foresee the utilization of technology goal as well as acknowledgment. Discoveries of significant examination uncover a way where apparent convenience affects the frame of mind positively for utilizing behavior goal for technology use (Davis 1989). Generally, observed effectiveness is estimated by four aspects, as follows: efficiency, adequacy, execution, as well as the new technology handiness (Taylor and Todd 1995).

Perceived Ease of Use: Perceived ease of use, in the reputation model era, is another component. It is depicted as "how lots a person trusts that using a specific framework is probably free from exertion" (Davis 1989). Albeit noted, helpfulness predicts expectancies to the use of, thereby perceived ease of use is non-obligatory and appears by means of seen particularity in reputation version era (Davis et al. 1989). Keil et al. (1995) revealed, usefulness is an extra essential issue than a consolation in deciding usage era. All of the greater strikingly, the few examinations do not reflect the consideration on perceived ease of use like the predicted future use determinant (Subramanian 1994; Hu et al. 1999). Further, perceived ease of use is envisioned via the means of the first model's six aspects, which are: facility to look as, controllability, accuracy, resilience, smooth to turn out to be practical, and fundamental ability to use in the late era (Davis 1989). In other words, helpfulness, Friendliness, and quickness of devices could be examples of the perceived ease of use. According to Chang and Wang (2008) and Stoel and Lee (2003), a positive relationship between perceived ease of use and favorable attitude or satisfaction was affirmed through previous studies (Shah and Attiq 2016). Therefore, various hypotheses could emerge regarding the usage of fitness technology innovative devices and customer satisfaction.

H_2: *A Positive relationship exists between friendliness of wearable fitness devices and customer satisfaction.*

H_3: *A Positive relationship exists between helpfulness of using wearable fitness devices and customer satisfaction.*

H_4: *A Positive relationship exists between quickness while using of wearable fitness devices and customer satisfaction* (Fig. 1).

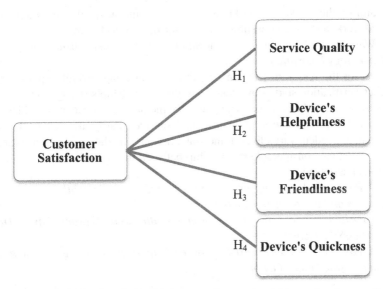

Fig. 1. Research model for the relationship between the tested variables and customer satisfaction

Attitude Towards Using Behavioral Intention to Use: Attitude is gestated as the character's advantageous or bad feeling approximated through using the brand recent technology; however, the behavioral goal belongs to the person's responsive plans to meet or not carry out a few exact subsequent behaviors (Venkatesh and Davis 2000). Specifically, the mindset assesses the user's assessment of the power of using the new era (Lederer et al. 2000). Moreover, the effect of behavioral assumption inclusive of perceived usefulness and ease of use on generation usage is assessed in phrases of customers' attitude closer to era, their goal to adopt the technology, and current usage of the technology (Baron et al. 2006).

3 Research Methodology

In the following section, the research approach will be discussed in addition to the study context, research problem and the taken steps to obtain the information and data.

3.1 Study Context and Research Approach

The aim of this study is determine the elements that affect customer satisfaction using fitness technology innovation. Based on the provided research and development theories regarding the fitness wearable devices, and it's the determinants that effect the customer satisfaction, the researcher built a methodological research. The research's model combined the independent variables (product's friendliness, helpfulness, quickness, and service quality after using the fitness devices) with the dependent variables – customer satisfaction. The data assisted in stating that there is a statistical considerable relationship between the compiled value of variables and customer satisfaction.

3.2 Research Problem

For the aim of the work and the knowledge stated and adopted assumptions of the theoretical work, a research question has been formulated as follows:

RQ: What are the determinants that would lead to customer satisfaction after using fitness technology innovation?

Answering the research question was through verifying several hypotheses. The hypotheses verification started by identifying the relationship's strength and statistical significance between the compiled variables, that included independent variables (product's friendliness, helpfulness, quickness, and service quality after using the fitness devices) and dependent variable customer satisfaction. The data assisted in stating that there is a statistical considerable relationship between the compiled value of variables and customer satisfaction.

H_1: A Positive relationship exists between service quality while using wearable fitness devices and customer satisfaction.

H_2: A Positive relationship exists between friendliness of Wearable Fitness Devices and Customer Satisfaction.

H_3: A Positive relationship exists between helpfulness of using wearable fitness devices and customer satisfaction.

H_4: A Positive relationship exists between quickness while using wearable fitness devices and customer satisfaction.

3.3 Measures and Procedures

For the prosperity and aim of this research, a quantitative methodology will be adapted. Quantitative data was collected, by the means of a questionnaire, to come-up with accurate information that represents the studied research question. The questionnaire was based on a Likert scale (7 Strongly agree – 1 Strongly disagree) since it is a well-known collecting data method and understandable by people.

3.4 Population and Sampling

The survey's sample was random since the usage of fitness technology innovative devices is becoming popular among people. The sample was chosen from North Lebanon in both urban and rural areas from both genders (males and females). The questionnaire was distributed over a 100 respondents who were mainly gym people, trainers and athletes in North Lebanon aged between 21 and 45 years. The sample size was limited to 100 respondents since it was a pilot research. The researchers chose this technique for its time and cost efficiency and many studies agreed on the increased honesty of responses collected using questionnaires.

3.5 Data Collection

The data was collected by researcher using the questionnaire technique. The questionnaire was divided into two categories: demographics, customer satisfaction toward wearable technology. The data was analyzed using SPSS. Chi-square and Pearson R correlation were used to verify the proposed hypotheses. The margin of error was calculated, where 4% was the margin of error and 95% confidence level.

4   Findings and Discussion of Results

The results from the collected data unveiled countless of findings that are generalized below. This study proved that there is a direct relationship between customer satisfaction and wearable fitness devices' friendliness, helpfulness, quickness, the service quality while using them. The four hypotheses were specified and are all revolved around this intention.

Hypothesis 1 was about the relation between "customer satisfaction" and "service quality". The results showed that there is a positive relationship between customer satisfaction and service quality of fitness wearable devices. The deduction was performed by utilizing Pearson Chi Square test and Pearson's R. After testing the correlation and significance of the dependent and independent variables "customer satisfaction" and "device's service quality", the sig = 0.000 and the Pearson's R value = 0.044. These results manifested a strong significant correlation between the tested variables. Thus,

H1 is validated; customer satisfaction is attained when the device's service quality is enhanced.

Hypothesis 2 was about the relation between "customer satisfaction" and "friendliness of wearable fitness devices. The results revealed that there is a positive relationship between customer satisfaction and friendliness of fitness wearable devices. The deduction was performed by applying Pearson Chi Square test and Pearson's R. After testing the correlation and significance of the dependent and independent variables "customer satisfaction" and "device's friendliness", the sig = 0.000 and the Pearson's R correlation value = 0.581. These results indicated a strong significant correlation between the tested variables. Thus, H2 is validated; customer satisfaction is strongly related to the customer friendliness of wearable fitness devices.

Hypothesis 3 was about the relation between "customer satisfaction" and "helpfulness of wearable fitness devices". The results showed that there is a positive relationship between customer satisfaction and helpfulness of fitness wearable devices. The deduction was performed through utilizing Pearson Chi Square test and Pearson's R. After testing the correlation and significance of the dependent and independent variables "customer satisfaction" and "helpfulness of wearable fitness devices", the sig = 0.000 and the Pearson's R correlation value = 0.768. This demonstrated a strong significant correlation between the tested variables. Hence, H3 is validated; customer satisfaction is achieved when the wearable devices are helpful.

Hypothesis 4 was about the relation between "customer satisfaction" and "device's quickness". The results exhibited that there is a positive relationship between customer satisfaction and quickness of fitness wearable devices. The deduction was performed through employing Pearson Chi Square and Pearson's R. After testing the correlation and significance of the dependent and independent variables "customer satisfaction" and "quickness of wearable fitness devices", the sig = 0.000 and the Pearson's R correlation value = 0.670. This conveyed a strong significant correlation between the tested variables. Thus, H4 is validated; customer satisfaction is attained when the wearable fitness devices are quick in use (Table 1).

Table 1. Hypotheses validation

Tested hypotheses	Results
H_1: A Positive relationship exists between service quality while using of wearable fitness devices and customer satisfaction.	Accepted
H_2: A Positive relationship exists between friendliness of wearable fitness devices and customer satisfaction.	Accepted
H_3: A Positive relationship exists between helpfulness of using wearable fitness devices and customer satisfaction.	Accepted
H_4: A Positive relationship exists between quickness while using of wearable fitness devices and customer satisfaction.	Accepted

The analysis of collected data revealed the acceptance of all the studied hypotheses. There is statistically significant relationship which is applied to studied variables:

between the independent variables (device's service quality, friendliness, helpfulness, and quickness) and the dependent variable (customer satisfaction). The relationship is relatively strong, where it was measured by Pearson Chi-Square test with sig $= 0.000$ and Pearson R' test. Therefore, a positive relationship exists between determinants related to the usage of innovative fitness technologies and customer satisfaction.

Referring to diffusion theory's customer satisfaction model, SERVQUAL is a leading model for measuring the customer's expectations a company meets. This model demands feedback structure and the gap between the customer's expectations and the service quality is the customer's satisfaction. Meanwhile, the revolution in customers' expectations and technology have to be deliberated, together with the variation of the evaluation method of service quality and thus customer satisfaction. It cannot be relied on the fixed evaluation of customer satisfaction for good decisions. Besides, growth and under-investment could be behind the customer satisfaction archetype (Yeon et al. 2006). The researcher investigated the relationship between service quality of wearable fitness devices and customer satisfaction. The results revealed a positive relationship between them. Hence, customer satisfaction of using fitness technology innovative devices can be determined by the service quality the company provides especially that these companies relies mainly on the change in technology that leads to growth, which is behind the satisfaction's archetype.

Besides, referring to the Technology Acceptance Model, prior studies proved a positive relationship between the satisfaction and perceived ease of use (Shah and Attiq 2016); thus, perceived ease of use can a determinant for customer satisfaction. However, the perceived ease of use is presented through various aspects as the facility to look as, controllability, accuracy, resilience, smooth to turn out to be practical, and fundamental ability to use in the late era (Davis 1989). These aspects could be exhibited in the shape of helpfulness, friendliness, and quickness of devices as the wearable fitness devices. The researcher conducted several hypotheses testing these aspects. The results demonstrated a positive relationship between customer satisfaction and helpfulness, friendliness, and quickness of the devices. Hence, these aspects (helpfulness, friendliness, quickness) included in perceived ease of use are determinants that lead to customer satisfaction.

5 Practical Implications

The research work is studying consumer satisfaction regarding the use of fitness technology innovation to understand how the consumer satisfaction is affected and reach the determinants that enhance this satisfaction. This study is vital for fitness technology devices companies since they have to track the customer's expectations and feedback to reach the customer satisfaction determinants. It is known that customer's expectation is not fixed yet changed with the change of technology and service quality, as well customer satisfaction. Thereby, this study could help in strengthening the companies' Research and Development to meet or exceed customer's expectations as product and service quality that is always in change. Also, as mentioned previously, according to FinancialBuzz (2020), the fitness technology devices' demand is falling due to the lack in capabilities. Therefore, enhancing customer satisfaction for such products is essential since it is capable of turning this fall into a raise in demand that leads to an increase in companies' growth rate.

6   Managerial Implications

Studying customer satisfaction is essential for better quality of service. The customer satisfaction is determined by the quality of the service. So, the quality of the service can be improved by attaining the customer satisfaction. Attaining customer satisfaction through the proved determinants and other determinants that recommended to be studied in the future would lead to a better quality of service provided by the companies. Therefore, customer loyalty would be achieved by the quality of service through customer satisfaction.

7   Conclusion

The customer satisfaction/fitness technology innovative devices were under study by different studies as the diffusion theory, theory of planned behavior, and technology acceptance model. The conducted research proved that the service quality the technology innovative devices companies provide determines the customer satisfaction since these companies depends mainly on the change in technology that leads to growth. Besides, generally, the perceived ease of use determines customer satisfaction; meanwhile, the helpfulness, friendliness, and quickness of devices that could be exhibited as elements in the perceived ease of use are verified as determinants that lead to customer satisfaction regarding the using of fitness technology innovative devices. Therefore, companies should take into consideration these elements while working on improving the wearable fitness devices in production.

Future studies would benefit from this analysis while using a wider sample in size. Forthcoming work should intend to include more determinants from the theory of planned behavior and technology acceptance model to come up with all the determinants that are cable capable of enhancing customer satisfaction in the fitness technology devices. Moreover, further research is required to generalize the results across all types of innovative technology devices through various theories since that the aim of this research is to eliminate the gap existing in the market research through studying the elements that would lead to customer satisfaction.

References

Baron, S., Patterson, A., Harris, K.: Beyond technology acceptance: understanding consumer practice. Int. J. Ser. Indu. Manage. **17**(2), 111–135 (2006). https://doi.org/10.1108/095642306 10656962

Davis, F.: Perceived usefulness, perceived ease of use, and user acceptance of information technology. MIS Quarterly **13**(3), 319–340 (1989). https://doi.org/10.2307/249008

Davis, F.D., Bagozzi, R.P., Warshaw, P.R.: User acceptance of computer technology: a comparison of two theoretical models. Management Science **35**(8), 903–1028 (1989). https://doi.org/10.1287/mnsc.35.8.982

Holden, R.J., Karsh, B.T.: Methodological review: the technology acceptance model: its past and its future in healthcare. Journal of Biomedical Informatics **43**(1), 159–172 (2010). https://doi.org/10.1016/j.jbi.2009.07.002

LaMorte, W.W.: Behavioral Change Models. Diffusion of Innovation Theory (2019a). 9 September. https://sphweb.bumc.bu.edu/otlt/mph-modules/sb/behavioralchangetheories/behavioralch angetheories4.html#:~:text=Diffusion%20of%20Innovation%20(DOI)%20Theory,specific% 20population%20or%20social%20system

LaMorte, W.W.: Behavioral change models. The Theory of Planned Behavior (2019b). 9 September. https://sphweb.bumc.bu.edu/otlt/mph-modules/sb/behavioralchangetheories/Behaviora lChangeTheories3.html#:~:text=The%20Theory%20of%20Planned%20Behavior%20(TPB)%20started%20as%20the%20Theory,ability%20to%20exert%20self%2Dcontrol

Lederer, A.L., Maupin, D.J., Sena, M.P., Zhuang, Y.: The technology acceptance model and the World Wide Web. Decision Support Systems **29**(3), 269–282 (2000). https://doi.org/10.1016/ S0167-9236(00)00076-2

Legris, P., Ingham, J., Collerette, P.: Why do people use information technology? a critical review of the technology acceptance model. Information & Management **40**(1), 191–204 (2003). https:// doi.org/10.1016/S0378-7206(01)00143-4

Mohd Din, N., Ismail, M.B., Nuh, R.: Consumer's satisfaction and behavior towards personal financing. Int. J. Entrepreneu. Manage. Prac. 61–79 (2019). https://doi.org/10.35631/ijemp. 27008

Shah, H.J., Attiq, S.: Impact of Technology Quality, Perceived Ease of Use and Perceived Usefulness in the Formation of Consumer's Satisfaction in the Context of E-learning. Abasyn Journal of Social Science **9**(1), 124–140 (2016). http://ajss.abasyn.edu.pk/admineditor/papers/V9I1-8. pdf

Spil, T.A., et al.: Are serious games too serious? Diffusion of wearable technologies and the creation of a diffusion of serious games model. Elsevier Public Health Emergency Collection (August 2020). https://doi.org/10.1016/j.ijinfomgt.2020.102202

Taylor, S., Todd, P.A.: Understanding information technology usage: a test of competing models. Information System Research **6**(2), 85–188 (1995). https://doi.org/10.1287/isre.6.2.144

Venkatesh, V., Davis, F.D.: A theoretical extension of the technology acceptance model: four longitudinal field studies. Management Science **46**(2), 169–332 (2000). https://doi.org/10.1287/ mnsc.46.2.186.11926

Yeon, S.-J., Park, S.-H., Kim, S.-W., Ha, W.-G.: Dynamic diffusion model for managing customer's expectation and satisfaction. Technological Forecasting and Social Change **73**(6), 648–665 (2006). https://doi.org/10.1016/j.techfore.2005.05.001

Zhu, Y., Dailey, S.L., Kreitzberg, D., Bernhardt, J.: "Social Networkout": connecting social features of wearable fitness trackers with physical exercise. Journal of Health Communication **22**(12), 974–980 (2017). https://doi.org/10.1080/10810730.2017.1382617

Digital Transformation

Changes in Global Virtual Team Conflict Over Time: The Role of Openness to Linguistic Diversity

Longzhu Dong[1]($\boxtimes$), Robert Stephens[2]($\boxtimes$), and Ana Maria Soares[3]($\boxtimes$)

[1] University of Wisconsin-Eau Claire, Eau Claire, USA
DONGL@uwec.edu
[2] Shippensburg University, Shippensburg, USA
RDStep@ship.edu
[3] University of Minho and CICS.NOVA.UMinho, Braga, Portugal
amsoares@eeg.uminho.pt

Abstract. This study examines global virtual team (GVT) conflict longitudinally. Specifically, the study compares changes in task conflict, relationship conflict, and process conflict over time in GVTs based on the level of openness to linguistic diversity (OLD) in the teams. We build on previous work by Guenter et al. [1] and use social identity theory to hypothesize changes in levels of conflict and conflict asymmetry in GVTs with high, medium, and low levels of OLD. Findings indicate that teams with low and medium OLD exhibit an increase in mean levels of all three types of conflict while teams with high OLD show decreases in mean levels of the task, relationship, and process conflict. It is also found that mean levels of conflict asymmetry decrease for high OLD teams but increase for medium and low OLD teams. We explore managerial implications and directions for future research.

Keywords: Global virtual teams · Task conflict · Relationship conflict · Process conflict · Openness to linguistic diversity

1 Introduction

A pre-COVID pandemic survey of 1,620 executives from 90 different countries found that 89% of respondents were on at least one virtual team and 27% were members of 4 or more virtual teams [2]. The effects of the COVID pandemic and the ongoing impacts of globalization have dramatically increased the use of international virtual work environments from these already high levels. In fact, it is not an understatement to say that in the global arena, virtual work is now the norm rather than the exception. Despite this significant shift in work modalities, many issues regarding GVT processes and outcomes remain poorly understood. This is particularly true when it comes to communication and conflict within GVTs. Global virtual teams are unique in that they usually include members from diverse national, cultural, and linguistic backgrounds. This diversity can be a strength but also poses numerous challenges which can make

M. A. Bach Tobji et al. (Eds.): ICDEc 2022, LNBIP 461, pp. 185–193, 2022.
https://doi.org/10.1007/978-3-031-17037-9_13

communication more difficult and contribute to increased levels of team conflict [3–5]. While the work of teams is always dynamic, research on teams is often static and generally relies on cross-sectional analyses. This study addresses that shortcoming by looking at changes in team conflict and conflict asymmetry over time.

Past research has looked at the impact of national diversity across several team outcomes including performance, creativity, and team conflict. In their comprehensive meta-analysis of diversity in teams, Stahl et al. [6] categorize diversity in teams by its convergent and divergent effects on outcomes. The authors find support for the hypothesis that increased national diversity in teams is associated with higher levels of conflict. Other research has shown that there is a lot of potential for conflict in GVTs due to the circumstances surrounding how they work, particularly the characteristics of space-time dispersion [4].

Openness to linguistic diversity (OLD), i.e. the acceptance of group members with differing levels of language proficiency [7], has been found to be relevant to understanding GVT's processes and outputs. For example, OLD may explain whether national diversity has a positive or negative impact in team conflict. One recent study found that openness to linguistic diversity weakens the positive impact of diversity in conflict and even turns it negative for teams with a high level of openness to linguistic diversity [8].

In this paper, we delve deeper into this question by further examining how team mindset towards linguistic diversity affects the dynamics of team collaboration. Previous literature on team dynamics and group development shows that teams may evolve in how they deal with the tasks at hand with the passage of time when a deadline approaches [9]. It is likely that the level of conflict experienced by teams varies along the process of collaboration. Specifically, we attempt to understand the role of OLD as team collaboration unfolds. Do teams with higher OLD experience differences in the changes of intragroup conflict over time?

2 Theoretical Development

Research looking at the impact of cultural diversity in a team's performance shows that this effect is not direct. Hence, to properly understand this relationship and reconcile opposing views on the nature of diversity consequences, it is necessary to consider the mediating and contextual variables that allow diversity to either become a source of richness or friction to teams [6, 10]. It is also necessary to outline the theoretical underpinnings of these relationships.

Social identity theory postulates that group membership is an important component and defining characteristic of personal identity [11]. The groups to which individuals belong provide a sense of meaning and context. These group identities are quite complex in global virtual teams. Members of GVTs identify with national, cultural, and linguistic groups as well as with the GVT itself. Diversity in-group identification can create an in-group/out-group dynamic.

We posit a dynamic model of GVT identity for time-limited temporary GVTs. In the early stages of group formation, membership in the team itself creates an immediately dominant identity. This shared group identity is often characterized by politeness and low levels of conflict as group members attempt to get to know each other. As the team continues to work together and has to begin negotiating tasks and setting process norms, team members begin to note differences which create a focus on out-groups due based on variations in culture, language, and national origin [12]. This sets the stage for potential conflict and helps explain the possible changes in conflict over time. In earlier stages of group formation, identification with the newly formed group provides an immediate sense of group cohesion [13]. As the group members begin interacting and learning more about their differences, deeper-seated social identities may begin to overpower identities created by GVT membership. These challenges may lead some group members to get overwhelmed by the challenges posed by geographical distance, communication obstacles, and cultural differences leading to further conflict.

2.1 Team Conflict

Team conflict is a relevant construct in GVTs due to coordination and communication difficulties enhanced by the fact that these teams work remotely. "There is much potential for conflict in GVTs as members work across cultural, geographical, and time boundaries" [4, p. 238]. Conflict in teams may lead to several negative outcomes such as decreased trust, cohesion, and performance [4, 5, 13].

Based on our reasoning above, we hypothesize that conflict in problem focused short-term GVTs increases over the duration of the team's existence. Due to differences in nationalities, cultures, and logistical and communication challenges task conflict, relationship conflict, and process conflict will become larger over the duration of a short-term, time limited GVT.

Hypothesis 1a: Task conflict in GVTs increases over time.
Hypothesis 1b: Relationship conflict in GVTs increases over time.
Hypothesis 1c: Process conflict in GVTs increases over time.

2.2 Openness to Linguistic Diversity

Openness to linguistic diversity refers to team members' attitudes toward multiple levels of language proficiency among other members of the team. Teams with high OLD have a higher tolerance for differing levels of language fluency [7]. Hence, the attitudes reflected in individuals and teams with high OLD are critical not only for facilitating better communication, but also for ameliorating potential conflict. Communicating with someone who struggles with language proficiency requires patience, tolerance, understanding and a willingness to work harder to be understood. These traits are not only necessary for improving communication effectiveness but are also useful in minimizing or preventing conflict. Thus, we hypothesize:

Hypothesis 2a: Task conflict in GVTs with high OLD increases more slowly than in teams with low OLD.
Hypothesis 2b: Relationship conflict in GVTs with high OLD increases more slowly than in teams with low OLD.
Hypothesis 2c: Process conflict in GVTs with high OLD increases more slowly than in teams with low OLD.

2.3 Conflict Asymmetry

Conflict is the tension among team members due to real or perceived differences. However, there may be differences in the amount of conflict perceived by team members. Jehn et al. [14] have proposed the construct of conflict asymmetry to refer to the "configural team property that reflects the variance in perceptions among team members" [ibid., p. 596]. Because teams with higher levels of openness to linguistic diversity work harder to understand and to be understood, it is more likely that these teams will share similar perceptions of the amount of conflict in the team.

Hypothesis 3a: Openness to linguistic diversity reduces task conflict asymmetry in GVTs over time.
Hypothesis 3b: Openness to linguistic diversity reduces relationship conflict asymmetry in GVTs over time.
Hypothesis 3c: Openness to linguistic diversity reduces process conflict asymmetry in GVTs over time.

3 Methodology

3.1 Sample

Hypotheses were tested using data from an ongoing large-scale international experiential learning project (X-Culture Project), which usually involves undergraduate and graduate business students from around 140 universities in about 60 countries on six continents every year. The students are placed in GVTs of about 5–7 team members from different countries and universities. Working with people from around the globe and dealing with cultural differences, time-zone dispersion, and global communication challenges, the teams complete a consulting project for a multinational company. The project involves the development of a solution to real-life business challenges presented by real-life companies and is centered foreign market entry plan for about eight weeks.

For the present study, we used data collected from all participants in the Spring 2018 which included 278 teams, with an average size of 4.25 members and about 42.43% of students are male.

3.2 Measures

Task Conflict. Task conflict was assessed using the three-item scale inspired by Jehn [14]. The survey questions for this construct are: "How much conflict of ideas is there in your work group?", "How frequently do you have disagreements within your work group about the task of the project you are working on?" "How often do people in your work group have conflicting opinions about the project you are working on?". Task conflict was collected twice (t1 and t2), with t1 in the middle and t2 at end of the project. Cronbach's alpha is 0.873 (t1) and 0.893 (t2).

Relationship Conflict. Relationship conflict was also assessed using the three-item scale from Jehn [14]. The questions are: "How much relationship tension is there within your work group?", "How often do people get angry in your group?", and "How much emotional conflict is there in your work group?". Relationship conflict was collected twice (t1 and t2), with t1 in the middle and t2 at end of the project. Cronbach's alpha is 0.841 (t1) and 0.880 (t2).

Process Conflict. Relationship conflict was also assessed using the three-item scale from Jehn [14]. The questions are: "How often are there disagreements about who should do what in your work group?", "How much conflict is there in your group about task responsibilities?", and "How often do you disagree about resource allocation in your work group?". Process conflict was collected twice (t1 and t2), with t1 in the middle and t2 at end of the project. Cronbach's alpha is 0.882 (t1) and 0.903 (t2).

Openness to Linguistic Diversity (OLD). Openness to linguistic diversity was assessed by a four-item scale adapted from Lauring and Selmer [7]. The questions used for this construct are: "My team members enjoy working with other people on the team despite language barriers.", "My team members make an extra effort to listen to people speaking different languages.", "My team members are eager to learn from people even when communication is slowed down by language barriers.", "My team members are more reluctant to communicate when faced with people speaking a different language." Cronbach's alpha was 0.600 with all four items. After a closer look, the last item was removed due to its low loading on the construct (0.051) possibly due to the reverse coding of the item. Cronbach's alpha of the abbreviated three-item scale is 0.824.

Conflict Asymmetry. The asymmetry of all three types of conflicts on a team was assessed as the standard deviation among teams members' perceived conflict levels, following Jehn [14]. The higher level of the asymmetry, the larger the differences among team members in terms of their conflict perceptions.

Controls. The study considered several control variables. These controls were: team size, the average age of team members, percentage of male teammates in a team, and readiness test score (a pre-project test for students' readiness to participate in a global virtual team) and self-reported English skill level.

4 Results

Descriptive and correlation results are shown in Table 1.

Table 1. Means, standard deviations, and correlations

	Mean	S.D.	1	2	3	4	5	6	7	8	9	10	11	12	13	14	15	16	17	18
OLD	2.034	.598	--																	
Team Size	4.251	.555	-.039	--																
English Skills	4.381	.325	.028	.074	--															
Male Percentage	.424	.245	.007	.081	.044	--														
Age	22.029	2.600	-.124	.225**	.079	.098	--													
Linguistic Diversity	.618	.093	.175**	.341**	-.121	.018	.054	--												
Nationality Diversity	.875	.053	.044	-.492**	-.055	-.155*	-.023	.082	--											
RCA @ t1	.537	.406	-.109	.138*	-.198**	.046	-.005	.030	-.135*	--										
TCA @ t1	.648	.369	-.018	.210**	-.111	.059	-.020	.106	-.105	.677**	--									
PCA @ t1	.623	.434	-.069	.151*	-.078	.081	-.024	.044	-.122	.678**	.665**	--								
RCA @ t2	.593	.457	-.223**	.230**	-.093	.039	.028	-.031	-.273**	.349**	.216**	.296**	--							
TCA @ t2	.671	.414	-.154*	.209**	-.076	.001	-.057	.031	-.139*	.222**	.205**	.210**	.709**	--						
PCA @ t2	.721	.501	-.193**	.150*	-.063	.034	.018	-.020	-.212**	.208**	.120	.210**	.728**	.664**	--					
Relationship conflict @ t1	1.524	.481	-.228**	.081	-.198**	.038	-.031	.007	-.132*	.691**	.485**	.483**	.286**	.192**	.240**	--				
Task conflict @ t1	1.687	.467	-.135*	.135*	-.187**	.024	-.045	.111	-.057	.449**	.586**	.431**	.197**	.191**	.139*	.612**	--			
Process conflict @ t1	1.597	.466	-.213**	.076	-.165*	.083	-.040	.051	-.133*	.564**	.566**	.727**	.244**	.169*	.195**	.662**	.690**	--		
Relationship conflict @ t2	1.662	.581	-.435**	.122	-.064	.038	.040	-.006	-.155*	.324**	.234**	.227**	.637**	.479**	.546**	.473**	.363**	.418**	--	
Task conflict @ t2	1.742	.523	-.325**	.138*	-.069	.043	.011	.026	-.083	.198**	.165*	.169**	.548**	.592**	.564**	.305**	.401**	.279**	.770**	--
Process conflict @ t2	1.726	.568	-.378**	.132*	-.032	.067	.009	.030	-.175**	.225**	.127	.208**	.534**	.490**	.677**	.322**	.248**	.352**	.805**	.727**

Hypotheses 1a–c predict that all three types of conflict will increase from t1 to t2. We tested the significance of the difference in mean of each type of conflict between two time points [mean$_{(t1)}$–mean$_{(t2)}$] and found that the level of relationship (−.138***) and process conflict (−.129**) increased over time, but the change in task conflict was not significant. Therefore, hypothesis 1 was partially supported.

Hypotheses 2a–c predict that openness to linguistic diversity hinders the development of all three types of conflict. We tested these hypotheses utilizing the Repeated Measures ANOVA approach. Specifically, we tested and compared the extent of each type of conflict increase from t1 to t2 at three levels of openness to linguistic diversity that operationalizes "low" (the 16th percentile), "moderate" (the 50 the percentile), and "high" (the 84th percentile). Three conditions (OLD) × two time points (Time) Repeated Measures ANOVA on three types of conflict revealed similar results. For task conflict, although the effect of Time was not significant (F[1, 228] = .099), the effects of OLD * Time was found significant (F[2, 228] = 4.498*). Overall, the results show that OLD does hinder the development of all three types of conflict (Fig. 1).

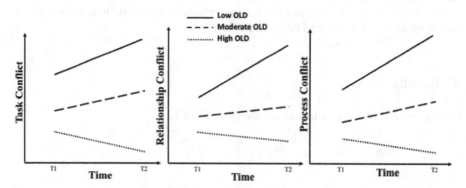

Fig. 1. Change in conflict over two time points.

Hypotheses 3a–c predict that openness to linguistic diversity can minimize conflict asymmetry in teams over time. To rule out the influence of initial level of conflict on the change of conflict asymmetry over time, we controlled conflict level at t1. Our results found that the level of asymmetry of all three types of conflict changed in a very similar pattern. For task conflict asymmetry, OLD * Time was found significant (F[2, 220] = 4.981**). A similar significance was also found for relationship conflict asymmetry and process conflict asymmetry (F[2, 220] = 4.758**). Our hypotheses 3a–c were supported as shown in Fig. 2.

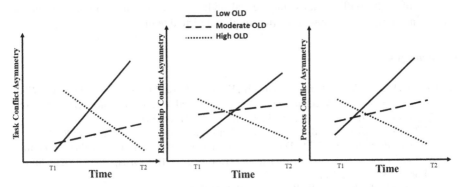

Fig. 2. Change in conflict asymmetry over two-time points.

5 Conclusion

This study aimed at extending the conflict literature by considering the role of OLD in the evolution of conflict levels in short term GVTs. Our results show that, on average, the level of all three types of conflict (task conflict, relationship conflict, and process conflict) increase over time within these teams. Teams with high levels of OLD, however, not only do not show increases in conflict but actually show decreases in all three types of conflict over time. This is a surprising and significant result, indicating that OLD has a significant impact on team dynamics and shows that teams high in OLD are much better at avoiding conflict. It is also found that mean levels of conflict asymmetry decrease for high OLD teams, while they increase for medium and low OLD teams. These results are noteworthy as they provide further support for the importance of diversity mindsets for leveraging team collaboration and are in line with Lauring and Selmer [7] seminal work on OLD. These authors emphasized that openness to diversity climate variables contributes to inclusiveness and tolerance. In fact, the role of OLD in mitigating the increase of conflict, and even decreasing it, is a valuable finding with rich managerial implications.

These findings make a case for the impact of adequate conflict management behavior in mitigating conflict. Skills evidenced by teams with high OLD, including patience, tolerance, and increased effort in communication, are not only important for enhancing communication but are also contributing to reductions in conflict. It is also possible that reductions in conflict are brought about by improved communication itself [7]. In either event, the importance of increased openness to linguistic diversity is evident. Managers should develop and implement training programs that lead to higher levels of openness to linguistic diversity when working in global settings, especially when much of the work is being done through virtual communication.

Directions for future research include identifying the circumstances in which higher and lower levels of conflict emerge. In particular, applying Qualitative Comparative Analysis (QCA) to these problems could provide additional valuable insights into why conflict increases in some teams and decreases in others. In addition, a more fine-grained analysis of high conflict teams may reveal additional dimensions to the phenomena underlying conflict and communication in global virtual teams.

References

1. Guenter, H., van Emmerik, H., Schreurs, B., Kuypers, T., van Iterson, A., Notelaers, G.: When task conflict becomes personal: the impact of perceived team performance. Small Gr. Res. **47**, 569–604 (2016). https://doi.org/10.1177/1046496416667816
2. RW3 Culture Wizard: 2018 Trends in High-Performing Global Virtual Teams (2018)
3. Stephens, R.D., Soares, A.M., Dong, L.: Leveraging language proficiency through cultural intelligence to improve global virtual team performance. J. Bus. Discip. 1–27 (2020). https://doi.org/10.35255/jbd1871.101001
4. Kankanhalli, A., Tan, B.C.Y., Kwok-Kee, W.E.I.: Conflict and performance in global virtual teams. J. Manag. Inf. Syst. **23**, 237–273 (2006). https://doi.org/10.2753/MIS0742-1222230309
5. Chiu, Y.T., Staples, D.S.: Reducing faultlines in geographically dispersed teams: self-disclosure and task elaboration. Small Gr. Res. **44**, 498–531 (2013). https://doi.org/10.1177/1046496413489735
6. Stahl, G.K., Maznevski, M.L., Voigt, A., Jonsen, K.: Unraveling the effects of cultural diversity in teams: a meta-analysis of research on multicultural work groups. J. Int. Bus. Stud. **41**, 690–709 (2010). https://doi.org/10.1057/jibs.2009.85
7. Lauring, J., Selmer, J.: International language management and diversity climate in multicultural organizations. Int. Bus. Rev. **21**, 156–166 (2012). https://doi.org/10.1016/j.ibusrev.2011.01.003
8. Stephens, R., Dong, L., Soares, A.M.: The impact of national diversity on task conflict in global virtual teams: the moderating effect of language factors. In: Jallouli, R., Bach Tobji, M.A., Mcheick, H., Piho, G. (eds.) ICDEc 2021. LNBIP, vol. 431, pp. 53–63. Springer, Cham (2021). https://doi.org/10.1007/978-3-030-92909-1_4
9. Knight, A.P.: Mood at the midpoint: affect and change in exploratory search over time in teams that face a deadline. Organ. Sci. **26**, 99–118 (2015). https://doi.org/10.1287/orsc.2013.0866
10. Stahl, G., Maznevski, M.L.: Unraveling the effects of cultural diversity in teams: a retrospective of research on multicultural work groups and an agenda for future research. J. Int. Bus. Stud. **52**, 4–22 (2021). https://doi.org/10.1057/s41267-020-00389-9
11. Tajfel, H., Turner, J.C.: An integrative theory intergroup conflict. In: Austin, W.G., Worchel, S. (eds.) The Social Psychology of Intergroup Relations, pp. 33–48. Brooks/Cole, Monterrey, CA (1979)
12. Vahtera, P., Buckley, P.J., Aliyev, M., Clegg, J., Cross, A.R.: Influence of social identity on negative perceptions in global virtual teams. J. Int. Manag. **23**, 367–381 (2017). https://doi.org/10.1016/j.intman.2017.04.002

13. Tuckman, B.W.: Developmental sequence in small groups. Psychol. Bull. **63**(6), 384–399 (1965). https://doi.org/10.1037/h0022100. PMID 14314073
14. Jehn, K.A., Rispens, S., Thatcher, S.M.B.: The effects of conflict asymmetry on work group and individual outcomes. Acad. Manag. J. **53**, 596–616 (2010). https://doi.org/10.5465/amj.2010.51468978

Readiness of Russian Companies for Digital Transformation: What's Changed?

Olga Stoianova[1] (ID), Victoriia Ivanova[1] (ID), and Tatiana Lezina[2](✉) (ID)

[1] Saint Petersburg State University, 7/9 Universitetskaya nab., Saint Petersburg 199034,
Russian Federation
{o.stoyanova,v.ivanova}@spbu.ru
[2] National Research University Higher School of Economics, 16 Soyuza Pechatnikov Str.,
Saint Petersburg 190008, Russian Federation
tlezina@hse.ru

Abstract. The article presents the results of the research on Russian companies' readiness for digital transformation in 2017–2021. The purpose of the study is to observe how the understanding and the attitude of the representatives of Russian business towards the digital transformation and the self-assessment of company's readiness for this transformation has changed. The source data are the results of surveys conducted in 2018 and 2021 among representatives of companies in St. Petersburg and the Leningrad region. The paper focuses on establishing in Russian companies the Corporate Culture essential to the success of digital transformation projects. It is shown that large companies have shifted towards greater employee engagement and management support for initiatives. However, in small companies, there is still a lack of employee belief in digital transformation and a top-down implementation of digital transformation.

Keywords: Digital transformation · Readiness for digital transformation · Corporate culture · Russian companies · Survey

1 Introduction

According to the BCG global survey [1], the world's most digitally mature companies are leading in value creation. Six months after the pandemic began, their value exceeded pre-crisis levels by an average of 23%, while the least mature companies were only able to grow by an average of 7%. BCG researchers classify the most mature companies as bionic because they base digital transformation on combining new technologies with human resource capabilities. Russian digital front-runners are driving the same strategy. But these are predominantly large corporations from the financial, mining and manufacturing sectors, including state-owned corporations.

To bridge the significant gap in the level of digitalisation between large corporations and other companies, since 2021 the focus of the government's digital economy programmes in Russia has shifted slightly towards small and medium-sized businesses. Therefore, the need for research on Russian companies' readiness to adopt digital

M. A. Bach Tobji et al. (Eds.): ICDEc 2022, LNBIP 461, pp. 194–202, 2022.
https://doi.org/10.1007/978-3-031-17037-9_14

changes has increased. The aim of the study is to trace how the understanding and the attitude of Russian businesses towards the digital transformation and the self-assessment of company's readiness for this transformation have changed between 2018 and 2021.

The study is based on the surveys conducted in 2018 and 2021 among representatives of companies in St. Petersburg and the Leningrad region from different sectors of industry. The obtained results look relevant for all Russian industrial companies. The practical insights of this study will allow to make justified decisions on the management of digital transformation at the state, regional and company management levels.

2   Related Work

Assessing digital readiness is still relevant for all companies. Many studies have analysed and ranked the existing frameworks for assessing companies' digital maturity/readiness [2, 3]. Some researchers note that global management consultants often avoid contextual factors in their digital transformation recommendations. For this reason, industry frameworks are in great demand [4–6]. Both universal and industry frameworks identify 5–7 domains for readiness/maturity assessment such as Business processes, Personnel, Management System, Data and others. Most of these models and frameworks are targeted at large, high-tech, project-oriented companies, such as telecoms or pharmaceuticals. Small and medium-sized companies require different approaches for readiness assessment [7]. This explains the emergence of frameworks with integrated domains. For example, criteria associated with the domain Data are often encapsulated in other domains.

The large number of criteria used in models and frameworks has been reduced to a minimum number of the most important criteria (the so-called success factors), which have appeared in online self-assessment tools [8, 9]. BCG specifies six critical success factors for transformation, which correlate with domains for assessing digital readiness, focusing on people, technology and data [1].

Some of the existing models/frameworks distinguish the levels of companies' digital readiness/maturity, which vary widely (see Table 1).

Criteria and procedures for assessing readiness/maturity levels also vary considerably between the models/frameworks.

Table 1. The models/frameworks with the levels of readiness for digital transformation

Model/frameworks	Levels
Forrester The Digital Maturity Model 5.0 [10]	Sceptics Adopters Collaborators Differentiators
PwC Industry 4.0 Self Assessment (Digital Operations Self-Assessment) [11]	Digital Novice Vertical Integrator Horizontal Collaborator Digital Champion
IDC MaturityScape [12]	Digital Resister Digital Explorer Digital Player Digital Transformer Digital Disrupter

3 Design of the Study

The study period is 2017–2021. The purpose of the study is to observe how the understanding and attitude of the representatives of Russian business towards the digital transformation of companies has changed. The source data are the results of surveys conducted in 2018 and 2021 among representatives of companies in St. Petersburg and the Leningrad region.

The first questionnaire was developed in 2017 on the basis of the existing models/frameworks for assessing companies' readiness for digital transformation, the standards of general management and IT management, and the results of analysis of Russian companies' best practices. In line with general questions aimed at profiling companies and respondents, the questionnaire included direct and indirect questions regarding attitudes towards digital transformation and assessments of various aspects of readiness by the respondents. Some examples of direct questions: "Whether the company requires digital transformation?", "How do you assess the level of the company's readiness for digital transformation?", etc. The indirect questions investigated the readiness for the digital transformation of companies' management systems, the commitment of employees, the maturity of business processes, the current level of information technology use, as well as data management and enterprise architecture issues.

The focus group survey revealed a lack of understanding of professional terminology among the respondents, especially in the issues of enterprise architecture and data management. For example, 43% of respondents answered that the concept of data management required further clarification. In response to these results, the questionnaire was modified. Unclear questions, special terms and concepts with an ambiguous interpretation were excluded. Meanwhile, several questions about expectations from the digital transformation and possible risks were added, e.g. "What are the measurable effects of digital transformation that the company wants to achieve?", "What risks do you consider digital transformation poses to your company?". The new questionnaire was used to conduct a survey among representatives of companies in St. Petersburg and the Leningrad region (160 respondents) at the end of 2018.

A new survey was conducted in 2021 to find out changes in the understanding and the attitude of representatives of Russian companies towards digital transformation and in their assessment of companies' readiness. Using the same questionnaire provides an opportunity to compare the results of the 2018 and 2021 surveys. Moreover, as the new study revealed a better understanding of digital transformation among the respondents, a supplementary calculation of companies' readiness was carried out. Based on the existing models of readiness/maturity described in the previous section, five levels of readiness were identified: Sceptics, Beginners, Adopters, Transformers, Disruptors. The scoring of the answers to the questionnaire for calculating an integral indicator to assign a company to a particular level of readiness is based on the Diffusion of innovations theory by Rogers [13]. The results obtained are presented below.

4 Results

4.1 General Characteristic

An analysis of Russian business representatives' attitudes towards digital transformation in the 2018 reveals: 33.75% of companies urgently needed digital transformation, 37.5% of companies felt the need for digital transformation although it was not a priority, 6.25% of companies were satisfied with the current state of affairs and did not need digital transformation, and in 2.5% of the companies, according to respondents, the activities didn't require digital technology. Moreover, 20% of respondents indicated their lack of understanding the essence of digital transformation [14]. Also, the majority of the respondents rated their readiness for transformation as low to medium, and about 90% of them stated the need for a methodology and tools to assess readiness and identify bottlenecks.

Many models and frameworks for assessing digital transformation readiness in 2018 considered the current level of IT use to be one of the key readiness criteria. However, our survey found that among the companies with a high current level of digital usage, only 33.33% considered the level of digital transformation readiness to be high. Moreover, we identified the dependency between digital transformation readiness assessments and such factors as employee engagement, proactivity, management maturity, and a range of others. These findings guided the development of the readiness assessment framework (the DTRA framework) [15], which includes the following domains: Systematic management, Enterprise architecture, Using of data, Maturity of business processes, and Corporate culture.

Using criteria from the DTRA framework and data of the survey conducted in 2021, the levels of digital transformation readiness of companies were assessed.

Among surveyed respondents, only 5% are familiar with the concept of digital transformation and do not consider their company to need digital transformation (Sceptics). 30% start to discuss possible digital transformation projects, although they do not rate their company's level of readiness as high (Beginners). 41% identify projects implemented in their companies as digital transformation projects and assess them as necessary (Adopters). 24% claim that their companies are in the digital transformation process and almost all business processes are driven by digital technologies (Transformers). At the time of the survey, none of the companies was categorized as Disrupters.

As the 2018 survey results revealed, most bottlenecks in all companies were concentrated in the domains of Systematic Management and Corporate Culture, we have focused on exploring the changes that have taken place in these areas.

4.2 Changes in Management System (the Systematic Management Domain)

The readiness/maturity of company management systems for digital transformation has improved significantly. This improvement is evidenced by the absence of negative responses to the question 'do you understand the company's strategy' compared with 27% in 2018. Also, the share of companies with a formalised description of goals and objectives increased from 47% in 2018 to 72% in 2021. The significant increase was due to large and medium-sized companies. Many companies have started using KPIs and cascading goals and objectives. The share of companies that do not use KPIs decreased from 32% to 9.7%. One more indicator of the company's readiness level in the Systematic Management domain is "Using modern technologies to analyse the external environment". The share of companies using such tools increased from 38% to 61% (see Fig. 1).

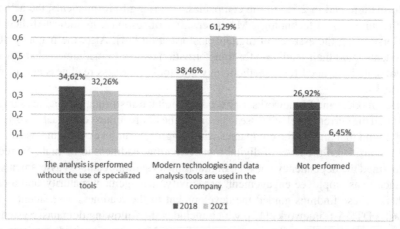

Fig. 1. Results of respondents' answers to the question "How the company analyses the external environment"

It is remarkable that the share of companies that use a closed form of feedback increased from 47% in 2018 to 68% in 2021 (Fig. 2). Understanding this phenomenon requires a detailed analysis of the changes that have taken place in companies' corporate culture.

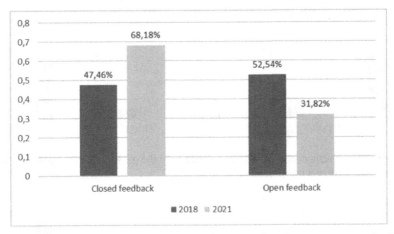

Fig. 2. Results of respondents' answers to the question "How does the company set up feedback?"

4.3 Changes in Corporate Culture (the Corporate Culture Domain)

The percentage of employees not understanding the core of digital transformation decreased from 45% in 2018 to 33% in 2021, in line with the growth by 18% of the share of companies whose employees are constantly improving their skills at company expense. The companies have increased their focus on training: the proportion of 'no training' responses has fallen sharply (from 19% in 2018 to 5% in 2021). Still the ratio of employees not interested in raising their skills remains stable (24% vs 25%), as well as employees' initiatives in professional training. Moreover, one-third of respondents in 2021 answered that there is no personnel development policy in the company. These results indicate a lack of gap in aspirations for learning and professional development.

The results of the comparison of employees' perception of digital changes in companies of different scales are rather interesting (Figs. 3 and 4). In large companies, in 2021 50% of employees have a positive attitude to changes vs 14.3% in 2018. In small companies one-fifth the most employees do not know what digital transformation is. These results may be explained by the fact that the large companies, on the one hand, support employee development and, on the other hand, substitute non-professional employees.

The readiness to change job functions under the necessity has increased (50% in 2021 vs 30.4% in 2018). A small number of respondents (10% in 2021) are ready to change their job functions proactively. Note that these indicators differ for companies of different sizes. In 2021, 23,8% of representatives of large companies said that their employees have a positive attitude for changing their job functions; no representative of small companies answered this question positively. It should be noted that the share of companies responding that "Employee attitudes are not analysed" decreased significantly (Figs. 5 and 6), as well as the neutral attitude of employees. The readiness of employees to change their job functions by necessity has increased, especially in large companies.

The conducted analysis indicates the growth of companies' corporate culture. Nevertheless, some passiveness of the personnel is identified. Employees are willing to develop

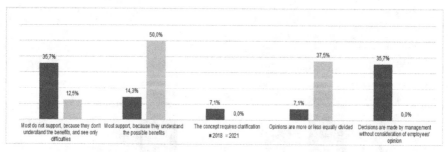

Fig. 3. Answers of respondents from large companies to the question "Do company employees support the idea of digital transformation?"

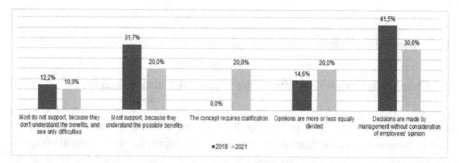

Fig. 4. Answers of respondents from small companies to the question "Do company employees support the idea of digital transformation?"

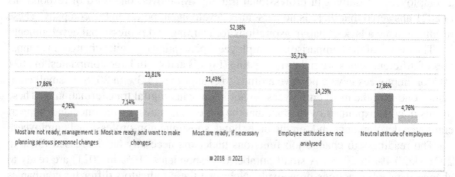

Fig. 5. Answers of respondents from large companies to the question "Are employees ready to change job functions?"

their skills and change job functions mainly at the initiative and with the support of management. For this reason, large companies may benefit from hiring new employees to implement digital transformation. These findings are consistent with the results of a survey conducted by KMDA [16] which found that 63% of managers are willing to hire new staff and 31% say they need to replace insufficiently competent employees with new ones.

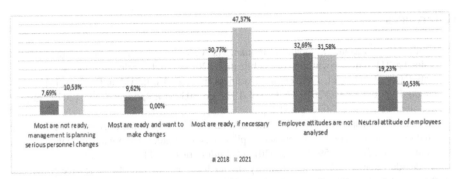

Fig. 6. Answers of respondents from small companies to the question "Are employees ready to change job functions?"

5 Conclusion

A comparative analysis of Russian business representatives' attitudes towards digital transformation reveals that in 2021 almost all companies understand the essence of digital transformation and admit its necessity. According to the survey 2021 only 5% of companies remain on the level of Sceptics vs about 29% of companies in 2018. In 2021, 41% of companies could be classified as Adopters because they are implementing digital transformation projects and these projects are underway.

The readiness study indicates that there have been significant changes in the management systems and corporate culture over the three years. The readiness of management systems has increased. Many companies have started using specific methods and tools to enhance consistency and transparency in management. In 2021, 72% (vs 47% in 2018) of companies have formal goals descriptions and only 9.7% don't use KPI's (vs 32% in 2018).

Significant changes have also taken place in the corporate culture of companies. However, these changes have been observed primarily in large companies. The large companies have shifted towards greater employee engagement and management support for initiatives. However, in small companies, there is still a lack of employee belief in digital transformation and a top-down implementation of digital transformation.

The surveys were conducted among representatives of companies in St Petersburg and the Leningrad region. This region is highly industrialised, so the values of the obtained indicators may differ for other regions. However, the main objective was to analyse the changes over three years. And in this respect, the results obtained look relevant for all Russian industrial companies and are consistent with the results of other studies. The practical insights of this study justify that the support of digital transformation of small and medium-sized businesses should be strengthened on the state and the regional levels. At company level, more emphasis should be placed on improving digital literacy and encouraging employee initiative.

References

1. Grebe, M., Rüßmann, M., Leyh, M., Franke, M., Anderson, W.: The Leaders' Path to Digital Value (2021). https://www.bcg.com/publications/2021/digital-acceleration-index
2. Voß, F.L.V., Pawlowski, J.M.: Digital readiness frameworks. In: Uden, L., Ting, I.-H., Corchado, J.M. (eds.) KMO 2019. CCIS, vol. 1027, pp. 503–514. Springer, Cham (2019). https://doi.org/10.1007/978-3-030-21451-7_43
3. Hanelt, A., Bohnsack, R., Marz, D., Antunes Marante, C.: A systematic review of the literature on digital transformation: insights and implications for strategy and organizational change. J. Manag. Stud. **58**(5), 1159–1197 (2020). https://doi.org/10.1111/joms.12639
4. Valdez-de-Leon, O.: A digital maturity model for telecommunications service providers. Technol. Innov. Manag. Rev. **6**(8), 19–32 (2016). https://doi.org/10.22215/timreview/1008
5. Digital Maturity Model. Achieving Digital Maturity to Drive Grow/Deloitte (2018). https://www2.deloitte.com/content/dam/Deloitte/global/Documents/Technology-Media-Telecommunications/deloitte-digital-maturity-model.pdf
6. Bilgiç, D., Akdağ, H.C.: Digital transformation readiness factors in healthcare. Hosp. Top. (2021). https://doi.org/10.1080/00185868.2021.2002745
7. Emmanuel Monod, E., Koester, A., Joyce, E., Khalil, S., Korotkova, N.: Digital transformation consulting: toward a human-technology performance model. Acad. Manag. Annu. Meet. Proc. **2021**(1), 12737 (2021). https://doi.org/10.5465/AMBPP.2021.12737abstract
8. Oden Technologies: Free Assessment (2021). https://oden.io/industrial-iot-digital-readiness/#gform_3
9. BCG: Digital transformation readiness assessment (2021). https://connect.bcg.com/digital-transformation-readiness-assessment/
10. Gill, M., Van Boskirk, S.: The Digital Maturity Model 4.0. Benchmarks: Digital business transformation playbook (2017). https://forrester.nitro-digital.com/pdf/Forrester-s%20Digital%20Maturity%20Model%204.0.pdf
11. PWC: Industry 4.0 Self Assessment (2018). https://i40-self-assessment.pwc.de/i40/landing/
12. Digital transformation: benchmarking assessment. IDC Recommendations (2017). https://equilibrio.si/wp-content/uploads/2017/01/Company_digital_transformation.pdf
13. Rogers, E.M.: Diffusion of Innovations, 5th edn. Free Press, New York (2003)
14. Stoianova, O., Lezina, T., Ivanova, V.: Readiness of Russian companies for digital transformation: how to evaluate? In: Vision 2025: Educational Excellence and Management of Innovations Through Sustainable Economic Competitive Advantage. Proceedings of the 34th International Business Information Management Association Conference, IBIMA 2019, pp. 5215–5221 (2019)
15. Stoianova, O.V., Lezina, T.A., Ivanova, V.V.: The framework for assessing company's digital transformation readiness. St. Petersburg Univ. J. Econ. Stud. **36**(2), 243–265 (2020). https://doi.org/10.21638/spbu05.2020.204
16. KMDA. Analytical report: Digital Transformation in Russia - 2020 (2020). https://komanda-a.pro/projects/dtr_2020

Towards a Better Digital Transformation: Learning from the Experience of a Digital Transformation Project

Houda Mahboub$^{(\boxtimes)}$ ⓘ and Hicham Sadok ⓘ

Mohammed V University in Rabat, Rabat, Morocco
{houda.mahboub,h.sadok}@um5r.ac.ma

Abstract. As a disruptive paradigm, especially with the Covid-19 emergence, digital transformation (DT) becomes a main area of interest for many organizations. From a trend perception to an obligation, digital transformation implementation requires many changes, adaptations, and updates. Its success depends on many levers, the most important of which remains the design and implementation of a digital transformation strategy (DTS). Indeed, lacking capabilities to embrace DT can lead to the disappearance of the company. However, and despite relevant research, the formulation, implementation, and evaluation of the digital transformation strategy as a key to successful digital transformation remain vague and blurred. Thus, this article aims to draw up a literature review on DTS with a general approach guiding the implementation of digital transformation. The focus on the experience of the AssetCo company as a monographic study will serve to concretely describe the formulation and the implementation of the digital transformation strategy, its stages, as well as a conclusion on the main key factors of success. Thus, this article intends to contribute to a better understanding of the stages of the digital transition of companies. While many recent works have proposed constructive models for the implementation of DT, these remain specific to a particular industry or business model. In this respect, the general approach proposed in this article is intended to be more generalist, and under certain contextualization, is also intended to be adaptable to any company.

Keywords: Digital transformation · Digital transformation strategy · Key success factors

1 Introduction

The remarkable growth of digital technologies, the increasing ubiquity and reliability of data have radically reshaped the business models of companies [1]. This has led to substantial changes in their activities, processes, and capacities [2, 3]. That's how more and more companies are embracing a digital transformation strategy to create and own more value. To this end, the key to successful digital transformation implementation is to overhaul business models so that they are consistent with business strategy [4].

© The Author(s), under exclusive license to Springer Nature Switzerland AG 2022
M. A. Bach Tobji et al. (Eds.): ICDEc 2022, LNBIP 461, pp. 203–214, 2022.
https://doi.org/10.1007/978-3-031-17037-9_15

According to the current state of managerial knowledge, it becomes palpable that digital transformation (DT) brings notable benefits for businesses, such as creating more efficient products and services that are more aligned with customer needs, providing an innovation process, shorter time-to-market, and the creation of related digital ecosystems [5]. In addition, DT promotes interconnection between various industries by guiding companies towards new opportunities for the creation and appropriation of value through digitization and connectivity [6]. It is through this connectivity that DT is reducing barriers between industries allowing companies like Google, Apple, and Uber to pay more attention to the automotive industry for the development of autonomous vehicles.

However, adopting DTS also comes with challenges [7]. Despite the progress announced, DT represents a challenge for companies, due to the ambiguities of its implementation. Some companies still have concerns about the definition conception and implementation of their digital strategy to benefit from it and ensure strategic positioning. This is the reason why the success of the DTS remains one of the most important challenges for the success of the DT. With this in mind, the main research question of this article is to help understand how companies can successfully implement digital transformation.

Therefore, this work attempts to shed light on the implementation of DT. Through its general approach, it aims to enrich subsequent work by proposing frameworks adapted to a particular business model. The epistemological recourse to the abductive method by focusing on the AssetCo monographic case can serve as a reference. It makes it possible to deduce some recommendations that can serve as a guide for companies wishing to take up the challenge of digital transformation.

To discuss this question, we structure the remaining part of the paper as follows: First, we present a brief literature review about the conception of digital transformation and its strategy, and we outline a general approach of its implementation. Second, we analyze the digital transformation project of the company AssetCo to bring out the most salient ideas, that we discuss before concluding.

2 The Digital Transformation: A Literature Review

As a key research area, the DT remains one of the haziest topics facing businesses. Before exploring its conduction, it therefore seems necessary to first specify its scope by sequencing it in three stages: it starts with the notion of digitization which consists in exploiting and converting data to the digital form [8–10]; then the digitalization referring to the transforming the business process into digital [9, 11] and finally the digital transformation which is a kind of implementation of a series of technological and human changes to restructure the existing managerial models and culture. It is to this conception used to describe the changes affecting business activities, processes, and skills through digital technologies [12] to which we refer in this article. The literature emphasizes that the achievement of DT depends on the success of the first two phases [10, 13, 14].

Indeed, the DT represents many advantages such as change facilitator [15, 16], value creation [13, 17], reducing costs [18–20], enabling new products [21, 22], generating new knowledge and business opportunities [9], seeking competitive advantage [23–25], better innovation opportunities and implementation [26–28], better connection with shareholders and economy [29]. In addition, DT affects enterprises through creating changes in business plans [30], competitive environment [31], value creation [32], process and products / services quality [11, 33, 34]. Hence, it is beneficial for the company due to more concentration on core activities and the development of new competences, helping therefore in competitive advantage creation [35].

For incumbents companies, the main objective in the beginning of DT is growth seeking more than financial concerns, contrary to digital entrants [8]. To reassure its stakeholders and ensure its survival, companies must balance between attending cost reduction through automation, and revenue growth via improved customer experience [36–38]. Giving the difficulty to keep the balance between this two goals (cost reduction and growth), the development of digital initiatives in new separate ventures as a digital start-up is highly recommended to keep focusing on development and digital transformation [10].

For the pre-digital companies, DT represents a holistic form enabled by information system (IS), with the support of economic and technological changes in the organizational and industry level [39, 40]. On this basis, the DTS is of great importance, due to its role of coordination, prioritizing, and implementation of efforts and to help in the achievement of the concretization of digital transformation [13]. The DTS give therefore insights and ameliorate the development and implementation of the digital transformation to meet the digital challenge [13, 41]. In general, the DTS is a roadmap helping with the implementation of organizational changes due to the digital transformation realization, with the support of technical and human competencies and tools, to attend value creation and strategic positioning [42, 43]. However, to succeed in DT, the formulation and implementation of a contextualized and appropriate DTS is important [44, 45]. A MIT study reconfirm the fact that the victory of DT is highly related to the DTS success [7].

In fact, setting a DTS involves proposing a plan to manage the changes caused by digital technologies in a sustainable and resilient way [13, 42], in order to optimize the transformation of processes, business models and the implementation of this new technologies [41]. Moreover, the success of this DT within organizations in general, and the digital transformation strategy in particular, requires the expertise in four main areas: use of technologies, structural changes, DT financial aspects, and changes in value creation [8, 13, 41, 46].

In the literature, many studies propose various approaches to successfully concretize the DT in companies. From the definition of blocks, to the formulation of DTS through the value creation and modification of business model and others aspects to the implementation of the digital transformation, five phases are proposed: digital reality, digital ambition, digital potential, digital fit and digital implementation [32]. Another study integrate three global phases: strategic vision definition, action plan elaboration and management strategy [47]. In fact, the key elements of DT concern two main areas: on the one hand, use cases regrouping the implementation of digital in products, services, value chain, business models and customer interaction, and on the other hand, enablers such as data management, human capital, partners, cybersecurity and technologies [48]. Thus, it is almost consensual in most of the literature dealing with the DTS that the formulation of the latter must take into account 4 major axes: objectives and perimeters, staff and collaboration, funding, governance and structure [49].

With much research and proposals focused on how to implement digital transformation in the organizational world, the lack of general approach remains a significant limitation to this enthusiasm [50]. In fact, numerous recent works have proposed models to deal with the DT challenge, but are generally specific to an industry or to a type of company. However, an approach attempts to provide some answers to this problem is summarized in the model below. The latter, based on several case studies [14], can serve as a transposition model for companies looking for an application benchmark (Fig. 1):

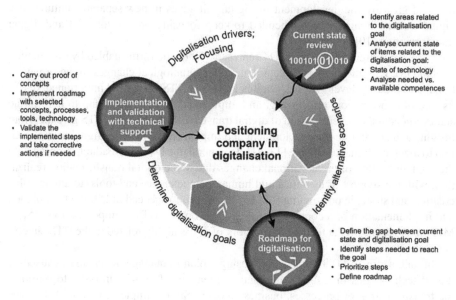

Fig. 1. Digital Transformation implementation approach. Source: [14]

As a general approach to DT implementation, the company starts with an analysis of its potential impacts to fix the future state to attend through several changes. Then, a comparison between the actual and future state is made in order to formulate adequate actions helping in digital transformation concretization. Finally, the implementation and validation of these actions take place to optimize the DT in the company. The model is used iteratively to gradually build the solution and fine-tune the digital goals and plans if needed. Its main steps are then examined in detail.

Step 1: Positioning the company in digital transformation
In order to know the positioning of the company in digital, four main elements are analyzed: the impact of the digital transformation, its goals, its drivers, and its scenarios. The impact study is conducted by detecting current and future digital trends, and their concretization in the company's business domain. It is possible to classify these trends using a SWOT analysis to take advantage of strengths and opportunities and to know how to respond to weaknesses and threats. Based on this trend analysis, digital transformation

drivers are defined and translated into major actions to guarantee the survival and update of the company, leading then to the formulation and study of the potential scenarios. Their analysis is related to possible benefits of each scenario, feasibility, costs, and risks involved in acceptance or rejection of each one. The main objective is to make the best alternative for the company. Then, digital transformation's process goals are defined to get a clear idea of the future path and indicators to evaluate the company's digital transformation success.

Step 2: Review of the current state

On the basis of the defined objectives, a diagnosis of the current state is carried out which puts in relation, on the one hand, the areas impacted internally such as tools, processes, and resources and, externally such as customers, the opportunities, the competitors, the processes, and the external resources, and on the other hand, the real situation to achieve. The main objective of this step is to determine the respect of the set objectives and the approximation of the success of the digital transformation.

Step 3: Roadmap for digital transformation

This step is so important since it concerns the translation of the goals set into instructions and a digital transformation strategy to achieve the expected results. First, the comparison between the current state and desired one helps in defining the main actions to reduce the gap between the two. Then, a feasibility study and classification of scenarios come to serve the roadmap formulation. Thus, the company formulates the necessary corrective actions and guidelines to get closer to its purpose of successful digital transformation. Indeed, if the problem concerns the internal aspects, the company must then correct and adjust its main processes and items causing the gap. If it's more related to external opportunities and disruptive goals, the company opt then for the definition and development of new offers, seeking new markets, acquiring new competencies, and rearranging internal resources. The definition of Key Performance Indicators (KPI) is also necessary to keep evaluating the main actions and areas of the company. In fact, the success of this stage can also be supported by a feasibility analysis. The latter can include a cost-benefit analysis, a change or impact on the organizational practices analysis, resources and risk analysis, and an analysis of constraints [14]. Moreover, the company must compare also the return on investment in digital with its costs such as training, recruitment, cultural and structural changes. This is the reason why the roadmap and main actions need to be validated by stakeholders in adequation with the organizational agility of the company.

Step 4: Implementation with the technical support

This phase concerns the implementation of the roadmap and the digital transformation strategy, moving from the strategic to the operational level, with the support of the technical team. Indeed, this stage is so important since it's related to the application of the main points of all the previous points. Under the continuous improvement logic, the company must keep in mind the idea of analyzing the gaps between forecasts and realizations, in order to formulate and apply the adequate corrective actions for the optimization of the success of the digital transformation in general and of the DTS in particular.

In general, the company analyzes the potential impact of digital to determine the strategic position needed. To achieve it, a comparison between the current and the desired state remains crucial, since it can help the company to emphasize the main actions to be taken and the main points to ameliorate to achieve the desired results. In fact, the model needs more of an update with more emphasis on the digital transformation stage than digitization, as the transformation incorporates organizational, process, and corporate culture changes. It is, therefore, necessary to take an interest during this transition in the management of cultural change in organizations in order to improve the quality of the approach.

3 Methodology

As an existential threat to the sustainability of organizations, digital transformation remains one of the most relevant challenges faced by managers. To help overcome this difficulty, our work aims to provide some answers to the following research question: **How can companies successfully implement digital transformation?**

As a methodological approach, and to reach our end, our article borrows an abductive method. The latter is an approach operating from a conceptual model or comprehensive theory of reality which makes it possible to prepare the observation or empirical work and to reduce the field to be studied. The place of the hypothesis is not a priori; it emerges from observation and/or data to then open up to a verification phase based on hypothetico-deductive and holistic-inductive approaches.

This third way of research methodology that we apply to a case study in the form of a monographic case certainly remains debatable and less popular. Admittedly, it makes it difficult to generalize and validate knowledge, but the choice of certain issues imposes it as the primary method for clarifying certain themes.

It was with this in mind that we used this research method to try to help companies better understand this phenomenon of digital transition which is in the process of imposing itself on all organizations. However, if each organization has its own characteristics, the general approach that we plan to put forward to better implement DT, remains a managerial reference for companies looking for a reference to implement their digital strategy in taking into account the particular situation imposed by the contextualization.

4 Digital Transformation Implementation Project: The Case of AssetCo

As one of the largest players in Europe in the financial services sector, especially real estate investments in urban areas, AssetCo (a pseudo name) has chosen to opt for the digital transformation in 2016. Despite the lack of competitive pressure, the enterprise wanted to take the challenge of digital transformation in order to experience and concretize innovation into its main processes. The formulation and implementation of the DTS were based on formal and informal interviews, observations, and internal and public data. To achieve this goal, six main phases were conducted: recognizing the need for digital transformation, setting the stage, initially formulating the DTS, preparing for DTS implementation, starting DTS implementation, finding a working mode, and enhancing the DTS [46].

First, the need for DT was a solution to the company sales declines, proposed by top management. Then, in the second stage, four main guidelines were approved to start the digital transformation project: opting for online and offline tools to increase customer benefits, end-to-end view on all processes, interfaces, and business models, ameliorating the existing technical infrastructure and platforms, and digitization of business and service processes. After that, the formulation of a target objective by the digital transformation strategy was made with alignment to the four-goal previously set (Fig. 2).

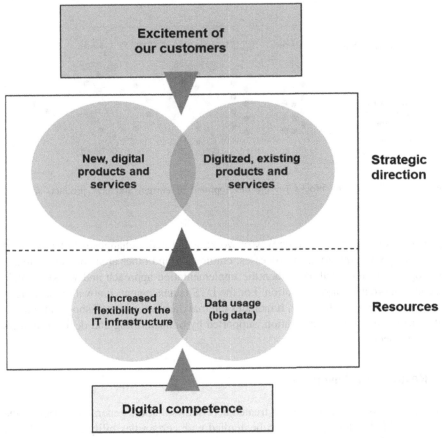

Fig. 2. AssetCo digital transformation target strategy. Source: [46]

Instead, it seems that this strategy formulation was vague and general due to the absence of the key digital transformation blocks rapprochement. The new DTS formulation was updated, by adding the building blocks and directions to digitalize the current products and services and the adoption of new ones, in adequation with the competencies and resources of the company, as shown in the 3rd figure below (Fig. 3).

Thus, once the formulation of the DTS is accepted, the budget allocation must follow for the implementation of the DTS and initiate the digital transformation of the

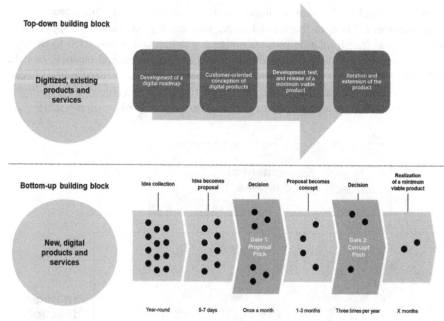

Fig. 3. AssetCo building blocks for the development of current and new products-services. Source: [46]

company. Consequently, an agile way of working and major changes is to be expected to accompany the mutation in processes, culture, IT, and other areas of the company. The top management validates then the implementation approach and working mode (agenda) in order to move to action. For the DTS enhancement, innovation-seeking is added as an important directive. It includes internal (targeted and workshops) and external (start-up investment) innovation, supported by brainstorming and decision-makers exchange meetings.

5   Results and Discussion

The case of AssetCo analyzed and treated here shows that the general approach of the phases of DT developed above can be applied with certain flexibility by the different companies taking into co-consideration the conditions and characteristics of each entity. In fact, and based on the experience of AssetCo, it seems that DT is a drastic and personal process and not a simple task to emulate and transpose. With many phases and consequent changes in all organizational aspects, the success of the challenge of DT is strongly linked, not only to the success of the formulation of the diagnosis of the characteristics of the company, of a roadmap and of the DTS implementation in line with the resources, skills and its proper implementation, but also depends on cultural fluidity and continuous evaluation to propose and apply the actions and corrections that are required. These iterative corrections are necessary because, despite the cognitive advance in the approaches and models identified in the literature to help the digital transition, contextualization remains one of the key success factors. The lack of alignment between the actions carried out and the characteristics of the industry and the company represents a major cause of corporate mortality.

In general, the analysis of the general approach and the AssetCo case study shows the difficulty of the digital transformation implementation. It is no longer a question of finding a model to follow but rather of implementing the key success factors of powerful digital companies and knowing how to adapt them to your company's situation. Moreover, the correct formulation and implementation of the DTS helps with future visibility and guidelines for the operationalization of digital transformation.

Therefore, the organizational culture fluidity and the disposition of IT skills and digital literacy are also other relevant elements for the success of the digital transition.

6 Conclusion

Being an element of managerial excitement in the business world, DT is on the minds of all decision-makers. The digital transformation thus remains a necessary, even existential challenge, when taking into account the effects of the cultural and socio-economic change caused by the Covid19 pandemic. Changing customer needs dictate improved business models and more flexibility at the organizational level. Digital transformation is then a kind of response to this change that is taking shape around us in the form of what we can call Glodigitalization.

Based on the analysis above, it is clear that its success remains a rather complex objective to achieve, requiring a coherent development and implementation of the digital transformation strategy. Despite the important models and approaches offered, the success of digital transformation in general and DTS in particular depends on the fit to the characteristics and context of the business. However, its implementation phases are not unified because there is no formal recipe for achieving this objective.

In this perspective, this article plans to enrich subsequent theoretical works since it presents a literature review on the link between the digital transformation and its strategy. For the managerial implications, our work clarifies the main directives and success factors to deal with the digital transformation. It can thus serve as a successful reference to address the challenges associated with implementing a DTS, help companies digitally transform their business, and reduce risk and uncertainty.

While the frameworks proposed so far clarify the implementation of DT from a specialized rather than a general point of view, our major contribution in this article is to holistically and methodically clarify the initial steps to be taken from inception to the end of the realization of the DT. This work can contribute to the ongoing construction to set up a digital realization roadmap for all companies.

Despite this attempt at cognitive breakthrough, the general approach presented in this work still remains perfectible in the sense that it does not sufficiently take into account other cases and factors such as the conduct of cultural changes in the organization. These limits will be the subject of other research perspectives aimed at better elucidating the issue of digital transformation.

References

1. Lanzolla, G., Anderson, J.: Digital transformation. Bus. Strategy Rev. **19**, 72–76 (2008). https://doi.org/10.1111/j.1467-8616.2008.00539.x
2. Ardito, L., Petruzzelli, A.M., Panniello, U., Garavelli, A.C.: Towards Industry 4.0: mapping digital technologies for supply chain management-marketing integration. Bus. Process Manag. J. **25**, 323–346 (2019). https://doi.org/10.1108/BPMJ-04-2017-0088
3. Fatorachian, H., Kazemi, H.: A critical investigation of Industry 4.0 in manufacturing: theoretical operationalisation framework. Prod. Plan. Control **29**, 633–644 (2018). https://doi.org/10.1080/09537287.2018.1424960
4. Warner, K.S.R., Wäger, M.: Building dynamic capabilities for digital transformation: an ongoing process of strategic renewal. Long Range Plann. **52**, 326–349 (2019). https://doi.org/10.1016/j.lrp.2018.12.001
5. Urbinati, A., Chiaroni, D., Chiesa, V., Frattini, F.: The role of digital technologies in open innovation processes: an exploratory multiple case study analysis. RD Manag. **50**, 136–160 (2020). https://doi.org/10.1111/radm.12313
6. Iansiti, M., Lakhani, K.: Digital ubiquity: how connections, sensors, and data are revolutionizing business. Harv. Bus. Rev. **92**, 19 (2014)
7. Kane, G.C., Palmer, D., Phillips, A.N., Kiron, D., Buckley, N.: Strategy, not technology, drives digital transformation. MIT Sloan Manag. Rev. Deloitte Univ. Press **27**, 26 (2015)
8. Verhoef, P.C., et al.: Digital transformation: a multidisciplinary reflection and research agenda. J. Bus. Res. **122**, 889–901 (2021). https://doi.org/10.1016/j.jbusres.2019.09.022
9. Dougherty, D., Dunne, D.D.: Digital science and knowledge boundaries in complex innovation. Organ. Sci. **23**, 1467–1484 (2012). https://doi.org/10.1287/orsc.1110.0700
10. Loebbecke, C., Picot, A.: Reflections on societal and business model transformation arising from digitization and big data analytics: a research agenda. J. Strateg. Inf. Syst. **24**, 149–157 (2015). https://doi.org/10.1016/j.jsis.2015.08.002
11. Li, F., Nucciarelli, A., Roden, S., Graham, G.: How smart cities transform operations models: a new research agenda for operations management in the digital economy. Prod. Plan. Control **27**, 514–528 (2016). https://doi.org/10.1080/09537287.2016.1147096
12. i-SCOOP: Digital transformation: online guide to digital business transformation. https://www.i-scoop.eu/digital-transformation/. Accessed 25 July 2021
13. Matt, C., Hess, T., Benlian, A.: Digital Transformation Strategies. Bus. Inf. Syst. Eng. **57**, 339–343 (2015). https://doi.org/10.1007/s12599-015-0401-5
14. Parviainen, P., Tihinen, M.: Tackling the digitalization challenge: how to benefit from digitalization in practice. IJISPM - Int. J. Inf. Syst. Proj. Manag. **5**, 63–77 (2017). https://doi.org/10.12821/ijispm050104
15. Agarwal, R., Gao, G.(Gordon), DesRoches, C., Jha, A.K.: Research commentary—The digital transformation of healthcare: current status and the road ahead. Inf. Syst. Res. **21**, 796–809 (2010). https://doi.org/10.1287/isre.1100.0327
16. Zhu, K., Dong, S., Xu, S.X., Kraemer, K.L.: Innovation diffusion in global contexts: determinants of post-adoption digital transformation of European companies. Eur. J. Inf. Syst. **15**, 601–616 (2006). https://doi.org/10.1057/palgrave.ejis.3000650
17. Li, L., Su, F., Zhang, W., Mao, J.-Y.: Digital transformation by SME entrepreneurs: a capability perspective. Inf. Syst. J. **28**, 1129–1157 (2018). https://doi.org/10.1111/isj.12153
18. Greenstein, S., Lerner, J., Stern, S.: Digitization, innovation, and copyright: what is the agenda? Strateg. Organ. **11**, 110–121 (2013). https://doi.org/10.1177/1476127012460940
19. Øiestad, S., Bugge, M.M.: Digitisation of publishing: exploration based on existing business models. Technol. Forecast. Soc. Change **83**, 54–65 (2014). https://doi.org/10.1016/j.techfore.2013.01.010

20. Kohli, R., Johnson, S.: Digital Transformation in Latecomer Industries: CIO and CEO Leadership Lessons from Encana Oil & Gas (USA) Inc., p. 16 (2011)
21. Saarikko, T., Westergren, U.H., Blomquist, T.: The Internet of Things: are you ready for what's coming? Bus. Horiz. **60**, 667–676 (2017). https://doi.org/10.1016/j.bushor.2017.05.010
22. Sebastian, I.M., Ross, J.W., Beath, C., Mocker, M., Moloney, K.G., Fonstad, N.O.: How big old companies navigate digital transformation. In: Galliers, R.D., Leidner, D.E., Simeonova, B. (eds.) Strategic Information Management, pp. 133–150. Routledge (2020). https://doi.org/10.4324/9780429286797-6
23. Berman, S.J.: Digital transformation: opportunities to create new business models. Strategy Leadersh. **40**, 16–24 (2012). https://doi.org/10.1108/10878571211209314
24. Kraus, S., Durst, S., Ferreira, J.J., Veiga, P., Kailer, N., Weinmann, A.: Digital transformation in business and management research: an overview of the current status quo. Int. J. Inf. Manag. **63**, 102466 (2022). https://doi.org/10.1016/j.ijinfomgt.2021.102466
25. Howard, M.: Digital ubiquity: how connections, sensors, and data are revolutionizing business. CFA Dig. **45**, dig.v45.n2.8 (2015). https://doi.org/10.2469/dig.v45.n2.8
26. Aubert-Tarby, C., Escobar, O.R., Rayna, T.: The impact of technological change on employment: the case of press digitisation. Technol. Forecast. Soc. Change **128**, 36–45 (2018). https://doi.org/10.1016/j.techfore.2017.10.015
27. Bourreau, M., Gensollen, M., Moreau, F., Waelbroeck, P.: "Selling less of more"? The impact of digitization on record companies. SSRN Electron. J. (2012). https://doi.org/10.2139/ssrn.2011854
28. Kolloch, M., Dellermann, D.: Digital innovation in the energy industry: the impact of controversies on the evolution of innovation ecosystems. Technol. Forecast. Soc. Change **136**, 254–264 (2018). https://doi.org/10.1016/j.techfore.2017.03.033
29. Gölzer, P., Fritzsche, A.: Data-driven operations management: organisational implications of the digital transformation in industrial practice. Prod. Plan. Control **28**, 1332–1343 (2017). https://doi.org/10.1080/09537287.2017.1375148
30. Pagani, M., Pardo, C.: The impact of digital technology on relationships in a business network. Ind. Mark. Manag. **67**, 185–192 (2017). https://doi.org/10.1016/j.indmarman.2017.08.009
31. Yoo, Y., Boland, R.J., Lyytinen, K., Majchrzak, A.: Organizing for innovation in the digitized world. Organ. Sci. **23**, 1398–1408 (2012). https://doi.org/10.1287/orsc.1120.0771
32. Schallmo, D., Williams, C.A., Boardman, L.: Digital transformation of business models—Best practice, enablers, and roadmap. Int. J. Innov. Manag. **21**, 1740014 (2017). https://doi.org/10.1142/S136391961740014X
33. Nadeem, A., Abedin, B., Cerpa, N., Chew, E.: Editorial: digital transformation & digital business strategy in electronic commerce - the role of organizational capabilities. J. Theor. Appl. Electron. Commer. Res. **13**, I–VIII (2018). https://doi.org/10.4067/S0718-18762018000200101
34. Reis, J., Amorim, M., Melão, N., Matos, P.: Digital transformation: a literature review and guidelines for future research. In: Rocha, Á., Adeli, H., Reis, L.P., Costanzo, S. (eds.) WorldCIST'18 2018. AISC, vol. 745, pp. 411–421. Springer, Cham (2018). https://doi.org/10.1007/978-3-319-77703-0_41
35. Liu, D., Chen, S., Chou, T.: Resource fit in digital transformation: lessons learned from the CBC Bank global e-banking project. Manag. Decis. **49**, 1728–1742 (2011). https://doi.org/10.1108/00251741111183852
36. Lemon, K.N., Verhoef, P.C.: Understanding customer experience throughout the customer journey. J. Mark. **80**, 69–96 (2016). https://doi.org/10.1509/jm.15.0420
37. Christensen, C.M., Bartman, T., van Bever, D.: The hard truth about business model innovation. MIT Sloan Manag. Rev. **58**, 31–40 (2016)
38. Verhoef, P.C., Kannan, P.K., Inman, J.J.: From multi-channel retailing to omni-channel retailing. J. Retail. **91**, 174–181 (2015). https://doi.org/10.1016/j.jretai.2015.02.005

39. Besson, P., Rowe, F.: Strategizing information systems-enabled organizational transformation: a transdisciplinary review and new directions. J. Strateg. Inf. Syst. **21**, 103–124 (2012). https://doi.org/10.1016/j.jsis.2012.05.001

40. Crowston, K., Myers, M.D.: Information technology and the transformation of industries: three research perspectives. J. Strateg. Inf. Syst. **13**, 5–28 (2004). https://doi.org/10.1016/j.jsis.2004.02.001

41. Hess, T., Matt, C., Benlian, A., Wiesböck, F.: Options for formulating a digital transformation strategy. In: Galliers, R.D., Leidner, D.E., Simeonova, B. (eds.) Strategic Information Management, pp. 151–173. Routledge (2020). https://doi.org/10.4324/9780429286797-7

42. Bharadwaj, A., El Sawy, O.A., Pavlou, P.A., Venkatraman, N.: Digital business strategy: toward a next generation of insights. MIS Q. **37**, 471–482 (2013). https://doi.org/10.25300/MISQ/2013/37:2.3

43. Braga Tadeu, H.F., de Castro Moura Duarte, A.L., Taurion, C., Jamil, G.L.: Digital transformation: digital maturity applied to study Brazilian perspective for Industry 4.0. In: García Alcaraz, J.L., Rivera Cadavid, L., González-Ramírez, R.G., Leal Jamil, G., Chong Chong, M.G. (eds.) Best Practices in Manufacturing Processes, pp. 3–27. Springer, Cham (2019). https://doi.org/10.1007/978-3-319-99190-0_1

44. Zaoui, F., Souissi, N.: Roadmap for digital transformation: a literature review. Procedia Comput. Sci. **175**, 621–628 (2020). https://doi.org/10.1016/j.procs.2020.07.090

45. Rêgo, B.S., Jayantilal, S., Ferreira, J.J., Carayannis, E.G.: Digital transformation and strategic management: a systematic review of the literature. J. Knowl. Econ. (2021). https://doi.org/10.1007/s13132-021-00853-3

46. Chanias, S., Myers, M.D., Hess, T.: Digital transformation strategy making in pre-digital organizations: the case of a financial services provider. J. Strateg. Inf. Syst. **28**, 17–33 (2019). https://doi.org/10.1016/j.jsis.2018.11.003

47. WHO, ITO (eds.): National eHealth strategy toolkit. World Health Organization [u.a.], Geneva (2012)

48. Kittelberger, D., Allramseder, L.-S.: The Digital strategy: the guide to systematic digitization of the company. In: Buttkus, M., Eberenz, R. (eds.) Performance Management in Retail and the Consumer Goods Industry, pp. 123–136. Springer, Cham (2019). https://doi.org/10.1007/978-3-030-12730-5_8

49. Fuchs, C., Barthel, P., Herberg, I., Berger, M.: Characterizing Approaches to Digital Transformation: Development of a Taxonomy of Digital Units, p. 16 (2019)

50. Korachi, Z., Bounabat, B.: General approach for formulating a digital transformation strategy. J. Comput. Sci. **16**, 493–507 (2020). https://doi.org/10.3844/jcssp.2020.493.507

Author Index

Printed in the United States
by Baker & Taylor Publisher Services